1980

Supermadre: Women in
Politics in Latin America

Latin American Monographs, No. 50
Institute of Latin American Studies
The University of Texas at Austin

Supermadre

Women in Politics in Latin America

by Elsa M. Chaney

Published for the
Institute of Latin American Studies
by The University of Texas Press,
Austin & London

International Standard Book Number 0-292-77554-7
Library of Congress Catalog Card Number 79-620012

To my mother,
Gulli Ingeborg Johnson Chaney

Contents

Tables

Acknowledgments

Special thanks are due to those who helped me along the way; only a few can be mentioned here. I am grateful to Charles W. Anderson, who encouraged me to do the research for this study before the topic became "fashionable." For their critiques of an earlier version, I thank Dr. Anderson, David Chaplin, Ximena Bunster, and Marion Neal Ash. I owe a special debt to Mary Lowenthal Felstiner for many helpful suggestions on a second draft; without her, there might not have been a final revision.

In Peru, Elsa de Sagasti was my first mentor—most generous and wise. Olga Gargate and Esperanza de del Busto in Peru and Monica González and María Eugenia Mesa in Chile helped me immeasurably through their warm friendship and their assistance in interviewing. The Facultad Latinoamericana de Ciencias Sociales gave me my Chilean roof in return for teaching a course.

In a very particular way, I acknowledge my 167 interviewees, so many admirable and vital women whose careers were cut short not only by their own understandable hesitations as the first generation of women political leaders in their countries but by the advent of military dictatorship. Still others to whom I owe a debt of gratitude include Isabel Alayza, Ruby Cabezas, Mónica Fabres, Elisa Flores Chinarro, Amelia Gaete, Olga González Garrido, Nora Scott Kinzer, Charles Lininger, Gregory Massell, Alicia Navarro, Marta Pajuelo, Ester Roa, Leonor Salazar de Ungar, Steffen Schmidt, Angélica Schreiber Duarte, Luz Vargas, and Donald P. Warwick. Mention here does not, of course, imply any responsibility for the analyses and conclusions presented in this study.

Next, I wish to acknowledge the help and assistance—through personal interviews and use of their libraries—of the founders of the suffrage movements in Chile and Peru, two valiant women, now deceased: Amanda Labarca Hubertson and María J. Alvarado Rivera. Finally, in a special manner, I want to thank the Familia Santolalla—and particularly Señora Irene and Señorita María Teresa—for their warm friendship, interest, and hospitality, not only during the time I was working on this study in Peru, but over many years.

Supermadre: Women in
Politics in Latin America

Introduction: Women and Development

Development is a word that has gone out of style in the Third World. To Asians, Africans, and Latin Americans, terms like "underdeveloped," "less-developed," and even the current "developing" imply a standard by which their societies have been judged and found wanting. Some reject the notion of "development" because they no longer wish to be measured in terms of Western progress nor to take on the values associated with modernization: individualism, competition, *Gessellschaft* replacing *Gemeinschaft*.

Today, leaders in many Third World countries are questioning the development paradigm borrowed from the West (whether in its capitalist or Soviet versions) with its emphasis on industrialization based on the rapid substitution of hand labor by machines, closely regulated by a centralized, bureaucratic state. Some are experimenting with alternative developmental models that stress, in the style of Castro and Nyerere, the honoring of the traditional (especially the peasant tradition and form of social organization) within a more productive economy. Here the emphasis is on national autonomy and on cutting the ties of economic and cultural dependency with other nations, along with a skepticism about the desirability of large, formal institutions, including those of trade and monetary policy, communications and education, associated with the West.

To stop using the term "development" entirely is difficult, however, and perhaps not necessary if one understands that development today is a process being determined by Third World peoples themselves according to their own criteria of cultural, social, and political progress. It is in this spirit that the word "development" will be employed here. Whether leaders talk of development or liberation, their goals are similar. They want to see their nations emerge as rapidly as possible from poverty, illiteracy, and disease and, externally, from their dependent relationships with the more developed nations.

This study does not, however, analyze or recommend a particular prescription for social, economic, or political change. Rather, it inquires into the paradox of nations becoming "modern" yet maintaining more than half their populations on the periphery of the development effort. As Ester Boserup (1970: 5) has noted,

> Economic and social development unavoidably entails the disintegration of the division of labour among the two sexes traditionally established in the village. With the modernization of agriculture and with migration to the towns, a new sex pattern of productive work must emerge, for better or worse. The obvious danger is, however, that in the course of this transition women will be deprived of their productive functions, and the whole process of growth will thereby be retarded.

In some places, it is true, increasing numbers of women are taking advantage of new educational and professional opportunities, especially in fields considered "feminine." Yet, at the leadership level, few women collaborate in policy making. Mead (1976-77: 151-153) believed this is a reflection of the nearly universal division of labor between men and women determined by their differing degrees of involvement in the process of reproduction:

> The confinement of women to activities compatible with child care is also reflected in the way in which public life has been steadily assigned to men. . . . Generally speaking, as soon as political decision making left the village level, the historic association between the male role and distance from home meant that women were excluded from participation at regional, national and international levels.

United Nations surveys repeatedly show that even in countries where women are active professionally, their level of responsibility as policymakers and planners is low even in certain sectors of the social field traditionally considered suitable for women. Women typically have not been involved in those larger economic activities that until recently have been considered the keys to development: international trade and finance, international lending and balance of payments negotiations, and production, buying, and selling of agricultural, mining, and other commodities and raw materials in the world market. Nor have women been part of the large-scale, male-dominated development "enterprises" that deal with health, sanitation, shelter, communications, rural electrification, technology transfer, agrarian reform, and rural development.

Even in those agencies, public and private, that deal with population, women are found in large numbers only at the lower levels of family planning and maternal health delivery systems: planners, policymakers, and upper-level administrators are with rare exceptions male.

Such an absence could be crucial at a time when we are discovering not only that women often derive little benefit from development gains but also that they may be adversely affected (Tinker 1974 and 1976). Quite simply, if women are not represented on policy and planning bodies, they will have no influence on the course of development. Gloria Steinem is cited in a comprehensive survey (UNITAR: 1975) on the lack of women in policymaking positions in the political and economic framework of the United Nations system: "Will the population planners and the decision-makers of the world ever agree—or be forced—to see women as powerful equals? As the group whose freedom holds the answer for us all? No one knows. At the moment women can't even get into the meetings."

This does not mean that women lack all influence. Rather, certain "boundaries" have been established designating women's legitimate professional and political activity. Women no longer are physically confined within the house, but in professional and public office they are generally confined to tasks analogous to those they perform in the home. The female public official often is forced to legitimize her role as that of a mother in the larger "house" of the municipality or even the nation, a kind of *supermadre*. The command echelons, however, are reserved to men.

There is no doubt that in some fields, especially literature and the arts, women have achieved eminence. The history of women in Latin America demonstrates that women there also have distinguished themselves in literary and artistic endeavors. But as Levy Cruz (1967: 221) observes in writing about women in Brazil, "it is doubtful that the term leadership can be applied to these cases." Moreover, these women always are "exceptional," and their activities do not affect the great mass of women in Latin America. Most women even of the privileged middle and upper classes might with some accuracy still sing an ironic verse composed by Mariquita Sánchez (Dellepiane 1923: 79), hostess of Buenos Aires's most famous salon in the first half of the nineteenth century:

> Nosotras sólo sabemos
> Oir la misa y rezar
> Componer nuestros vestidos
> Y zurcir y remendar.

> The only things we understand
> Are hearing mass, reciting a prayer,
> Arranging our ensembles,
> And patching and repair.

But perhaps women do not need to hold office to exercise political power.

Certain students of oligarchies contend that behind every ostensible political elite stand, in the shadows, those who actually referee the political game. Observers who do not understand the boundaries of women's influence sometimes make this mistake. They admit that women may not hold many official public positions, but, on the basis of discovering influential women whose advice is heeded in some spheres, they leap to the conclusion that many societies are governed by a "matriarchy."

Such a contention is not unrelated to a favorite North American myth, that of women's "unseen power." Since women in the U.S. buy most of the consumer goods and are the owners of savings accounts, stocks, and real estate in greater proportions than men the conclusion often drawn is that they exercise secret political power. In Latin America, too, title to lands, stocks, and property is often vested in women. At another class level, Latin American women produce subsistence and often other crops, and in some places monopolize the marketing of goods.

Yet formal ownership or economic activity must be distinguished from actual control over resources. In the Latin American case, it is interesting that female market traders in the Andes and the Caribbean are the only women ever singled out as having political clout—and then no assertion is made that such influence extends beyond the local level. As for upper-class women, putting property in the names of wives and daughters has been a common ploy of male relatives to escape limitations imposed by land reform or tax laws. In any case, to claim that women as a group—either in the United States or Latin America—exercise hidden political power because they formally appear as owners of economic resources is to fail to understand that such potential influence is scattered in dozens of conflicting directions.

Evelyne Sullerot cuts through the myth that indirect influence can compare with direct participation. Certainly we need more research here, to try to uncover *why* most women are satisfied to choose what in Colombia is designated the "wife-counselor" role over running for office themselves (Harkess and Pinzón de Lewin 1975: 460). As Sullerot puts it,

> It is certainly true that the wife of a politician has a role to play in politics and is an important element in her husband's success or failure. But who is to believe that there is no difference between this gentle creature who backs up her husband and decorates his publicity campaign, and the female candidate running her own campaign, assuming full responsibility for her acts and beliefs, and finally winning a seat for herself? [1971: 228]

What about women's influence at the polls? In a few cases—Italy and Chile under the influence of strong Christian Democratic parties are the best examples—women at times wield a certain political power through their vote. In electoral politics, the gaps between proportions of men and women voters have been narrowing; women form from one-third to one-half the electorate in many countries. It is here that male leaders of developing nations face a dilemma: evidence from older political systems demonstrates that women's increased participation in elections often acts as a brake on change (whether women's clear tendency to pull politics toward the right as they gain the franchise is more a result of the class status and age of the new voters than of their sex will be examined in the first section of chapter 5, "Women and the Vote").

Nor has increased participation in elections opened the way for women's greater participation in political leadership anywhere in the world. Chapter 5 explores in greater detail the fact that voting is often regarded not as "political" but as the civic duty of every citizen. Thus women now routinely vote in many cultures in which women in political office are still exceptional. The participation of women in electoral politics and their assumption of political leadership roles must be analyzed as distinct phenomena.

Should leaders in the developing world be concerned that women today play so small a role in any government, political party, private agency, or movement promoting reform? At some point in the development process, might feminine leaders be expected to appear in the ranks of those politicians, economists, social scientists, and intellectuals working to restructure their societies? Will there be feminine experts in agrarian and tax reform, housing, city planning and transportation, employment and human resources, labor organization, and rural development? Granted that women are working today in almost all these fields, why are they so few in number? Why are women almost always encountered at the lowest levels of the bureaucracy or academia, and almost exclusively in the feminine section of political parties? Why are they so rarely involved in over-all planning and decision making?

All these questions lead us to the central concern of this study: If women *did* participate in greater numbers at the leadership level, what difference would it make? Is there a feminine dimension to development and social change? Do women have anything distinctive to contribute to the modernization process and, if so, how would a feminine perspective alter current models of development? Are "women's issues" (revolving around such concerns as the changing family and the increase in the woman-based household, abortion and contraception, inflation and the food supply, shelter, schooling, and peacemaking) inherently revolutionary, and is women's apparent greater conservatism more in the eye of the beholder? Jane Jaquette (1974: 2) has cautioned that the categories and paradigms used to analyze female participation in the developing world are biased by North American cultural and methodological perspectives and by a feminist bias (also a product of North American ideology) that evaluates sex role differentiation negatively and designates women's issues as "moralistic," "peripheral reforms," or not "political" at all. As women's interests move to the center of the political arena, will women gain political power? Will women have what Sullerot (1971: 248) calls their "unwitting revenge for being left out," as leaders realize that female collaboration is necessary for the solution of all the great "new" world problems: underdevelopment, overpopulation, starvation, the environment, the very survival of the species?

This study seeks to answer these questions not only through exploring the differing roles most societies assign to men and women but also by looking at women in two specific but contrasting political cultures—the Peruvian and the Chilean—supplemented by information on women in other Latin American countries where it is available.

The survey depends on a questionnaire administered to eighty-one women leaders in Peru and eighty-six in Chile who held political or administrative office at the municipal or national level. Much supplementary material was gathered as well in a fourteen-month initial stay, seven months in each country, and in two extended visits afterwards. The main consideration in going to do field work in Peru and Chile was to have an opportunity to study women in two countries at different stages of development but with a common heritage, language, and colonial history in order to control in a rough way some of the variables of the social and cultural environment.

There was also a desire to investigate two groups of women who exhibit different political behaviors. Chilean women are recognized by many observers as the most active in the Americas in terms of professional and political involvement, whereas Peruvians usually are classed among the least active. Peru is still a closed, conservative, Hispanic society in which men and, sometimes in even greater degree, women view an active political role for women as inappropriate and unfeminine. In Peru, writes the distinguished Peruvian philosopher and educator Nelly Festini (1968: 59), it still is a common belief that "women belong in the home and need only certain domestic skills and a minimal education."

So far as Chilean women are concerned, as early as 1939 the Peruvian Aprista leader Magda Portal (1945: 10), exiled in Santiago, wrote admiringly of their progress in comparison to those in the rest of "colonial and semi-colonial" Latin America and particularly in her own country. Before the military coup of 1973, traditional attitudes toward women had changed to some extent, permitting a notable group of Chilean professional women, bureaucrats, and politicians to come forward in numbers not equaled in any other countries with the possible exceptions of Sweden, Yugoslavia, and the

Soviet Union. In absolute terms, 1967-1968 was the high point in the numbers of Chilean women in political or public office.

Even in these countries, however, women have assumed few top policy positions, and the total shrinks to insignificance when compared to males in leadership roles. That is why this inquiry, even though it focuses on women political leaders, should not be classified as a political elite study. Most women operate with so little share of power that they are "leaders" only in a relative sense. For the first time, a particular cohort that became active in the late 1950s and early 1960s in several Latin American countries stood out—in stark contrast to the almost complete invisibility of women in the political sphere.

What may advance our understanding of women in the political process is to consider women leaders as "deviant cases" among society's largest marginal group. Viola Klein (1965: 4-5) has suggested that

> in a society in which the standards are predominantly masculine, women form an "out-group" distinguished from the dominant strata by physical characteristics, historical traditions and social role. . . . Members of "out-groups" are subject to collective judgments instead of being treated on their own merits. While such stereotypes may encourage certain qualities in the member of a group, their general effect tends to be inhibitive. To be judged, not as individual, but as a member of a stereotyped group, implies an incalculable amount of restrictions, discouragement, ill-feeling and frustrations.

So far, not only the women leaders in my sample, but women generally who take on public roles, would seem to be more intimidated by the experience than otherwise. My cohort of interviewees, even before the respective coups in their countries, had encountered so much opposition and male prejudice that the traditional image of women's proper role appeared to be reasserting itself even among this exceptional group. Most intended to withdraw from public life or at least to return to the practice of their regular professions after the one experience.

This propensity to withdraw will be treated at length—see particularly the discussion in the next chapter—and ought to be kept in mind in interpreting all the other data. Indeed, discouragement among the first cohort, hindering them from venturing forth in search of political power, appears to be a worldwide phenomenon. The first leaders of the neo-feminist movement in the United States, the founders of the numerous professional and academic women's caucuses, and the first women in public office (except for isolated cases here and there) do not seem to generate a successor cohort. Younger women come along and make significant gains, but in some sense they reap where the initial cohorts have sown. Rather than taking over the movements, or going into government and public life, they make advances through pursuing individual professions in the private sphere.

Yet the lessons of recent history tell us that the strengths forged in struggling against the frustrations of minority status and the strategies learned from operating on the periphery of power may, in the end, be keys to women's advancement. That is why case studies of such cohorts are valuable, and why an attempt is made here to put the experience of the Peruvian and Chilean leaders in a wider framework.

This study begins with a general assessment of the difficulties of mobilizing women for development, and several current explanations for the lack of feminine participation are rejected. An alternative theory is proposed: that women's universal task of motherhood has profoundly influenced the boundaries and style of their interventions in public life. Chapter 2 analyzes the image of woman in Latin American society generally and how it has influenced her contribution to social, cultural, and economic life from colonial times to the present.

The next two chapters discuss the feminist movement in Latin America and the experiences of the first women to join political parties and to hold office. The final chapters present the findings of a questionnaire survey of 167 women in government and politics in Peru and Chile, tracing their recruitment and career histories, and exploring their views on women's role in society, their attitudes toward women's participation in the professions and political life and their commitment to social and economic change.

The original interview material, gathered in 1967-1968, was updated in 1972 through reinterviews with many of the women in the original survey. Military coups in both countries have, at this writing, removed virtually all these women and most civilian men from political decision-making. In Chile, women active in conservative politics with whom I talked in April 1974 (six months after the Pinochet government came to power) appeared reconciled to the probability that women would play no active part in government "while this *macho* military junta is in power, perhaps for the next twenty years," as one former prominent National party member put it. Some women on the left, particularly those of the MIR and the Communist party, were active in the underground, if they were not in exile.

These events in no way invalidate the fact that women in Chile made notable political advances in the 1960s and early 1970s, while Peruvian women were making tentative beginnings. In choosing political or government careers, these women defied the conventional image and the weight of culture and history, going against traditions not unrelated to those under which most women live. An insight into what the struggle cost the "deviants" and an exploration of the women leaders' characteristics and motivations may tell us a great deal about why most women are absent from the policy-making process. Such an analysis may also provide some clues to the terms and conditions of a greater involvement of women in the future.

Lest it appear that once again an outsider is attempting to analyze and prescribe for a reality not her own, let me make clear at the outset that the ideas expressed in this monograph grow out of hundreds of interviews and conversations not only with Latin American women leaders but also, in 1975-1976, with poor women in marginal occupations in Lima. My objective is to articulate the situation of women in Peru and Chile from their perspective. Indeed, some of the conclusions originally were difficult for me, as a North American feminist, to accept.

Latin American women probably will not replicate United States or Western European patterns of women's liberation. They have their own reality. North Americans would do well neither to expect nor to advise Latin Americans to copy the style of women's liberation in this country. Whatever they do, Latin American women themselves will decide their own course of action in the context of their own culture and aspirations.

1. The Inferior Role of Women in Public Life: Some Theoretical Speculations

Toward an Explanation: The Universal Motherhood Role

How are we to account for women's virtual absence from the councils of the decision-makers in every country and at every level of society? What theories might be advaned to explain women's inferior status and lack of participation at the command echelons, not only in Chile and Peru, but all over the globe?

Certainly we cannot complain that modernizing nations lack philosophical guidance on the emancipation of women. Whether our model of modernity is built on the liberal values of the West or on Marxist philosophy, we identify a cloistered place for women with traditional society and an emancipated place with modern society. In the West, serfs are emancipated and feudal privilege ends. Women's rights become the logical extension of the claims to individual liberty and autonomy that have provided the foundation for the whole process of transformation in the West over the past two centuries. In the socialist state, there is no ideological basis for denying equal rights to one-half the comrades because of their sex. Lenin returned more than once to the notion that mere legal equality is only a first step; it is not "bourgeois feminism," he said, to suggest that women must form their own organizations to achieve complete emancipation because "the building of socialism will begin only when we have achieved the complete equality of women and undertake the new work together" (1934: 111 and 69).

Despite the logic of their ideologies, however, in neither East nor West has woman reached equality. If we define emancipation to mean equal access for women—in law and in fact—to responsible roles through which they bring a feminine perspective to political, economic and social life, then it is obvious that women are not emancipated even in developed societies, whatever the types of regimes or the nature of their guiding ideologies.*

This situation leads us to ask what is holding women back. Before we can answer this question with any certainty, we may need to devise entirely new frameworks and theoretical concepts to deal with women's behavior. Women in most societies do not, for example, fit any of the current models through which political scientists attempt to analyze the phenomena of politics. They are not an elite; they do not, as a group, seek power; they are not a cohesive minority; they do not form coalitions to bargain with other power contenders. Women are so unorganized and ill-defined as a group and command so few political resources that to regard them as forming an interest group in the same sense as industrial laborers, the military, or landowners would be misleading. (For an extended discussion of the inadequacies of group theory applied to women, see Blachman 1974.)

Nor does a simple economic/class explanation of women's inferior position appear adequate. It would be superficial and shortsighted to ignore the effects of economic relations within societies on women or to deny that women's position in dependent economies is affected by the needs of the world's industrialized centers. As Heleieth I. B. Saffioti (1969a, 1969b, and 1974), Brazilian sociologist, demonstrates, women's inferior status is functional for the world economic system. (Saffioti probably has the most complete discussions of the effects of international dependency relations on women of the "naciones periféricas," nations on the periphery: see also Marianne Schmink 1974 and Helen Safa 1974b.) Women are socialized to a tremendous ambivalence about their roles, says Saffioti, and oscillate between the model of housewife and the model of worker or professional. This ambivalence serves well the needs of economic systems that swing from prosperity to depression; unsure of their role, women are maintained as the most significant component in the "reserve army of labor." They are especially vulnerable in the dependent economies of Third World countries. My disagreement with

---

*In Spanish, the term *emancipación* is generally not used in relation to women's rights, since in legal terminology it has another meaning: it denotes a young person's freedom from parental authority, granted by the courts before the young man or woman reaches legal age. Voting rights for women are generally called *derecho a sufragio* or *voto femenino* (female suffrage), and other legal rights (such as those that permit a married woman to administer her own property or to dispose of her salary) are called *derechos de la mujer* (women's rights) and their absence *incapacidad de la mujer*, literally, woman's incapacity. Emancipation, reserved here to denote liberation in the full cultural as well as legal sense, has no exact equivalent in Spanish, although the term *liberación* is sometimes used and, indeed, was in use many years before the phrase "women's liberation" was employed in the United States.

Saffioti is that she attributes women's marginal position to capitalism, whereas I see much evidence of women's secondary status in the economies and polities of socialist countries, too. As Margaret Mead (1976-77: 154) notes, the combination of the slaughter of World War II and an egalitarian ethic has made it possible for Soviet women "to work closer to their potential than American women. Yet they still are not freed from household responsibilities, and this fact blocks their fullest contribution to their country's development."

Some analysts believe that a "feminine consciousness" cannot develop in highly stratified societies. Moreover, because of the urgent problems facing Latin American and other Third World countries from both within and without, many say that peasant and proletarian women *should* not become concerned over specific problems that appear to affect only themselves, but should first join the men in changing economic institutions oppressing men and women alike.

Such a position no longer appears tenable, however, in the face of overwhelming evidence that expanded participation in the labor force and in mass political activities does not bring about an automatic expansion of women's participation in decision-making, even in socialist societies. Moreover, women's relative position often worsens as a modernized agriculture and industry take over the production of goods once manufactured in the home and as the centralized bureaucracy takes over many of the services performed by family members. Most women, left only with a residue of household tasks and used as a reserve labor force at the lowest levels of industrial production and the service sector, become victims of the modernization effort—even though, paradoxically, their participation rates in the labor force may continue to rise.

As a consequence, some Marxist women analysts (see Benston 1969, Larguía 1973 and 1975, Mitchell 1966, Bambirra 1971, and Dalla Costa 1972) have joined up with their bourgeois sisters in refusing to accept any longer the thesis that women will be available for a full political and intellectual contribution as soon as they can be drawn into paid work outside the home. They all agree that doing such work is a precondition for changing women's status, but they insist that obstacles in the socio-cultural superstructure must be *directly* attacked if women are to improve their position.

Attempts to explain women's inferior status through sociological concepts prove as unsatisfactory as political and economic analyses because they imply that all women are uniformly oppressed. Yet countries vary dramatically in the options they offer women, and even within countries, regions, and cities there are great gaps between the privileged and the poor. Women as *women* therefore cannot be classed as "marginals"; neither are they "castes" or "second class citizens," although substantial numbers of them may form part of all these groups in a given country.

Women are not a "caste," because by definition caste fixes forever a person's position in society. A woman suffers disabilities of caste not because of her sex but because of her family's status. If her father is lower caste, she will inherit his status in exactly the same way as her brother. She may not marry into a higher caste, and many opportunities are closed to her not simply because she is female (her brother lives under the same restrictions) but because of the limitations imposed by the caste system. This does not imply that there are no inequalities between men and women within castes.

Nor are women a "class"; rather, they are attached to and derive their position from a "significant male." They share the honors, perquisites, and class position of the men on whom they depend, acquiring more status if the significant males in their lives are upwardly mobile and losing status if these males fail to maintain their class position. Historically, women never were able to improve their position through their own brains and effort but only through marrying upward, just as they lost status by marrying downward. On their own, with the exception of the high-status woman who could fall to the level of prostitute, women could neither improve nor worsen their social class. In traditional societies, it is true, the situation of the male was not much different; yet as modernization began to break up the stratified class system, some males achieved mobility.

Not all women are by any means "marginals." Alice S. Rossi (1965: 101-102), in what still is a landmark article on woman's emancipation, points out that women are the only group that lives on intimate terms with its oppressors and is accorded a nominal status equality. No other type of social inequality, whether racial, class, religious, or ethnic, permits representatives of the unequal groups to live in closer association with each other than with members of their own group. As Steffen Schmidt (1974: 8) perceptively notes, the woman has been sister, spouse, mother, and grandmother to her own oppressor.

Although Rossi does not mention the comparison specifically, my own objection to the "woman as nigger" parallel—often drawn by feminists in the United States—lies here. No other members of a minority group except women are taken into the house of their oppressors as their nominal equals, to share their tables and their beds. Perhaps in even greater degree, the tradition of *caballerosidad,* the Spanish version of "gallant" behavior, gives honor and respect to the upper- and middle-class woman, and even to women of the lower classes if they are hardworking and "decente."

What must be noted is that from the most "in" to the most "out," from the most marginal to the most integrated, from the highest to the lowest in caste or class, women are discriminated against not only by all the men and women of higher groups, castes, and classes but by the men of their *own* status as well. Thus the woman of the highest status suffers unequal treatment at the hands of at least one group of significant males: her own father, uncles, brothers, and husband. Conversely, as Fidel Castro (1966: 7) has pointed out, the woman of the working class is in a desperate situation not entirely explained by her class status: she is not only oppressed (as also are the males of her class) by all the men and women of the classes above her; she is exploited and depreciated by the men of her own class as well.

It is interesting to note here, as Randall Collins (1971: 5) has done, that the reverse is never true: even though an upper-class woman may indeed give orders to and oppress lower-class men (for example, male servants), it is not her sex but her class status that allows her to do so. Her class privileges tend to mitigate the disabilities of being a woman; still, she rarely commands in political or professional spheres. And, as Camilo Torres observed (quoted in Schmidt 1974: 37), the privileged woman busy at her cards and social visiting is in some sense oppressed because of the opportunities denied her for the full development of her potential as a human being.

This short review by no means exhausts the rich theoretical literature on the situation of women. Yet none of the usual concepts employed quite explains the persistence of female powerlessness. An alternate explanation, one that may be more valid because it accounts more completely for the inferiority of women in every caste and class, is that for centuries only one approved role was open to women: motherhood. Whatever her social position, the woman's major validation lay in producing children. The woman who married and failed to achieve motherhood was pitied; the woman who did not marry was despised. Because she broke the link in the generations, in many societies the single woman's life was counted a waste, and her very existence became a tragic burden to herself and to her family.

One can readily comprehend why motherhood has been the only possible option for most women since the early centuries of humankind's existence. Women had little choice but to passively receive children up to nature's biological limit (although some controls, including infanticide, appear to have existed in most primitive societies). Moreover, demographic realities demonstrated the wisdom of bearing many children as a guarantee of seeing some of them survive to adulthood so they could provide for parents in their old age. Certainly it is nonsense to demean woman's role in primitive society; in terms of humankind's long fight for survival, she performed essential tasks. Anthropologist Eleanor Burke Leacock (1972: 33-35) shows how fascination with matrilineal descent systems (in which power to rule is passed through the female line but not exercised by women) led students of primitive societies to neglect the important contributions women actually made "in the large collective household . . . within [which] both sexes worked to produce the goods necessary for survival." Not only was it her exclusive role to bear children, but as inventor of cultivation and as food-gatherer the woman probably made a more important contribution to the food supply than the male, who often returned empty-handed from the hunt (women, incidentally, also hunt in some cultures).

Yet woman's life was quite unlike that of the male because of her motherhood vocation. For most women their adult life coincided with the span of their fertility, and childbearing literally wore them out. In peasant societies, woman's work role remains more nearly equal to man's; as societies modernize, however, many of woman's tasks are taken away from her—and rarely does she share an equal authority with the male either in or outside the walls of the home.

The male is not limited in the same way. In earlier societies his life may have been brutish and short, but fatherhood probably was even less significant a role than it later became. Certainly not then or later did anyone suggest that fatherhood was the only possible role for a man. The male from earliest times combined and subordinated his fatherhood role to the hunt, to war, and to politics. Very early, man was occupied in trades and professions that made it necessary to organize and engage in competition, differentiation, the drive to excel.

Meanwhile, women were isolated in their individual families or clans, often guarded to guarantee the legitimate paternity of sons. The tasks of motherhood were hidden, unspectacular, unchanging, unconnected to any power nexus. Many preindustrial societies venerated woman's reproductive capacities, celebrating them in the cults of the fruitful earthmother goddesses, but modern man long ago lost his awe of women's mysterious powers. Now that we know more about biology, it is clear that no special talents or abilities or magic are necessary to produce babies.

In contrast, as Simone de Beauvoir (1953: 58) has argued, although the male lacks the power to reproduce the species, he is seen as transcending women's natural functions with his goal-oriented, meaningful activities. This leads to Beauvoir's famous observation that "superiority has been accorded in humanity not to the sex that brings forth but to that which kills." As Sherry Ortner (1974: 75) points out, this formulation

> solves the great puzzle of why male activity involving the destruction of life (hunting and warfare) are often given more prestige than the female's ability to give birth, to create life. Within de Beauvoir's framework, we realize it is not the killing that is the relevant and valued aspect of hunting and warfare; rather it is the transcendental nature (social, cultural) of these activities, as opposed to the naturalness of the process of birth.

In discussing the relative contributions of men and women in different cultural systems. Michèle Zimbalist Rosaldo (1974: 19-20) demonstrates that male activities always are defined as more important, even though in some societies males perform tasks that Western observers would call "female." Yet no matter "how trivial or picayune" an activity might be, as Mead (1976-1977: 152) said, "if it was performed by males, it was more prestigious than if performed by females." Sullerot (1971: 245) sees the problem as a question of the power to define, not of innate differences in ability. The male group,

> having early taken the lead . . . now has the authority to define which activities carry prestige and which do not. . . . They can even impose the type of advancement they will allow women to have, in rather the same way that industrialized countries influence the rate of modernization of the underdeveloped.

The dichotomy between man's and woman's world/domain/place has often been drawn. Jessie Bernard (1973: 20-21) contrasts the female "status world," in which bonds are on a love/duty basis, and the achievement-oriented, competitive, and emotionally-neutral "cash-nexus" male world. The inhabitants of the female world are all but invisible for history and social science, Bernard says. "Men are furiously interacting with one another, but one hardly catches a glimpse of any woman." Margaret Benston (1969), like Bernard, sees most women (along with serfs and peasants) still inhabiting a preindustrial world; in her analysis, domestic work has "use value" but not "exchange value"; thus women's contribution is not esteemed. As Nancie L. González (1973: 51) sums it up, "*work* is defined as that which occurs outside the household and which in one way or another contributes to the Gross National Product: . . . only those who work, as defined above, may be accorded full status as normal and honorable adult members of the society."

What happens is that women are not "seen" to be working but are visible only in their proper housewife role. Often women's paid work is part-time, sporadic, and/or low in status. At other times women work long hours in subsistence agriculture, yet identify themselves as housewives (see discussion in Deere 1977: 7-12). Saffioti (1974) attributes this situation to women's own ambivalence about whether to view themselves primarily as workers or as "dueñas de casa."

Marirosa Dalla Costa (1972: 26) adds an important insight. Even though giving birth to, raising, disciplining, and servicing the worker for production are absolutely essential to the continued functioning of the modern industrial state, since this work is considered "unskilled" it is neither valued nor paid. Benston and Dalla Costa both attribute the denigrated position of woman in the household economy to capitalism. It seems clear, however, that women's exploited position differs only in degree in socialist countries. The isolated family unit and the system of unpaid housework and childrearing have evolved to support the modern bureaucratic and industrial state, whatever its ideological underpinnings.

When women begin to move out to the larger society, the boundaries and style of their participation are profoundly influenced by their traditional roles as mothers and preservers of the race. As Rosaldo (1974: 23) puts it, the fact that most women spend a good part of their adult lives in giving birth to and raising children "leads to a differentiation of domestic and public spheres of activity that can . . . be shown to shape a number of relevant aspects of human social structure and psychology."

If women's primary destiny is motherhood, then no special distinction is possible to women except to become outstanding mothers or to seek a surrogate motherhood in a "womanly" profession. Most women go into fields analogous to those tasks they perform in the home, preeminently education and the welfare of women and children. But women do not improve their inferior position very much by turning professional. Feminine fields are neither prestigious nor powerful because they are associated with the depreciated tasks of birth and nurture.

Women in political life are no exception. They, too, tend to gravitate toward "feminine" tasks and to define their political responsibilities in maternal terms. This is the particular focus of the next section, as we turn from this general discussion to the case study of women in Latin America.

Women in Political Life

At least two major theses about women's political participation emerge from the historial, socio-economic, and political analysis in the first part of this study and are confirmed by the survey data from Peru and Chile in chapters 5-7. First, traditional images of woman's proper activity still are so strong in Latin America that, when women do enter government, they (and the men) almost invariably appear to consider their intervention as an extension of their family role to the arena of public affairs. Many envision women in public office (to use descriptions originated by Talcott Parsons [1956: 47] to characterize current male-female roles) as carrying out the nurturant and affectional tasks society assigns to women, rather than in the instrumental male role, which is defined as more aggressive, authoritarian, and achievement-oriented.

We touch here on the basic conceptual question of this study: Does the sex status "female" explain or associate more strongly with women's behavior in the economy, society, and polity than do other characteristics such as class, age, marital status, race, religion, and urban or rural residence? To say it another way, do women's perceptions of their proper role in politics (and their behavior) relate more to their social class, age, or any of the other "intervening variables" mentioned above, or are most women alike in accepting and acting according to similar feminine stereotypes of their political roles?

My own survey shows that women overwhelmingly agree to a division of labor in the polity that parallels the traditional, unequal roles of men and women in the family. Both men and women believe that women should participate in politics, but in a style that is a "reflection in the political institution of the division of tasks in the family" (Blachman 1973: 11). These attitudes cut across all class and political divisions. A woman official most often defines herself as a kind of supermadre, tending the needs of her big family in the larger *casa* of the municipality or even the nation. Thus Eva Perón, perhaps the most formidable female politician Latin America has ever produced, explained her public role in terms of woman's eternal feminine tasks:

> In this great house of the Motherland, I am just like any other woman in any other of the innumerable houses of my people. Just like all of them I rise early thinking about my husband and about my children . . . and I go about all day thinking about them and a good part of the night. . . . When I go to bed, tired out, then instead of dreams, marvelous projects occur to me and I try to sleep before I burst. . . . It's that I so truly feel myself the mother of my people. [1951: 313-314; translation mine.]

In this context, it is interesting to note that at the first Inter-American Congress of Women, held in Havana in 1923, the women's movement in Latin America was characterized as "maternidad social," social maternity (Aguirre 1948: 106). In analyzing the texts and resolutions prepared for this and subsequent women's congresses, it is striking to note how they center almost exclusively on themes related in one way or another to the home and family and to the enforcement of public morality. It is almost as if women believed that they had no right or competence to deal with other issues facing society. This concern with moral questions indeed may have a positive side, as Cynthia Little (1975: 386) has argued; moral reform movements "often have indicated women's active presence and concern about the direction of a nation's social policies."

Certainly the whole struggle for the vote, just emerging as an issue at the time of these meetings, often was viewed almost exclusively as a vehicle for obtaining social reforms in favor of women, children, the old, the sick, juvenile delinquents, and prostitutes.

Nothing is more natural than that women's first ventures into the public arena should have been put in the framework of their traditional vocation of wives and mothers and should stress moral values. As Little herself recognizes (p. 387), moral reform movements do not attempt to make structural changes; rather they concentrate on making legal, constitutional, and educational modifications within the existing systems. My own study will demonstrate that moral reformism may foster a conservative outlook and an ambivalent attitude toward change on the part of many women leaders. Historically, the image of the active woman as supermadre has prevented many women from joining the vanguard of movements advocating profound political or social reform.

González (1973: 49, 52-53) has noted the same tendencies: she sees political activities divided into two spheres, the "jural," those activities that relate one unit to another in the larger society, and the "domestic," or the internal affairs of the unit. When women begin to break into the public realm, she says, almost always they concern themselves with domestic issues. Socialization of the young, she points out, now includes school board politics, school taxes, busing. Welfare and health matters, once household concerns, now are public issues. González (p. 54) suggests we need a new concept to fill the gap between the familial-domestic world and the jural domain proper. She has used the term "supra-domestic" to cover those activities now at least partially controlled by the state. It is precisely here (and only exceptionally in the jural domain proper) that women in politics find their field of activity. As González puts it (p. 53), "there are more and more out there [in the labor force and government], but a closer scrutiny shows that most are not doing the same things men do."

Collins (1971: 5), as noted above, thinks women's subordinate position in the world of work and politics also may be explained by the peculiar command system linked to her subordinate position in the home. The principle of this system, he says, is that women take orders from men but do not give orders to them; hence only men can command other men, and women can give orders only to other women. Certainly the division of public life and professions into masculine and feminine spheres facilitates the preservation of the command echelons for men. Blachman (1973: 7), too, points out how the subordinate position of women in the family automatically relegates them to a similar position in the political system. "Man the husband [or father, we might add] is the mediator," he says, "the link between the family and the outside."

At this stage of research, we do not know to what extent men act as gatekeepers, excluding women from policy positions, and to what degree women's exclusion is self-imposed by their own ideas on spheres proper to women officials. Robert A. Lane (1959: 212) observes that quite aside from women's primary responsibility for the young in most cultures and their consequent pre-occupation with the moral training of the next generation, there is some evidence that the custody of moral values often is bestowed as a "consolation prize" for exclusion from other activities more highly valued in a society. In this respect, Latin American women differ only in degree from other Western women. Once again, however, it is important to suggest that the solution may not require women to take on the values or plead for the issues that men have defined as important. They might instead begin defining for the polity concerns related to care, nurture, and preservation that sound profoundly "conservative" but may in fact be revolutionary in the destructive wake of men's aggressive push to modernize and industrialize this fragile planet.

The ideal, in a world without traditions and prejudices, certainly would be that men and women would fill the posts in government and elsewhere for which their talents and training prepared them, without any special note being taken of their sex. Men and women would dedicate themselves to primary or secondary institutions as their own particular capacities and bents dictated. Men would serve in child welfare without doubts being cast on their virility, and women would be scientists or administrators without being considered "marimachos," castrating females. The ideal justly asks: Why should not both men and women, according to their own particular bents, concern themselves with improving the lot of the woman, the child, the old, the sick, the juvenile delinquent—and with planning, industrialization, balance of payments, inflation, monetary reform, agricultural development, and outer space?

But the ideal "modernized" world is not yet, and tradition has designated (or stereotyped, if you will) certain concerns as feminine. This study hypothesizes that most women carry over these same concerns to politics when they become active—and it asks what difference a feminine perspective might make in policymaking.

A second thesis underlying this study relates closely to the first. Women's active political intervention in Latin America (as elsewhere) in any numbers has always occurred at the crisis points in their nations' histories. Women tend to become active only in times of extreme challenge, then sink into apathy when the emergency is over. Women's "propensity to withdraw" appears to be a universal phenomenon; as Elizabeth Mann Borgese (1963: 64-65) points out, in times of crisis throughout world history women often take an active role in public affairs but afterwards have no opportunity to organize and consolidate their gains. The typical pattern of involvement is one of entry/retirement. In a crisis, behavior outruns belief; when normalcy returns, the image of women's role has not changed sufficiently to allow more than a few to remain active at a responsible level.

The conquest and independence movements in Latin America, the winning of the West and the abolition movement in the United States, and the two world wars and the peace movements are some of the events that called women forth to share the risks and tasks of society side by side with men. But, in each case, women's participation was provisional and tentative, often indirect and anonymous, and almost always justified in terms of the feminine image, that is, it was allowable for women to agitate publicly for peace because they were mothers. Society accepts woman's help in an emergency, but her permanent collaboration on an equalitarian basis has yet to be legitimized or institutionalized anywhere in the world.

Thus, the self-sufficient pioneer woman of the North American West was succeeded not by the woman entrepreneur, senator, or professional, as might have been expected, but by the fainting, sheltered Victorian lady. In Latin America, the *criollo* heroines who conspired alongside their menfolk in the wars of independence against Spain did not follow them into the legislatures and governments of the new republics but disappeared into another full century of silence. In Brazil, as Gilberto Freyre (1963: 75) records, "in the rugged early days of the settlement of the coast, when men and women were confronted with an awe-inspiring virgin land waiting to be conquered, women enjoyed greater freedom of action." But the capable and energetic early plantation or ranch mistress became in the succeeding patriarchal period an artificial, morbid being, "a sickly person deformed by her role of servant to her men and doll of flesh and blood to her husband" (Freyre 1963: 74).

Extraordinary events may also awaken large numbers of women to political responsibility and encourage them to make the tremendous effort political office demands. Then when their country returns to "business as usual" they abdicate.

After World War II, for example, Europeans entered a period of political ferment and idealistic fervor as they rebuilt their political systems. There were 40 women in the assembly of 630 members that drafted the 1946 constitution in France, and 23 in the senate. By 1970, the numbers had dwindled to 8 and 5 of an assembly reduced to 487 members. Italy had only 5 women senators and 25 deputies in 1970 (of houses with 249 and 596 members, respectively), but immediately after the war there were 45 Italian women in parliament. (In justice, one must point out this still is more than the British or American representation, although Sullerot [1971: 225-226] says these women were an isolated cohort without successors.) Nowhere is the trend more striking than in Japan, where 39 women were elected to the first postwar diet (of 410 positions); by 1970 their number had declined to 8 of 467. (Figures from Gruberg 1968: 76-77 and United Nations Secretary General 1970, Annex: 1, 8.)

A study by Barbara Jancar (1972: 37) of all the top Soviet decision-making bodies since 1917 shows that even in the Soviet Union there is an extremely high rate of turnover for women officials. The study shows that of 4,600 top positions available since the revolution, women have filled only 84. Moreover, few of the *same* women remain from one party congress to the next; only 5 women now in the top hierarchy go back beyond 1961. (See also Jancar's discussion of women's situation in other Communist countries [1978].)

Sometimes the novelty of the right to vote and to hold political office pushes women into politics even in countries with very old political systems; again, they abdicate as the excitement declines—or when they find the political game a rough one. This apparently happened in Peru, where 8 women were elected to the *cámara de diputados* in 1956 and 1 to the senate, in the first election after women received the right to vote. In the next congress (and the last one before the present military government took over), there were only 2 survivors. In Chile women reached a high mark of 12 congresswomen and 3 senators during the Frei administration; the numbers went down to 7 and 2 in the Allende period.

There may be another reason women do not attain high posts: they appear unwilling—or unable because of family responsibilities—to serve the long years that appointment to major assignments in government requires.

No single finding of the present study illustrates women's entry/retirement pattern more graphically than the fact that the first generation of women to hold government posts in Peru and Chile lacked any further aspirations. Many of the 167 women interviewed became active in the late 1950s after the vote and the right to hold office were extended to women. For a time, a climate more favorable to women's intervention in public affairs was created, and the duty of women to become involved was discussed everywhere. Then the novelty wore off, opposition and male prejudice were encountered, and the traditional image of woman reasserted itself. Of the 167 women interviewees, 104 disclaimed any interest in continuing in politics or advancing to a more responsible post in government; only 34 wanted to rise in the future. The remaining interviewees (N = 29) said they were content or did not know if they wanted to advance (5 cases). This propensity to withdraw is a factor that ought to be kept in mind in interpreting all the other data in this study.

Woman's Emancipation and Development: The Future

The preceding sections have dealt mainly with women's response to the challenges of the past. What about the future? From the perspective of development, is not women's full and active collaboration essential to the development process? From the perspective of the women themselves, will not economic, social, and political change automatically assure their liberation?

The first question has, of course, been addressed—principally in pointing out that almost all women are involved in some kind of productive activity (and hence in development, whether they are formally "incorporated" or not), yet they are hardly ever involved in development in a political or technical sense, either at the local level, in national governments, or in international development agencies (see, for example, Papanek 1977: 14-15 and Mead 1976-77). Western countries did not have any significant number of women in leadership positions in their periods of greatest industrial expansion, and Japan is only the last and most conspicuous example of a newly-developed power with low indices of feminine participation in education, the professions, and political life. If we continue to view development as a narrow economic issue, then very likely not many women will be involved at decision-making levels.

Neither does it follow that economic development necessarily liberates women for meaningful participation in public and professional life. It is obvious that only exceptional women have achieved equality even in "developed" countries. In the Soviet Union, for example, where prospects for entering and succeeding in a career probably are the best for women anywhere, Norton T. Dodge (1966: 214-215), an expert on women in the Soviet economy, found that women had not achieved full equality:

> The proportion of women in the administrative and professional jobs . . . tends to decrease with each successive increase in rank, even in such fields as education and health, where the role of women is dominant. . . . There appears to be an undeniable tendency for female specialists in all fields to congregate in the lower and middle echelons. Perhaps the most striking instance of this is the small number of women among the [Communist] party professionals.

Even crude economic activity rates for women (in contrast to those for men) do not seem clearly affected by degree of industrialization, as some have supposed. Indeed, economic progress sometimes correlates negatively with levels of women's activity outside the home. David Chaplin (1969) has suggested that women's participation goes through two stages in relation to industrial development. In the first industrial revolutions in the West, when new occupations opened up that initially were "sexless" or unattractive to men, many women entered the labor force. Later (midway in the industrialization process, according to Chaplin), when relatively less labor was required and development brought more prosperity, women "retreated" to specialized roles as homemakers and consumers.

There is evidence to support Chaplin's contention that in a consumer-oriented economy "it takes time to spend money, more time than the average man can afford." Prosperity reduced Italy's labor force by more than one million women during the past decade. In 1961, 25 percent of all Italian women were working; by 1968, the number had dropped to 19.7 percent because husbands were earning larger salaries and their wives could give up their jobs. Several other observers have noted similar tendencies among the middle classes of industrializing countries; a prestige factor may also be involved—the male's demonstration of his ability to maintain his family without the salaries of his wife and/or grown daughters (see Germain 1974: 15 for additional citations).

In the United States, the move back to the family may also have been influenced by what has been widely referred to as the "feminine mystique" (but which Jessie Bernard [1968: 8-14] perhaps more aptly has characterized as the "strange interlude of the Motherhood Mania"). It is important to note that the "move back to the home" probably was confined principally to the upper class (which sets the norms for women), since women's participation in the labor force continued to rise at the lower-paid levels. Professional women, however, declined from about one-half of all employed professionals in the 1930s to one-third by 1960 (Alpenfels 1962: 74).

Other evidence appears to call into question the contention that economic development is related to women's participation. Collver and Langlois (1962: 370-374), reporting on twenty countries around 1950, show that women's work participation rates vary greatly from country to country, regardless of the level of economic development. In Peru and Chile, as well as in other Latin American countries, women workers in factories decreased not only proportionately but numerically from high points in the 1950s and early 1960s, when Latin American countries embarked on "import substitution industrialization" in order not to be caught short again as they were when imports of consumer goods were cut off by the Great Depression and the two world wars (Chaplin 1967: 187-195). As factories become more mechanized, even the proportion of males employed in the industrial sector has been shrinking because of capital-intensive development strategies. These and other obstacles to women's participation in employment will be discussed in depth in chapter 2. We might note here Ester Boserup's (1970) study, which shows that in most world regions men usually are recruited for modern activities, whereas women tend to be left behind in traditional tasks; not only does modern industry overwhelmingly favor the employment of men, she says (p. 139), but in Africa and Asia, "the inferior position of women in urban development is exacerbated by the strong preference for recruitment of men to the clerical and administrative jobs." For a further discussion, see Chaney and Schmink 1974.

There is also evidence to support the view that alternatives offered to women must be meaningful and challenging before women will incorporate themselves permanently into the labor force. Women will not find in low-level, repetitive, and underpaid jobs anything more than a temporary means of earning money, unless they are the sole support of their families. Paid employment may indeed be a first step for a woman toward widening her horizons and securing a certain economic independence, but there is no infallible guarantee that paid employment will lead to permanent emancipation. Economic development based on industrialization thus may play an indirect role in the progress of some women, but it does not automatically free them to enter careers on an equalitarian basis with men or to participate in the decisions affecting the economy and the polity.

We touch here on the revolutionary changes required in the structures of work, changes that will affect men and women alike. Such changes may also hinge on the willingness of governments to sacrifice some percentage of economic "growth" and adopt less capital-intensive development models in order to create employment, distribute income more justly, and widen opportunities for everyone to participate in the economy and the polity. Such rethinking of basic development strategies is already under way in many countries as they face hordes of young men and women reaching working age because of rapid population growth. In Latin America, where the economically-active female population has fluctuated during the past two decades between 16 and 20 percent of all women, women remain particularly vulnerable in the abundantly-supplied labor markets of countries whose traditions dictate that women should remain in the home.

Some evidence exists that feminine rates of activity in the developing areas might be influenced more strongly by demographic change than by economic progress. Jeanne Claire Ridley (1968) has explored the influence on women of sharp demographic transitions in countries that do not register high on indices of economic development. Her data show that a decline in mortality is highly correlated with an increase of women in the labor force and that a decline both in mortality and the birth rate pushes women's activity rates even higher. If women live longer and (because of declining mortality rates) realize that they do not have to bear so many children in order to see some live to adulthood, they are far more likely to seek employment outside the home. Hunt (1965), in a study of feminine occupational patterns in the Philippines, Japan, and the United States, also finds no direct relation between industrialization or urbanization and female employment patterns; along with other observers, he concludes that cultural and educational influences are much more effective in determining women's occupational roles in these countries.

All these facts point to the conclusion that only within the context of a total mobilization effort are women given important tasks outside the home. As with Blacks, the labor reserve of married women is tapped only in cases of acute labor scarcity. During the two world wars many women were drawn into work outside the home. Shortages of males in the Soviet Union after World War II brought large numbers of women into the labor force and, in addition, broke down sex stereotypes attached to certain jobs. Viola Klein (1965: 85-88) found that married women in Britain—who for the first time in any country constituted the only labor reserve—finally were beginning to command equal pay, status, and promotions. In present-day Cuba and China, labor-intensive modernization efforts are giving women new opportunities for productive work.

It remains to be seen if these newer mobilizations of women will result in lasting advances. In all these cases there is strong evidence that women are drawn out of the home and into paid productive work only when the male political elites consider women's participation essential to other (and higher) priorities.

A United Nations survey on women in economic and social development (1970: 3) remarks that trends in many countries make it appear that measures taken to increase the participation of women "are prompted not so much by the desire to bring about a fundamental change in the role of men and women in society, but rather by the realization that over-all development requires a greater utilization of the potential labour force." One can make a good case that not even revolutionary Marxist governments promote equal participation of women in economic activity unless women's involvement is necessary to a higher priority goal—for example, in the Soviet Union after World War II, in Castro's Cuba (see Purcell 1973), where women were needed desperately in the labor force, or in Soviet Central Asia, where the Communist party attempted to break up the traditional Muslim society by forcing local Communist officials to unveil their wives and daughters and send them out to work (Massell 1974). Shelah Leader (1973) confirms the same tendencies in China, and Rae Blumberg (1976) for women of the kibbutz in Israel.

Must we then conclude that at present only the developed nations can afford the "luxury" of creating alternatives for women? Except in situations of labor scarcity or national emergency, are women allowed to assume only supermadre roles in the supra-domestic realm? Could women leap from their traditional status to an as yet undefinable and significant neo-feminine role in a post-industrial world? Are there any features of Hispanic society that might lead us to expect for women in Latin America a different development and a different pattern of emancipation? Might the key be in redefining the goals of development?

As Blachman (1973) suggests in his conclusion to his study of Brazilian women in politics, two crucial areas must be explored in answering such questions: the ideological and the institutional, the image and the reality. The two chapters following, which discuss the feminine stereotype as it developed in Latin America and explore how women lived up to the feminine image as they began their political life, suggest that the answer to all these questions may be a qualified "yes."

2. Women in Latin American Society and Polity: The Image and the Reality

This study asks if a more egalitarian participation of women as policy-makers and planners in development would make any difference to policy outcomes; it asks particularly if their participation in other activities would be enhanced. The study asks this question, moreover, in the specific setting of two contrasting political cultures, with a view to extrapolating at least some of the answers to women in other developing countries.

Clearly, if women aspire to (and win) places in the existing male hierarchy, and if they then go on doing only what men do, their presence will not alter the direction of development. If, on the contrary, women want to participate in development on their own terms, acquiring more of its benefits, blunting some of its negative effects on themselves and other women, and emphasizing women's issues, then another strategy is indicated.

Lest it appear that, once again, an outsider is analyzing and prescribing for a reality not her own, let me emphasize that the ideas expressed here grow out of hundreds of interviews and conversations not only with Latin American women leaders but also with the poor and powerless. Leaping over, for the moment, the question of how they would acquire some power for themselves, Latin American women who want to participate in development on their own terms face two problems at the outset: (1) overcoming the negative features of women's image in Latin America and building on the positive aspects of their role; and (2) exploiting the advantages of the Latin feminine culture, perspective, and domain.

The Feminine Image in Latin America

When one probes into the image of women in Latin America, one at first is dismayed: how can such a negative view ever be overcome? Yet this image, so dismal at first glance, has a positive face. Women's behavioral norms are complex; they were not formed simply as negative reactions to affirmations of male virility. The exploration will take us well beyond the now fashionable concept of *machismo,* the cluster of male traits related to masculine honor.

All the predominant images forming what might be called the "feminine myth" in Latin America consistently place woman in a subordinate, inferior role; the images are constantly reinforced and perpetuated by the secondary role she has in fact always played in social and political life within harsh patriarchal systems whose endurance is rivaled only in the Arab world. (For an interesting discussion of the similarities and contrasts between Latin American and Arab women, see Nadia Youssef 1973. Youssef demonstrates that Latin American women are relatively better off than women in the Arab world, since women in many Latin American countries have made significant educational and professional advances, even though formal norms of women's secondary status are maintained; in Muslim countries, she says, women's behavior coincides much more closely with the subservient image. My own data tend to support this thesis, although I think that in making her case Youssef paints too rosy a picture of the Latin American woman's position.)

It is difficult indeed to break a cycle in which the feminine myth and the reality have for centuries nurtured each other. In such an ascriptive system, a woman is judged "successful" not on her individual capabilities and accomplishments as a *person* but on how faithfully she reflects the prevailing image of womanliness. This ideal tells her she will be happy only if she fulfills a complementary and subordinate role in relation to the male. To do so she has internalized norms that establish a division of labor in society, giving males supremacy in assuming work and political roles outside the home, especially at the supervisory levels.

An important clarification in this discussion of woman's image must be stressed: the difference between subordinate or dependent status, and passivity. The ideal of feminine submission in Latin American culture does not mean that women are expected to do *nothing,* as the stereotype often seems to imply. No doubt, many women in Latin America and elsewhere have accepted their subordinate status with resignation and passivity; others, however, have thrown themselves into energetic fulfillment of their assigned roles. As investigators probe more deeply into the social history of Latin America, they are discovering active, innovative, and influential women in every era. So long as they respect the boundaries set for women's "proper" tasks, active women do not violate behavioral norms. The dominant behavioral model in some historical periods has indeed been the passive female (for example, in the Victorian era), a model also exported to Latin America. Moreover, the passive model is necessarily class related; working women never have had the "luxury" of playing such a role, since a certain income level is necessary to maintain a wife in decorative idleness.

In modifying my own somewhat narrow view of the Latin American woman's "passivity" and in coming to understand why unequal relations between the sexes might be maintained because they undergird a system in which both sexes have a stake, I am indebted to insights gained in discussions with and to the research of four scholars in particular: Jane Jaquette (1974 and 1976), Nora Scott Kinzer (1973 and 1974), Steffen Schmidt (1975), and Evelyn P. Stevens (1973a and 1973b).

This effort to dissociate passivity and subordinate status is not a denial that Latin Americans consider abnegation, obedience, and submission to be desirable female virtues. But it would be a mistake to confuse these actions with the behavior denoted by the term "passivity." Servility demands constant awareness and activity; the completely passive slave invites the lash. Inferiors have always had to expend large amounts of energy on the strategy of survival. What W. E. B. Du Bois has called "double consciousness" aptly describes the dependent person's situation: the subordinate must attend to the task in hand but must also remain aware of the master's reactions. June Nash (1975a: 85), with much insight, has applied this idea of binary consciousness (which, she says, is "womanly intuition" by another name) to woman's situation. The woman's glance is, as it were, always directed over her shoulder to gauge how her performance is affecting her superiors.

It is beyond the competence of the author and the boundaries of this study to enter into the long controversy over whether the dominant masculine and subordinate feminine roles in most cultures result from men's and women's distinctive biology and psychology or whether the feminine character simply is itself the product of history and environment. (Simone de Beauvoir [1953] has written the classic work setting forth the latter view, and Judith Bardwick [1971] has reviewed the psychological theories about women's role.) Perhaps we are dealing with nothing more (this is the author's view) than a matter of physical tendencies, culturally reinforced. The question cannot be answered, however, because neither the biological sciences nor psychology have enough evidence to determine whether woman has a "special nature"—and, as Sullerot points out (1971: 244-245), genetics (which may give us some surprises) is still in its infancy and cannot offer any solid clues.

What can be documented, however, are the expectations society holds in relation to women's role in the family, the community, and government, the image of woman that forms the basis for her own as well as the male view of proper womanly behavior.

Traditional ideas on womanly behavior are so decisive that they appear to influence Socialist and Communist women (and their men) almost as strongly as women in general, a fact demonstrated in the responses of leftist women in the questionnaire phase of this study, as well as by observation of their style

of political activity. In spite of abundant socialist rhetoric on the necessity
for complete equality of men and women in building a socialist society, the
Latin American male is macho first and político second; hence he apparently
expects very little shoulder-to-shoulder comradeship from the women of his
party. There are outstanding exceptions, but on the whole the few Communist and Socialist women in public office define their political role in terms
of *respaldo* (backing up) of the male and concentrate on typically feminine
activities within their parties. This is true even though leftist parties in Latin
America do not generally segregate women in separate feminine sections.

Thus, home and family responsibilities typically are put first even by
women of the left in Chile and Peru. Dr. María Elena Carrerra de Corbalán
has been a Socialist from her university days, and in Chile this meant being to
the left of the Communist party. In 1967 her party asked her to run for her
husband's senate seat after his death in an auto accident, and she won it
easily in a by-election. But Dr. Carrerra was very definite about the role of a
revolutionary wife; until that time, she said, she purposely had taken on only
short-term political responsibilities because of her home and profession (she
is a medical doctor): "While my husband lived, I felt I could best make my
contribution to the revolution by backing him up, relieving him of home
responsibilities, making a tranquil atmosphere for him to come home to."

My own survey shows that such attitudes are widespread among Peruvian
and Chilean women, no matter what their political persuasion: home and
family come first, even for professionals who have worked all their lives, and
many believe that the married woman should not work if she does not need
to do so and that most women who work do so from economic necessity.
(Blachman [1973: 7-8] cites several surveys showing that the Brazilian woman
generally agrees that women's entry into work and political roles should be
highly qualified by the sexual division of labor in society.)

If one were required to single out one term to characterize desirable female
behavior in Latin America, it might well be the ideal embodied in the word
decente. Decency is a key concept in any description of desirable womanly
deportment; moreover, it is a word one hears very often not only about
women but about anything that is capable of passing public muster. A house,
a neighborhood, an article of clothing, an occupation, all can be *decente* and
hence deserving of respect.

It will be obvious that the word, in Spanish, means a great deal more than
simply "decent"; it connotes honesty, decorousness and gentility, modesty,
reasonableness, seriousness, appropriateness, even neatness and order! —in
sum, the virtuous and the proper. Probably the most fundamental classifica-
tion a Latin American (whether male or female) makes of women is their
division into *decente* and *no decente.* It is a distinction that cuts across class

lines and determines how one acts toward individual women. A poor, uneducated *pobladora* may come to do the washing in a Chilean home, but if she is *gente decente* she will be treated with respect by the *dueña de casa* (mistress of the house), and she will accept such respect as her due. But a woman who is not considered *decente,* especially if she is of a different race or social class, is considered fair game by a man.

The *mujer decente* (I am speaking here of the image, the myth, and not necessarily of everyday reality) is preeminently the *madre* and *dueña de casa.* Ideally, a girl passes without any detours from the house of her father to the house of her husband, there to fulfill her destiny as the mother of children and the dutiful wife who carefully performs all her domestic tasks with a view toward her husband's comfort and convenience. As Blachman (1973: 5) points out, the importance of the image is not that the majority of women ever lived according to the intricate rules of the patriarchal family, since this ideal was approximated only in the upper and middle classes, but that the patriarchal family was the dominant model of family life.

The *madre* and *dueña,* again in the ideal, is characterized by her submission to her husband's authority and by her abnegation, her resignation in the face of the inevitable sufferings that are the lot of woman in this life. Not the least of these will be her stoical acceptance of the fact that her husband is inclined, in rhetoric if not in practice, to put her on a pedestal: she is *la esposa,* the wife, and must be protected from any hint of dishonor and scandal. Precisely because she is *decente,* the guardian of his hearth and the mother of his children, the wife must also accept the fact that her husband often does not consider her the proper object for his sexual satisfaction. She understands that he will seek to fulfill such needs elsewhere, and she will be expected to accept this behavior as perfectly natural, especially since in the ideal view she herself is too pure to take pleasure in sex. What every woman knows in Latin America is that "los hombres son así"—men are like that. It should be stressed again that living women only approximate the ideal!

The only other kind of woman (aside from the nun) whom a Latin American man generally can envision is the *mujer de mala vida,* the woman of doubtful reputation who somehow has escaped the careful tutelage of priest, father, brother, and husband, and in whom woman's weakness and propensity to evil therefore have been allowed to go unchecked. There seemingly is no alternative, at least at the conceptual level. If a woman is not actively exercising her role as mother and homemaker, or fulfilling her apprenticeship under her father's roof for woman's universal vocation, she must perforce be dedicating herself to a life of immorality and even wild license. Octavio Paz characterizes the Spanish attitude toward woman as "very simple":

It is expressed quite brutally and concisely in these two sayings: "A woman's place is in the home, with a broken leg" and "Between a female saint and a male saint, a wall of mortared stone." Woman is a domesticated wild animal, lecherous and sinful from birth, who must be subdued with a stick and guided by the "reins of religion." [1961: 36]

Thus, other images fill out and complement (and do not basically contradict) the image of the Latin American wife and mother in her submission, self-sacrifice, and purity: the woman as physically and morally weak, as lacking judgment and reason, as prone to evil, as a *peligro*—a danger to herself and to man unless she submits herself to his guidance and authority.

Even today, among the lower classes, a girl often is protected with as much vehemence as in any ancient Islamic harem. Julia Toro Godoy paints this picture of the daughter in the peasant's or fisherman's hut in present-day Chile:

Her brothers, just because they are men, will have over her an authority without limitations. They will oversee every one of her acts, they will censure her conduct, and in some cases they will be permitted to dictate even the way she dresses. In the provinces there are many cases of girls who waste away in a corner of the house, because the brothers don't wish her to go out, much less work outside the home or talk with a man. [1967: 14]

This supervision, traditionally exercised not only by the menfolk but by the mothers of the young, unmarried girls, goes on in more subtle form in the cities. One of my interviewees, with a wide knowledge of the upper and upper-middle classes of Lima, remarked that until the age of eighteen or nineteen, a Peruvian girl often must still ask if she can go out onto the street or into the center of town. "Then her mother will ask, 'Who are you going with? Who is she (or he)? Who is the mother? Do I know her?' If the mother doesn't know the family, she is likely to say, 'I prefer that you not go.'"

Another modern version of purdah: in Lima, and to a lesser degree in Santiago, a single woman—no matter what her age, professional status, and official position—risks her reputation if she lives alone. When one finally has some friends *de confianza* in Peru one learns about an interesting alternative—the "penthouse." Girls joke among themselves that if their families do not let up on the supervision, "I'm going to get my penthouse." This is, of course, not anything so pretentious as the name suggests, but a secret apartment where a girl can decorate to suit her own tastes, keep books and records, and receive trusted friends. But she does not sleep there; she locks up and goes "home" to her father's house, and the existence of the apartment never is revealed to family or relatives. Sometimes friends share the cost.

Recent inquiries suggest that secret apartments are no longer so prevalent, because of the economic conditions.

But the reason more women do not become independent is only partly economic; many are psychologically bound to family. In Santiago, one of the top women in the Frei government, a professional well into her fifties, told me:

> No, I definitely do not think that the Chilean woman is completely emancipated. It is true that she now can study and work at nearly anything, but in herself she is not really free yet. For example, many professionals I know—single women—continue to live at home with their families. We are psychologically bound to them.
>
> I myself am one of these: I live with my mother and aunt. It is often very inconvenient; I end up entertaining my friends and business acquaintances in a *salón de té*. I could afford to have my own place, to live apart from my family. But I do not.

An authoritative corroboration that traditional norms of behavior for women still prevail is the study of women in Chile by the Mattelarts (1968: 59-60). This study shows that, in spite of the modern ideas often enunciated, especially by young professionals and university students, traditional views still lurk very near the surface of the most modern-appearing attitudes. (A later study by the same authors [1970: 133] confirms the fact that old ideas about the mother and spouse still predominate in these groups, although "a small proportion is beginning to be won over by new notions on the relationship between spouses.")

The dominant quality both men and women of all social classes look for in married women (and marriage is confirmed overwhelmingly by the respondents throughout the study as the only appropriate feminine vocation) is that they be "de su casa," that is, dedicated totally to their role of wife and mother.

No ser salidora, that is, not be a gadabout, is a reply that continually emerges in the replies of the lower-class women in the Mattelart study. "Not out in the street amusing herself," "Busy herself only with her house, her husband and children," "Stay at home"—such is the program for the married woman outlined by the country women, the wives of workers, and the wives of fishermen.

Women of the upper classes, though certainly not physically confined to the home, express notions of wifely duty in their own terms in the study: to be well organized, to save and to budget. The overriding ideal is identical among women of all social classes. "Ser buena madre," "Ser buena esposa"— to be a good wife and mother. They join, say the Mattelarts (1968: 60), in "a universal language that erases class differences" to affirm that the married woman's major concern should be to behave well and be attentive to her husband and to help him. In the lower classes, the notion that the woman ought to respect her husband is much emphasized.

In another part of their study, the Mattelarts (1968: 72-75) query men about their ideas on man's authority in the home. There are strong tendencies among all social classes for men to declare in theory that authority in the home ought to be shared between husband and wife, ranging from 75 to 80 percent in the lower rural classes to about one-half the urban men (although—probably because they are the most traditional—90 percent of the men of the upper class think the man should be boss in the home).

However, when actual behavior is investigated, in this case management of the family finances and participation in decisions on how the family budget will be spent, the man emerges overwhelmingly as the decision-maker. In all social classes, women generally make decisions on daily expenditures; however, when it comes to important purchases of furniture or equipment, payment of income taxes, rent and home maintenance outlay, and funds for vacation and amusement, then the man decides, often without consulting his wife. Because traditional images of women actually still prevail, there is a lack of congruence between what the more modern sector declares ideal and its actual conduct. Thus "in principle the man admits that the woman may work, but not that his own wife exercise a profession. The woman, for her part, will agree on the necessity of a professional integration for the feminine sex, but nevertheless the only aspiration she will have for her own daughter will be matrimony" (Mattelarts 1968: 19).

Moving from the home to the public arena, the Mattelarts (19-22) show how overemphasis on the role of wife and mother seriously limits women's contribution to and integration in modern society. Men and women of all social groups in Chile believe a woman may become a doctor because women have an innate sympathy for suffering humanity (but they should specialize in obstetrics or gynecology). Dentistry is appropriate for women because they can have their offices in their homes and oversee the care of house and children. Architecture is a good career for women because they have an inborn understanding of housing. My own survey shows similar beliefs in relation to women officials in government: they are appropriate only if they concentrate their energies on administration and legislation related to health, education, social welfare of women and children, or the arts and culture. Even women who handle budgets and expenditures in government often say they have been appointed to these "neutral" posts (in the sense that they are not stereotyped as either masculine or feminine) because women have had much experience in keeping household accounts and because "women are more honest than men."

Evelyn P. Stevens links male dominance in the political sphere to the cult of machismo and the subordinate image of woman. Not only in Mexico but in other parts of Latin America, politics is considered to be the business of men:

> This is not to say that women do not participate in political activity; a small number of them do, but they are the exception rather than the rule. . . . In the main, politics remains a "man's world" and male values are regarded as appropriate. Role expectations in politics, as in other spheres of action, require that a man must get his own way; he may brook no opposition nor share his power with anyone else. To do so would be to show traits of femininity, of submissiveness and of passivity. [1965: 849]

The Latin American male is not now so overtly opposed as formerly when he encounters women in public office. However, formal acquiescence to female collaboration in theory does not necessarily mean that the individual Latin man would approve of his own wife's participation. María Correa Morandé, who was in the Chilean congress in 1957-1961 and remained active politically for many years, remarked that the majority of men look with a "great deal of sympathy on the participation of women in politics—always supposing that their own wives are not involved." This attitude, she continued, puts women in a dilemma because "they must choose between giving full satisfaction to their desire to participate . . . and the generous renunciation of political responsibility so that they will not compromise the harmony of their home."

The Image of Woman: Religious Sources

Sources of the prevailing images of woman in Latin America are well worth investigating in some detail not only for their intrinsic interest but because only by understanding where the ideas about women originate will we be able to estimate their power to influence the behavior of present and future generations.

Images and their sources vary, of course, from region to region and among classes. Because this study focuses on the educated, middle-class woman and her role in government, those influences operating among the educated classes will be emphasized. The similarity in culture, outlook, and taste of the Latin American educated classes—who are said to differ more markedly from the *pueblo* of their own countries than among themselves—often has been noted. Sources and examples from Peru and Chile will be emphasized whenever they are available.

The principal influence forming the image of woman may have been the reactionary Roman Catholic Christianity found in Latin American countries that baptized and confirmed Greek ideas of male supremacy. This groundwork laid, later philosophical movements not much more sympathetic to woman re-enforced the image, while all through Latin American history, literature contributed powerfully to the feminine myth of women's inferiority and unfitness for a role in social and political life. Only the first and last of these sources will be explored here.

The earliest influence delineating woman's role in Latin America may well have been Scholastic philosophy. Spain had imposed Scholasticism throughout her colonies as the one official philosophy; although challenged, it remained powerful for generations after the influence of the Schoolmen in Europe had waned through the assaults of the Renaissance and the Reformation. At the dawn of independence, throughout Latin America there were, of course, movements inspired by the revolutionary ideas of eighteenth-century rationalism and the French revolution. But many historians doubt the deep or lasting impact of these ideas outside the limited circles of those who led the political emancipation movements. Moreover, as Simon Collier (1967: 361) has pointed out, it now is a "gigantic commonplace" to say that the Latin American revolutions for independence were mainly political in character and "clearly were not social revolution in the sense that the French and Russian revolutions were."

One powerful reason for the limited effects of 1789 and 1848 on the culture and society of Latin America is the fact that most universities began as theological seminaries. One estimate (Diffie 1967: 549) puts the number of degrees granted throughout Latin America in the first three centuries after settlement at 150,000, "the vast majority in theology." Whether founded by the crown or the church, all the universities remained under the powerful influence of the proponents of the Thomist theological and philosophical system. As Diffie points out, the Scholastics avoided the application of Newtonism to religion, economics, and society, and the philosophers who did so—Voltaire, Locke, Diderot, Montesquieu, and Rousseau—were anathematized. Contemporary students of education in Latin America emphasize that the influence of the Schoolmen remained strong until very recent times.

What predominates in the Scholastic pronouncements about women is the certainty of her inferiority to the male. Thomas Aquinas and Bonaventure, the most famous Schoolmen of the thirteenth century, were alike in basing their views on the mistaken biology of Aristotle, who viewed the woman as a deformed or "stunted male" (Smith and Ross, eds. 1912: Book II.3, 737[a] 27). In the Aristotelian view, if everything went well during generation, the resulting child would be male; if something went wrong, then a daughter would be the unfortunate result. Neither Aristotle nor the Schoolmen knew anything of the ovum, and they believed the male seed was the active life principle. The woman indeed was needed in generation, but her contribution was passive, nutritive, vegetative. She provided only the material component, the receptacle for life. Thomas (citing Aristotle) minces no words in describing the inferior nature of woman:

> As regards the individual nature, woman is defective and misbegotten, for the active force in the male seed tends to the production of a perfect likeness in the masculine sex; while the production of woman comes from the defect in the active force or from some material indisposition, or even from some external influence; such as that of a south wind, which is moist, as the Philosopher observes. [*Summa Theologica*, I, q.92, a. 1]

The Schoolmen thus believed that a daughter was an inferior being, a living demonstration of her father's lack of vital capacity, and it is striking how this image of woman has lived on to this day in Latin American culture. This view of an exclusively male role in generation may explain, in part, the psychology of the macho. If woman is only the receptacle for the male's life-giving force, then women have less to "prove" in the sexual sphere and less ego involvement in producing a large family. Once they have proved their fecundity by producing a firstborn, women by and large remain fertile until menopause. The man, on the contrary, affirms his more fragile virility in an unmistakeable way with each child he generates.

Bonaventure agrees with Thomas that the formation of Eve from Adam's rib is in perfect keeping with the nature of man, who "excels woman in dignity of origin, in power to act, and in authority to govern" (Healy 1956: 13). The Seraphic doctor, whose influence was widespread in medieval Spain, goes so far as to declare that the image of God is less distinct in woman because man is virile and strong, woman weak and frail. Man's biological superiority thus has an influence on his intelligence. There are two functions or faculties of the intellect; the superior faculty directs the soul toward God and higher things (the *superior portio rationis*); this faculty is virile, masculine, and predominant in the male. The inferior reason turns the intellect toward external and changeable sense objects; inferior reason therefore is effeminate and imperfect, predominating in the female sex (Healy 1956: 22-23). This duality comes very close to the Greek ideas from which the Scholastics took their major inspiration.

Among the practical consequences of these views, according to the Schoolmen, is the ability of the man to grasp abstract ideas more readily, while woman clings to the concrete and the personal. And since the world of the senses is by definition lower and carnal, woman also is weaker and more inclined to evil than man. All this has a direct bearing on the teaching of theologians that man fell into original sin through Eve, that Eve's sin therefore was greater than Adam's, and that woman ever since has been, on the whole, a source of sin, evil, and misfortune to man.

What is to the point here is the fact that the Schoolmen's views were not only set forth in their philosophic purity in the universities but also widely disseminated at the popular level. For the uneducated there were sermons and cathechism lessons, and for all the demonstration effect of woman's second-class status in both church and school. As family expert Virginia Gutiérrez de Pineda (1963: 156) points out, for generations throughout Latin America the catechism has admonished the woman "that her principal work should be *in the house,* and that of her husband should be in the fields and outside the house."

In the Catholic view, the duties of wife and mother have always been related to the work of Mary at Nazareth. Until recent times, girls were told by their teachers and pious female relatives to pattern themselves after the silent, modest Virgin, who for thirty years made a home for her Son and only once ever questioned his strange mission or her own role in it.

It is true that in Catholic theology Mary becomes Queen of Heaven after her work on earth is completed. Yet it would be a mistake to suppose that this position gives her any authority in her own right. Her major work is defined not as that of ruler but as "intercessor." As Virgin, untouched by man, she is considered fit to intercede for sinful mankind and turn away the wrath of a just God. As Mother, she is thought to have special influence over her Son, who also is God in the Catholic scheme. Always emphasized as virtues are her submission and her unquestioning surrender to "God's plan" as announced by the angel in the biblical account (in Catholic theology the conception of Christ takes place at this moment of blind acquiescence to the unknown future).

Nor has the Catholic church, still an influence to be reckoned with, ever really changed its ideas on the differential role of men and women. Now it generally couches its teachings in more courteous language than that of Thomas and Bonaventure: "Man is the head, woman the heart of the home" is perhaps the most widespread Catholic cliché. Most Catholic pronouncements on woman deplore the attitude of Thomas and scold him for his "curious blind spot" concerning woman. They admit that woman is equal to man in her human nature, in her sharing in the redemptive merits of Christ, and thus in her eternal destiny. But they insist that woman is not to be considered identical to man, her characteristics being different and complementary to his so that she can be "his companion and helpmate." The popes stress that woman's place should be in the home, that "the sphere of woman, her manner of life, her native bent is motherhood" (Faherty 1950: 169-170).

As late as 1930, the encyclical letter of Pius XI on Christian Marriage (Werth and Mihanovich, eds. 1955: 42), widely disseminated through the Catholic world at a time when the generation of educated Latin Americans now in power were forming their ideas, strongly reaffirmed the married woman's home duties as her exclusive occupation and roundly condemned what it termed the three-fold emancipation of woman: first, the physiological, by which "the woman is to be freed at her own good pleasure from the burdensome duties properly belonging to a wife as companion and mother" by "the prevention or suppression of offspring," condemned as "not an emancipation but a crime"; second, the economic, which "gives woman the power to conduct her affairs quite independently"; third, the social, by which "the wife being freed from the cares of children and family, should, to the neglect of these, be able to follow her own bent and devote herself to business and even public affairs."

These attitudes were somewhat counteracted by the allocutions of Pius XII (ibid. 1955: 135-136) in the late 1940s and early 1950s on the duties of women in public life, influencing this generation of women leaders—among them, a number of my own interviewees. But these pronouncements envision for woman a role directed exclusively toward a "feminine" politics—improving the conditions of the family, the woman, and the child—rather than participation in public affairs according to each woman's personal competence and training. Most recently, the Second Vatican Council made no specific mention of women at all, and only toward the end of the second session were a few women (most of them nuns) finally allowed to attend the meetings as non-participant observers.

Religious instruction is optional in the public schools of Latin America today, but current textbooks approved for use in the schools faithfully reflect the same images of woman as the encyclicals and the popular catechism. One secular text designed for the seventh year, when all students in Chile study the family, society, and government, does point out that many women today are employed outside the home and pictures one woman, a nurse, among the 112 illustrations of people at work. No text shows any other woman engaged in any occupation except domestic tasks. Even the sales clerks and teachers are pictured as male. *Regidores* (local elected officials in the municipalities, many of whom are in fact women) are males. National leaders are males (cf. Godoy Urzúa 1971 and Valenzuela and Haeberle n.d.).

Literary Images of Women

Robert E. Lane (1959: 212) has suggested how powerful the literary heritage of a nation is in defining woman's role as nonpolitical. The classics, "reread by every generation," he says, create images of woman in domestic, or perhaps artistic and literary, or even career roles—but never in political positions. Nor, he says, is television, radio soap opera, or other entertainment any better. Thus "there is little reinforcement for the image of 'political woman' in this area."

As early as the sixteenth and seventeenth centuries, the Hispanic new world possessed in abundance the epic of the Cid, the novels of chivalry, and the pastoral poetry and novels of the Golden Age, as well as the plays of Lope and Calderón. Lima and Mexico City, especially, were centers of culture with leisure and money enough to indulge in a wide variety of reading. Amadís de Gaula and his descendants—the knights Esplandián, Amadís, and Lisuarte de Grecia—led in popularity the tales of *caballería*. The *Diana* of Jorge de Montemayor was the pastoral novel most often shipped to the colonies, so loaded down with references to Greek mythology that only a specialist could unravel them all. (See Leonard 1964, especially chapter 9 on favorite fiction and chapters 13 and 14 on the book trade.)

Spanish literature, in common with the continental, whose main currents it eventually takes up and occasionally inspires, for many centuries saw women only in two dimensions: the noble lady (occasionally a nun), impossibly idealized and remote, the object most often only of platonic love; and the common woman, destined to satisfy man's physical desires. In both cases, the woman remains passive; it is the man who ventures forth, carries out brave deeds, and returns to his waiting love.

Modern literary scholars speculate that the platonic love ideal had its origin in eleventh-century Spanish Arab poetry. If so, the ideal of an exalted, exaggerated, and (on the part of the woman) passionless purity, not unlike the standard set for the "good" woman today, has roots that go deep into the Spanish soul. Gerald Brenan (1957: 26), in his definitive history of Spanish literature, makes a good case for the theory that the theme of courtly love, first diffused by the Provençal poets and later taken up by Dante and Petrarch, came to southern France from Moslem Spain. "Laura and Beatrice, Angelica and Una," he says, "first combed their hair on the banks of the . . . Guadalquivir." Brenan and Sánchez-Albornoz (1960: I, 390) both point out that such an idea of love would fit the customs of peoples among whom the sexes did not mix and woman was restricted by the harem and the veil.

The Latin tradition of *caballería,* celebrated in the chivalric and pastoral novels and in romantic poetry, is intimately linked to the cult of the Virgin Mary. The pure love and respectful treatment the knight gave his lady were directly related to the love and respect he was also supposed to have for Mary.

Indeed, when the knight did not have a special lady, he could dedicate himself and his deeds to the Virgin.

It sometimes is argued that the chivalric code and its diffusion through literature may have tempered the harsh view of woman and sex engendered by the Church. Still, the bloodless lady on the pedestal is no more involved than Eve's weak daughters in the affairs of society. As Moll (1967: 101) remarks, the courtly love ideal "which removes woman from the companionship we demand today is just as much removed from what society needs as is woman seen by Tertullian as the 'gate of hell.'"

The chivalric ideal was revived in the great dramas of Spain's Golden Age, especially by Calderón. The image of woman remains generally the same; in the classic Spanish theater, as Martínez Estrada (1942: 178) points out, the women are generally of two types, "wives who play the part of mistresses and maidens of brutal virtue." As he also notes, the distorted image of woman is heightened by the nearly complete absence of mothers and children from the artificial, highly contrived Spanish drama formula. The figure of don Juan, originating in the play *El burlador de Sevilla* by Tirso de Molina and revived in what probably is Spain's most famous drama, Zorrilla's *Don Juan Tenorio,* has in the several hundred years since their first stagings epitomized in the starkest fashion the images of the male as conquering macho and the female as sacrificial victim.

Images are conveyed not only in the classics but also in contemporary fiction and the popular press, as well as by movies, radio, and television—and through that interesting invention, the *fotonovela,* which uses posed photographs in sequence to tell a story in terms simple enough for those with low reading skills. Jaquette (1973: 4) observes that the few female characters in contemporary Peruvian fiction (the relative absence of female characters in Peruvian literature is itself, she thinks, an interesting commentary on the position of women in Peruvian society) are used as symbols of nature or the indigenous culture or as stereotypes. She discerns three recurring images that, she says, represent the female role alternatives in Latin American society: woman as Mother, "Witch," or Wife/Concubine.

Cornelia Butler Flora (1973) and Michèle Mattelart (1970) both have done content analyses of women's magazine fiction, demonstrating, as Jaquette suggests, that the media not only mirrors traditional role images but also socializes women into their roles. In 202 randomly-selected short stories of Mexico and Colombia, Flora found few females actively controlling their own lives. There were only a small number of women in public roles, and male authority was accepted and reenforced. Flora thinks the consequences for society are negative if such images are the only models presented to women. "Until woman can begin to act on her own life," she says, "her major societal efforts will be toward maximizing short term security and maintaining the status quo." Jorge Amado's lusty heroines are much more in control of their destinies, but still find their greatest fulfillment in their lovers' arms.

There is also the tendency of males, whatever their political ideology, to define woman in terms of the "hot chick"—the chorus girl of the Bim Bam Bum (a burlesque house in Santiago)—as Vania Bambirra (1971: 7-8), a Marxist analyst, has observed. She accused the leftist press in particular of systematically diffusing the symbol of the "mujer-objeto," the woman as sex object, and pointed to the persistence of traditional institutions and values in relation to woman that, she says, leftist organizations were not in fact even worried about, much less making any effort to overcome them through the communications media they control.

The most casual perusal of the leftist press confirms Bambirra's contentions. Illustrated comic books, published by Unidad Popular in Chile (particularly *La Firme*), pictured leggy women militants, their exaggerated breasts encased in tight sweaters, and wearing the briefest of skirts. Leftist publications routinely carried cheesecake; this reached truly grotesque levels as in an issue of a leftist youth magazine, *Ramona* (1972), printed at Editorial Quimantú, the Allende government's publishing house, and listing males as both director and editor. This particular issue proclaimed 1972 as the "decisive year of the woman" and illustrated the theme with a photo of a shapely, naked girl draped in the Chilean flag.

Even well-intentioned efforts to give women a positive view of themselves founder on the stereotype. During the Allende years, Quimantú published a generally excellent collection, "We Chileans," to acquaint the Chilean people with their culture and heritage. The volume on the Chilean woman (Puz 1972), however, deviated hardly at all from the image of woman as trivial and dependent, yet instinctively the self-sacrificing and heroic mother. The picture painted demonstrates in stark fashion how the traditional image of woman persists even in the most politically and socially advanced sectors of Latin American society.

The Chilean woman, we are told (p. 5), is attached to the place where she lives because she loves "the sure, the perennial"; she "lacks the adventurous and nomadic spirit of the man who one day burrows down into the mine and the next casts forth his fishing nets." We also learn (p. 11) that the Chilean woman likes "the big drama of Mexican films, songs that talk of lost loves, lachrymose love novels, the troubles of other people," as well as "talking about illnesses, 'Simplemente María' [a soap opera], and the stories lived by the heroines in the women's magazines." Chilean women are "incorrigibly romantic," and are "always ready to fall in love, again and again; for them, love is the fundamental, primary thing." But the Chilena "never reasons out the selection of her mate"; rather, "she is guided by hunches and . . . gives herself completely without demanding any guarantees." Nor is there any woman who can resist "prophesies, palmists, card readers, mind readers, and all types of love sorceries" (p. 36).

Yet, paradoxically, this silly creature is, more than anything else, a mother:

Self-sacrifice for her children characterizes the woman of all social groups. In the poor *población*, in the peasant *rancho*, in the mining camp, in the residences of the *barrio alto* [the upper class districts], the Chilena-Madre puts the happiness of her children before her own. The house, her husband, her friends, her social life, her personal fulfillment, everything else comes afterwards. [P. 51]

This characterization of woman as sacrificial mother sums up what Latin Americans consider the most positive aspect of the image of woman. Yet the picture drawn so far would be one-sided if the description ended here. The dependent, subordinate, and sacrificial mother has an alter ego. It is to the positive aspects of the mother-figure that we now turn in order to round out the model of the ideal woman in Latin America.

The Heroic Mother and the Boundaries of Her Influence

The situation of the Latin American woman has many facets. For example, the position of legal wife (unlike that of married women in societies where wives are bought as chattel) is an honorable estate in the middle and upper classes, and the home is considered sacred. Men, especially of the older generation, were taught to look upon their wives and mothers almost literally as "other Marys," and if they pursued active sexual lives, they did so outside the holy marriage bed. Women in a curious way appear to gain from what Stevens (1973a: 91) has named "*machismo's* other face, *marianismo.*" That is, women gain power to influence and manipulate through "the cult of female spiritual superiority which teaches that women are semi-divine, morally superior to and spiritually stronger than men." Jane Jaquette (1973: 5) goes so far as to assert that women have an important stake in maintaining the status quo since machismo and traditional role differentiations are functional for *both* women and men. "Male 'immorality,'" she says, "is basic to female legitimacy and influence."

Despite the limitations on woman's role outside the home, then, it will be evident from the foregoing discussion that something more remains to be said on the very complex subject of the image of the Latin American woman and her role. Paradoxically, Peruvian and Chilean women sometimes wield formidable power within certain restricted spheres, principally behind the high walls and closed doors that guard the sacred and private family circle.

Such a contention is difficult to document, however, because woman's ascendancy, where it exists, is so subtle and hidden, and because formally and publicly the superiority of the male almost always is maintained. The Mattelart study suffers somewhat because a questionnaire cannot get at this reality, and women come out looking uniformly oppressed. As anyone who truly knows the reality will attest, however, women in Latin America are not completely powerless. They know how to "defend themselves," as they put it, within certain well-defined limits. What is important to note are these *boundaries.*

Many times I have watched in admiration as an experienced Latin woman got around her menfolk. Rarely does she oppose a husband or a grown son openly. She may even appear to go along on an issue that she has not the least intention of agreeing to in the end. With patience and silence, with stubbornness and charm, she subtly leads the man to another opinion while letting him believe it was he alone who reconsidered the matter and changed his mind. Latin American women know very well how to win these kinds of battles. They wait and keep silent, and then they let the generals claim all the medals. As Chester Hunt (1965: 417) remarks about the Filipinas, they conspire to maintain the formal superiority of men while in actual fact women in the Philippines now often enjoy real authority and power, even in the public arena.

A Latin man will generally not carry a baby or push a baby carriage in public; he will not allow a woman to drive if he is in the car—"Por qué soy yo hombre? " (Why am I a man?). He will not bestir himself to remove a plate from the table or to serve the coffee if the maid is having her night out. The women give in gracefully on these issues because they believe the real terrain of battle is elsewhere and they do not like to waste ammunition. For example, as Amanda Labarca (1952: 12) notes, it is often the woman who selects the schools for both daughters and sons.

As a woman grows older, her prestige increases. Especially in the middle and upper classes, there are cases of veritable matriarchs who preside over the extended family with a certain degree of despotism. Some widows retain control and management of the family business or fortune. The respect and attentiveness accorded to older women by husbands and sons alike would astonish many a North American grandmother. Married sons and daughters long removed from the maternal roof would not dream of making a major decision in their own lives without consulting *la mamá.* Nor will a single major holiday, or the mother's birthday (or in Chile, saint's day), pass without all the sons and daughters coming, with their children, to greet the old mother.

Certainly much of this "consulting" has a ritualistic quality, and many old matriarchs possess no power to sanction courses of action already decided on. But there is no doubt that some exercise real authority. Determined opposition from a mother will sometimes cause a decision to be modified or a project to be dropped altogether—or perhaps postponed until the old mother dies.

In another context, no one who reads of the salons, or *tertulias,* literary and political alike, in which women of earlier times played a prominent part can doubt that women have had a certain power and influence not confined to home and family affairs. As Tamayo Vargas (1965: II, 523) notes, the *tertulia* provided woman an opportunity to take part in cultural and educational activity while "maintaining appearances and not offending against the norm"; she "complied with the custom of 'puertas adentro,'" he says, a phrase meaning withindoors. A woman belongs in the house and the only doors she opens are those within her own home; she does not touch the outside doors that lead to the street. There is an old Spanish saying that puts the matter succinctly: "La mujer en la casa, el hombre en la calle"—woman in the house, man in the street. In days gone by, this was literal. Today, of course, the doors are symbolic, but the tradition of public affairs as man's exclusive domain remains strong.

Because these matters are so subtle and so difficult to measure scientifically, it becomes difficult indeed for a foreign observer to judge the extent of female influence. Outsiders do not always catch the nuances. They do not realize when deference accorded a woman is mere form. In many cases they do not understand the significance of the doors, the boundaries. They imagine that women who are so patently in charge of certain areas of life must be highly emancipated in all. For example, two very intelligent North American social scientists (both of whom, however, know Latin America only superficially) declared that my study of women made no sense because in Chile, in any case, women were doctors, lawyers, congresswomen, and journalists and were "completely emancipated." But *90 percent* of my 167 interviewees among women leaders do not agree with them!

Yet the intervention of the revered mother figure in certain spheres gives some women undeniable power to manipulate and coerce (if rarely officially), a power that they and society, paradoxically, recognize and respect. When women do break out of the normal boundaries set by the ideal image, they do so most successfully when they emphasize the positive aspects of the womanly image depicted here. Ximena Bunster, Chilean anthropologist, says that women in her country approach their professional and public roles in a style quite different from what she perceives as the North American woman's attitude:

What happens is that we extend matrimonial roles to work. . . . We tend to treat the man as a mother would, and not as if he were the husband, the lover, or the colleague. The Chilean is a *mamá* who approves, sanctions, corrects, quite different from the North American environment where professional relations are marked by the sense of competition. [Quoted in Vexler 1968: 40]

Latin American women's first ventures into public life followed this pattern, and the next two chapters document how women ventured into the public arena in the guise of the supermadre: understanding the revered mother-image and recognizing how to use it.

3. Women in Public Life: Precursors of the Emancipation Movement

In Latin America, in keeping with the traditional boundaries set for women, feminine political activity most often has been indirect and tangential, a re-enforcement of the masculine struggle. Few women have acted on their own; almost all notable women were wives, mistresses, or daughters of notable men involved in the public affairs of their day—or occasionally sisters, as in the cases of such diverse women as Javiera Carrera, Chile's formidable "woman of iron," as Francisco Encina (1954: I, 526-527) calls her, who left husband, children, and aged parents to accompany her brother on his military campaigns, or Irene Frei, former Chilean President Eduardo Frei's closest political associate until her death in an automobile accident. It is by now common-place to observe that most women prominent in political life—and not only in Latin America—are related to male politicians (see Schmidt 1975: 468). Jahan (1976) suggests that women leaders emerge only in "oligarchical politics," linked to family and kin networks.

Only the present generation (and only in certain sectors of society) has seen progress toward a more autonomous role for women in public life. As Rosa Signorelli de Marti (1967: 194) observes in her study of Spanish American women, the world wars that profoundly altered women's situation in the United States and many European nations had only slight and indirect effects in South America. Sánchez's observation (1963, II: 176) about the duality of nineteenth-century Latin American life—cosmopolitan in the street, traditional in the house—also holds good in many respects to the present day.

Yet women with aspirations to liberate themselves began to appear in the last century. It is to these precursors of emancipation that we first turn; after that, the development of women's educational opportunities from these beginnings will be traced, as well as the evolution of their intervention in the world of work and professions. All this is necessary background for a discussion of the Latin American suffrage movement proper, which is reserved to chapter 4.

The first women actively interested in women's rights were markedly different types in Peru and Chile. In the first country the precursors of emancipation were, with few exceptions, novelists and poets, whereas in Chile woman's emancipation from its beginnings in the 1870s was tied to the entrance of women into higher education and the professions. In both countries the most successful women carefully maintained the boundaries set by woman's universal mothering role and legitimized their activities as forming natural extensions of it. When they overstepped the boundaries, as we shall see in the two following chapters, they paid dearly for doing so.

The sharp difference between women's early activity in Peru and Chile may account, at least in part, for the significantly greater progress Chilean women later made in public life. At the time the first women medical doctors were receiving their degrees in Chile, Peruvian women had not yet emerged from the privacy of the salon. There, however, through a revival of the *tertulia,* they began to participate in shaping ideas of social and political renovation.

Women of the Salons: Precursors of Modernity in Peru

In Peru, new ideas about women's emancipation were first articulated in the 1870s by a remarkable group of women writers. Literary and journalistic endeavors were the first professions open to women because they could be carried out within the house. These Peruvians contributed significantly to the literary and political developments of their day, not only through their writings but also through a revival (in the 1870s and 1880s) of the *tertulia,* which had existed in creole society a hundred years earlier, often as a "cover" for revolutionary plotting.

The *tertulia* (or *salón* or *velada,* as it also is called in Latin America) deserves more detailed comment. The large literature, particularly on the Argentine and Peruvian salons, gives evidence that the *tertulia* provided the only opportunity Latin American women have ever enjoyed for intellectual exchange on an organized basis with men who were shaping the destinies of their countries. Never before nor since have women been so closely identified with the national destiny, not even in today's political parties, where women are segregated in their own divisions and have little contact with men, except for the "token" woman on the national executive council. When women began working for political emancipation, they formed groups consisting exclusively of women; many also trained for "feminine" careers, further isolating themselves from the centers of political power.

The revival of the *tertulia* in Peru meant that women were again exposed to political ideas because, as so often in Peru's history, the literary and political movements of the time engaged the same people (Tamayo Vargas 1965:

II, 520-523). In this second flowering of the *tertulia,* there was no parallel activity in Chile, where, as Vicente Grez remarks (1966: 113), "no great literary figures existed among women."

The "woman problem" was only one among the many social and political concerns that engaged them. They also talked and wrote about the plight of the Indian and the peasant, the corruption of political leaders, the indifference of the landowning class and of the church. Manuel Cuadros (1949: 142-143) records the participants and themes of the series of *tertulias* held in Lima in the late 1880s, presided over or attended by these "literary women." The most prominent male literary and political figures of the day came to discuss the Peruvian novel, the abandoned and suffering Indian, the novels of Flaubert, Zola, and Fernán Caballero. Meeting every two weeks, the evenings would draw up to fifty participants: thirty men and twenty women.

Most of the women involved were of the upper class and had little personal contact with the poor and oppressed. In their literary efforts, they were greatly influenced by *costumbrismo,* the fashionable literary current of their times, and in keeping with the general spirit of romanticism they tended to moralize on the evil landowners and on the innocent charm of Indian life rather than to focus on specific programs for social reform. Nevertheless, theirs were upsetting and radical ideas for those days, and some of the women were perceived as overstepping all bounds of propriety. They became the object of popular derision and the butt of cruel verses and cartoons in an "environment hostile to women's education and which had for them only judgment and suspicion" (Tamayo Vargas 1965: II, 537). Several were exiled for their association with liberal politics in the repressive era of Piérola.

In such an atmosphere, the women were prevented from exercising much immediate influence on their female contemporaries, and they never succeeded in launching any significant social or feminist movements. Nevertheless, the women of the Amauta group around José Carlos Mariátegui were their direct heirs, and these women in turn had a share in unleashing the ideas that in the next generation were to become embodied in the Aprista party with its programs for integration of the Indian and other social and economic reforms.

Not all these women can be introduced here. However, a sketch of the lives and activities of two outstanding women of the last century in Peru, Clorinda Matto and Mercedes Cabello, will give at least some idea of what this group of women contributed to the political and social movements of their day and to those that followed.

Clorinda Matto de Turner presents, as Juan Gonzalo Rose (1968: 138) characterizes her, "the incredible case of a woman who initiated the novel of social and realistic tendency in Latin America and, at the same time, contributed to the founding of the novelistic form in Peru."

Women's rights was only one of Clorinda's many interests, as *Cuadros* documents (1949: 112-113). Her principal social theme is the exploitation of the Indian by the great landowners with the connivance of the corrupt government and church officials, whom she pictures as conspiring to keep the indigenous population in subjection. She managed a farm at Tinta (near Cuzco), and thus was the only woman in her circle who knew conditions in the sierra at first-hand. Two of her novels have churchmen as principal villains. In *Aves sin nido* (1889, published in English in 1968), a future bishop, while he is curate of Kíllac, fathers two children, one of whom is placed in a poor Indian home, the other with the wife of the governor. As young adults, they meet and fall in love, not realizing they are brother and sister. Clorinda uses this device to show the bitter life of the Indians, but her prescriptions for their incorporation into national life lack any revolutionary content. Her main formula is books and schools. She was much ahead of her time, however, in her other recommendation—marriage for the clergy. When one notes the date of this novel (1889), one understands why Clorinda earned for her outspokenness the antipathy of many powerful people, especially among the *gamonales serranos* (landholders of the sierra), whom she attacked. Ciro Alegría (1967) criticizes Clorinda for blaming the "famous trinity" (the landowners, the government, and the church) for "a problem which actually is social and economic"; nevertheless, he says, her novel deserves much praise because it was written and published "with nobility and courage in the midst of an epoch in which to accuse the oppressors of the Indian was a delirium . . . always bringing on unfortunate consequences to the authors." The novel was translated into many languages and recently was reissued in Spanish.

A native of Cuzco, Clorinda came to notice when she began to write her *Tradiciones cuzqueñas* in the style of Ricardo Palma's famous *Tradiciones peruanas*. In the late 1870s, on a visit to Lima, she participated in the *tertulias* of novelist Juana Manuela Gorriti, where discussions ranged from the romantic poets and Wagner to modern philosophy and socialism (Cuadros 1949: 139-140). In 1887, after moving permanently to Lima as a young widow, Clorinda began presiding over her own *veladas*, which brought together the literary figures of the day. Many were members of the Ateneo de Lima, dominated by the figure of Manuel González Prada, and of the Círculo de Literatura, whose members fostered the first stirrings of Peruvian radicalism (Tamayo Vargas 1965: II, 523).

At Clorinda's, Tamayo Vargas tells us, the talk most often turned on how a nation could be formed that would include not only Lima but the wild mixture of tiny, unnumbered communities scattered along the desert coast and through the high sierra valleys, the haciendas covering thousands of miles, the Amazon jungles rich in unknown woods and minerals and "savage" peoples.

Many of the discussions took on a definite political character. The War of the Pacific had just been concluded, and the Chileans had returned home after occupying Lima for three years. The intellectuals of the postwar period, says Cuadros, gathered at the home of the young widow "to talk about leaving behind them the rancorous and fruitless internal divisions, and to organize a group to work for the realization of national aspirations" (Cuadros 1949: 141). This was the era of bitter struggle between the militarist and civilist factions in Peruvian politics, and a small group of radical insurgents from the Ateneo and Círculo joined with González Prada to found the Party for National Union. This movement, though too theoretical to have much practical effect on politics, nevertheless strongly influenced two future Peruvian reformers: Mariátegui and Haya de la Torre (Owens 1963: 51).

Late in 1889, Clorinda became editor of *El Perú Ilustrado,* a periodical closely linked to both the political and the literary movements of her day. In the revolution of 1895, she was forced to flee to Argentina as the Piero-listas attacked her home and destroyed the commercial press she ran with her brothers (Matto de Turner 1902: ch. I).

Contemporary with Clorinda Matto de Turner—and sharing the honors of inaugurating the realistic novel in Peru—was Mercedes Cabello de Carbonero. Her novels were centered in Lima rather than in the sierra and dealt with the decadence of the upper class. Her last work, *El conspirador* (1892), is a polit-ical novel that, in the judgment of Tamayo Vargas (1940: 61), perfectly captures the politicking tradition of Peru. Mercedes Cabello was a regular participant in the *veladas* of Juana Goritti and of Clorinda Matto, and stored up a great deal of political shoptalk. Tamayo Vargas notes a Mexican critic's appraisal of this novel:

> Not admiration but surprise is the reaction I feel in contemplating that a woman shows such an exact, highly developed sense for political questions. No masculine pen has better characterized this dangerous social element constituted by the ambitious, vain and egoistic public man. [Tamayo Vargas 1940: 69]

In the *veladas* she once gave the results of a "comparative study" she had made on intelligence and beauty in women; on another occasion she lectured on the improvement of women's education and social condition (ibid.: 30).

In spite of these distinguished women of letters, however, women's admis-sion to the university in Peru was delayed; as late as 1907, one of my inter-viewees recalled, her aunt, "the sister of the then-Rector [president] of the University of Cuzco, received her degree, to the consternation of the townspeople, who, on occasion, threw holy water as she passed." On the educational opportunities of other women in the Americas, we know little as yet, but see JoAnn Aviel (1974), Nora Scott Kinzer (1973), Vivian Mota (1974), Heleieth Saffioti (1969b), and Steffen Schmidt (1974) for information on women's education in Costa Rica, Argentina, the Dominican Republic, Brazil, and Colombia. In the next section we look at the situation in Chile.

Precursors of Emancipation in Chile: The Educators

During the three centuries of the colonial period, secondary education in Chile, as in the rest of Latin America, had been reserved for boys, usually in *liceos* and *colegios* (secondary schools) directed by Jesuits and Dominicans who were not allowed by their rules to educate women. At the dawn of the Republic, the great revolutionary general, José Miguel Carrera (was he perhaps influenced by his sister Javiera, who had ridden to battle by his side?), decreed that all monastic establishments must set aside a large room for teaching girls "religion, reading, writing and the duties of a housewife, the state of life for which the Fatherland must train them, the teachers' salaries to be paid by the municipality" (Labarca 1952: 15).

Compliance was, however, far from universal, and most girls went unlettered (Paul 1966: 6). The state in its early years opened several *liceos* for boys, mainly in the provincial capitals, but was unwilling to devote any of its scanty resources to girls' education. A few primary schools for girls were conducted under private auspices, but none survived its foundress.

The true precursors of women's emergence in Chile are two remarkable and enterprising young women, Isabel Le-Brun de Pinochet and Isabel Tarragó, who became highly dissatisfied with the state of women's education. In the 1870s each opened a private high school for girls and "rivaled each other in giving their students the best and most complete education of the time" (Labarca 1934: 142). It was their work that influenced the minister of education, Miguel Luis Amunátegui, to issue the decree permitting women to present themselves for the university exams (Paul 1966: 6). From that moment, at least legally, all professions have been open to Chilean women. Amunátegui founded that same year (1877) the first public *liceo* for girls at Copiapó, and the first trade schools for girls were inaugurated soon afterwards.

The University of Chile was the first in the Americas to open its doors to women, and ten years later, in 1887, the first two female graduates, Ernestina Pérez and Eloísa Díaz, received their degrees as medical doctors (in gynecology and pediatrics), followed in 1892 by Matilde Throup Sepúlveda and Matilde Brandau in law. Paulina Starr became Chile's first woman dentist in 1884, and Glafira Vargas was graduated in pharmacy in 1887 (Labarca 1934: 142, and 1947: 191).

In the liberal period between 1880 and 1890, there was much public expenditure on education in Chile. A mission of German educators arrived to organize teachers' training colleges, until that time in the hands of nuns, and women's normal schools became state institutions. From that date on, public education has been dominated by a more secular spirit than was ever the case in Peru.

Amanda Labarca Hubertson (who later would pioneer the suffrage movement in Chile) was herself a precursor of women's progress, beginning in 1916, when she was appointed director of the girls' Liceo Rosario Orrego of Santiago. As Paul records (1966: 24-29), she was already marked as a secularist and positivist through her study at Teacher's College of Columbia University and her subsequent writings, which reflected the influence of William James, John Dewey, and William Kilpatrick, all of whom were at the height of their influence during her years in New York. The conservatives characterized her appointment as a "threat to Catholic precepts and practices in Chile," and before the furor subsided, the cabinet had resigned (Paul 1966: 25).

The president stood behind his appointment, however, and Amanda Labarca was able during the next six years to carry out many new practices in women's education designed to ease the rigidities of the traditional Spanish system, which still prevailed in public education, and of the German system, which had been superimposed on it. She introduced a system of electives, seminar courses in which students participated, courses in domestic science and commercial subjects, extracurricular activities, and student government. The directress, moreover, was accessible to the students, ate lunch daily with them, took them on field trips, and kept her office door open to them for personal counseling.

In 1922 Amanda Labarca became the first woman appointed as a regular professor of the University of Chile when she accepted an appointment to the Faculty of Philosophy and Education. She wrote widely on pedagogy and was the author of several textbooks. In 1931 she became director of secondary education, the highest government post ever held until that time by a woman. While serving in the Ministry of Education, she inaugurated the Liceo Experimental Manuel de Salas, now known as the Institute of Educational Research of the University of Chile, which became a model for similar experimental schools in Latin America (Paul 1966: 27-31).

Women's Progress and Education Today

Building on earlier secularizing tendencies in Chilean education, Amanda Labarca played a large part in making the public *liceo* acceptable and respectable for Chilean girls of the middle and upper-middle classes. In both Chile and Peru, education at the primary and secondary levels is still segregated by sex in the cities; in Chile, however, since the beginning of the century the curriculum in the public *liceos* has been identical for boys and girls.

Middle-class Chileans thus could choose between good private and good public instruction for their daughters, with no stigma attached to graduation from a *liceo* if it had a good reputation and was located in a good neighborhood. Peru opened its first public secondary schools for girls only in 1927, nearly fifty years after public education for women was inaugurated in Chile. Before this time, however, because so many girls who could not afford private schools wanted to study, some had been allowed to matriculate in the boys' high schools. Four *colegios* were created, in Lima, Arequipa, Cuzco, and La Libertad. The first director of Rosa de Santa María, the girls' school at Lima, was a North American (Pajuelo Eduardo 1965 and 1968).

In Peru, girls' education for the middle (and upper) classes is still carried on almost exclusively in institutions run by nuns or in expensive private schools under secular auspices that offer a traditional "genteel" girls' education. To a far greater degree than in Chile, the *mantel blanco* (white smock) of the public school students was a sign of the common people. Since about the mid-1950s, as more children of the lower-middle and working classes have moved into the public schools, private schools in Peru have proliferated.

Some, especially the boys' schools, are excellent institutions with long waiting lists; others are money-making enterprises of doubtful educational value. They are, nevertheless, patronized even by parents who admit that public education in some instances is superior in quality. Girls of the lower middle class who ten or fifteen years ago might have attended a good public school like Rosa de Santa María are now placed in a private school of as much standing as their parents can afford. They are placed there not only for reasons of social prestige and for the friendships important in their future lives but also because parents do not want their daughters to mix with workers' children, who they say know little of culture and good manners.

Today, one-half of all secondary school students in Latin America still attend religious schools run by the Catholic church; in several countries, the figure reaches 80 percent (Houtart and Pin 1965: 220-224; Vallier 1970: 223). What effects has sex-segregated education had on women's ability to make their way in the professional and political worlds dominated by men? Is woman's slow progress partly explained by the fact that many middle-class women are educated by nuns, who only in recent times began to orient and prepare girls for careers outside the home?

As yet, too few data are available to allow us to ascertain if less traditional vocational patterns of girls are correlated with public secondary education, but one may at least speculate that the relatively greater progress of Chilean women might be related to the fact that so many of them have a secular

secondary education and that such education has been available to them for
so much longer. In my own study, two-thirds of Chilean women political
leaders had attended a state secondary school, whereas only one-third of the
Peruvians had done so. Middle-class Chilean girls whose parents could afford
higher education for their daughters may have been less inhibited by their
secondary education than Peruvians; what is certain is that for some reason
Chileans have been more open to the idea of study at the university level. We
must not forget an elementary fact here; there simply *are* more Chilean
middle-class women than Peruvian; their greater "statistical" progress may
very well be class related.

By 1970, women had reached 46 percent of the university population at
the University of Chile, one of the highest percentages in the world. Peruvian
women form a much smaller proportion of the total university population in
their country—30.4 percent (Universidad de Chile, Instituto de Investigaciones,
Estadísticas 1970, and Consejo Nacional de la Universidad Peruana [CONUP]
1972: 3. The educational statistics below depend mainly on the publications
of these two institutes).*

The large numbers of women university students in Chile in relation to men
can also be attributed primarily to the fact that all legal and most traditional
barriers to enrollment of women are down and that university admission
depends on successfully passing a "national aptitude test" and on secondary
school grades: women tend to outscore men on both. In both Chile and Peru,
the annual percentage rate of increase in women matriculating is now greater
than that for male students, according to the publications already cited. A
closer analysis of these statistics shows, however, that even among the more
professionally inclined Chilean women, vocational choices are confined overwhelmingly to feminine careers. For example, only 5 percent of engineering
students in Chile are women, whereas at least 94 percent of all future kinder-
garten teachers, nurses, and dieticians are women. In 1970, only 14 percent
of economics students were women, and only two women studied economics
and one political science at the graduate level (in the ESCOLATINA, the
Estudios Económicos Latinoamericanos para Graduados, and the FLACSO,
the Facultad Latinoamericana de Ciencias Sociales). Peruvian figures are
almost the same (5 percent for engineering students, 15 percent for economics).

More "traditional" fields formerly dominated by males are, however,
opening up to women, especially in Chile: by 1971, women students represented 25 percent of those studying law and 30 percent of those preparing for

---

*This discussion relates to Chile in 1970-1972. Trends in Chilean universities today
are unknown.

a medical career (although most of these were in the feminine specialties of obstetrics and gynecology). Figures for Peru were smaller—16 percent of law students and 14.7 percent in medicine. Dentistry in both countries also has become a feminine field.

Peruvian careers remain more sex segregated than the Chilean: for example, only 2 percent of social work students in Peru were male, whereas in Chile, with efforts to "de-feminize" this career, 24 percent of the students of social work were male. Students of nursing among males in both countries remained at about 6 percent. Overall, however, young women in the two countries elect feminine-stereotyped professions in about the same proportion as their mothers' generation—about 75 percent in each case, as Appendix IX shows.

In Chile, about one-half of all men and women have completed primary school and about one-quarter have gone on to finish their secondary education (Bussi de Allende 1972: 14). Interestingly, the percentages of women completing primary and secondary education are slightly *higher* than the male percentages, demonstrating that women lack neither the intellectual interest nor the preparation for a university career.

In Peru, statistics show larger differences between men and women: 53.5 percent of men but only 44.6 percent of women have completed their primary education; 19 percent of men and 15 percent of women have finished secondary school (Villalobos 1975: Anexo II-20). More alarming, while the percentage of illiterates in Peru has *decreased* (from 58 percent of the total population in 1940 to 27 percent in 1972), the absolute numbers and the proportion of women illiterates *increased* in those years, from six out of ten persons in 1940 to seven out of ten in 1972 (Villalobos 1975: 1-19). This increase in female illiterates follows trends noted recently in many Third World countries. There are twice as many Peruvian and Chilean male university graduates as there are female—although totals for both sexes are low: 5 percent and 7.4 percent of the Peruvian and Chilean populations respectively have graduated from a university (Villalobos 1975: Anexo II-20; Plandes 1971: 155).

Gains may not come for women of the lower classes for a long time—and not only because they lack economic resources for education. The Mattelarts' study (1968: 161, 180) documents the terribly restricted view the lower classes retain of woman's present prospects and future possibilities—perhaps a realistic view of what those prospects really are. In relation to perceptions of change, there are many women and men of the lower classes who are unaware of *any changes at all* in the position of women in Chile. Thirty-six percent of rural women (there were 555 women in the total sample) and 50 percent of fishermen's wives do not note any alteration whatever in woman's status and prospects. The image of unchanged status is re-enforced by the fact that not a single one of the rural women selected was employed outside the home (although many did dressmaking or laundry for pay inside their own four walls). As for their daughters, the women's aspirations "are always faithful to the traditional occupations; the desire to see them participate in a technical and modern society appears only in a very few cases. A preponderant percentage (40 percent on the average) of the women of all [lower class] categories limit the girl to the work of dressmaking."

But what "deeply surprised" even the Mattelarts were women of the lower classes in the city who on this same revealing question "do not show aspirations for their daughters very different from the rural area."

> One could say that urbanization has not widened the gamut of choice for woman. For example, there is not one mention of employment in industry in the replies of the women of the lower class.

> Just as in the rural environment, the women [of the city's lower class] only refer to that profession with which they are in direct contact. This explains the higher proportion of lower class women who would choose social work and paramedical careers for their daughters. In fact, they simply are more in touch with these professions than rural women.

> One would have thought that office work would have been more frequently mentioned by women of the urban lower class, but only 14 percent cite the secretarial career. [1968: 183]

The upper-middle-class women show the greatest diversity in their choice of an ideal profession for their daughters but still center on the traditional womanly professions: medical careers are mentioned by 32 percent; architecture and teaching by 10 percent each; and social work, journalism, psychology, and secretarial work are all cited. The upper-class woman has, in her own way, as limited a horizon for her daughters as the poorest *campesina:* half would choose architecture for their daughters, and 20 percent would wish their daughters simply to marry. (In another place, the Mattelarts show how architecture is regarded as ideal because many women are unaware of its technical aspects and think women would naturally be good at it through some instinctive feminine knowledge about houses.) The others mention one of the feminine professions. Outside architecture, a career most mothers probably do not understand, and very slight mention of sociology and psychology, not one woman of the total sample mentions either a technical, a modern, or a "masculine" career (even law) as ideal for a daughter (1968: 183, 190)!

For sons, Chilean women have no such limited horizon. Even in the rural areas, the Mattelarts report, "to the women it seems easier for a young man to integrate himself into the modern, technological world and into the urban environment, although university professions are appreciated less for the status they confer than for the fact that through them one 'makes money.'" Among the urban upper and middle classes, the women consider many possible careers as ideal for their sons, although doctor and engineer outstrip others by far (65 percent of the upper-class women, 72 percent of the higher-middle-class women, and 48 percent of the lower-middle-class women mention one or the other) (1968: 185). Data from a 1970 study in Peru on desired professions for eldest sons and daughters show the same patterns (Villalobos 1975: Anexo II-30).

The recentness and tentativeness of woman's participation is reflected in my own study: of 167 women leaders concerned, only 34 had mothers who had trained for a profession and/or had actually engaged in employment outside the home. Of these 20 were trained as primary school teachers, but several had never worked. Because women lack role models and are socialized toward traditional undertakings, their professional progress is all the more remarkable when it occurs.

Women in the Labor Force

If elite women have problems in breaking through the traditional barriers that still segregate them in certain career and professional areas considered to be "suitable," their peasant and proletarian sisters are in an even more difficult position. Although the present study focuses on the professional class from which the potential female leaders and policy-makers have so far been drawn. nevertheless several trends noted in relation to other women in the labor force should be mentioned here because they bear very directly on the development process. These are among the issues that women researchers and policy-makers have already begun to address.

For one thing, several small-scale studies that have probed behind the national statistics on women's economic activity demonstrate decisively that women contribute far more to agricultural production in Latin America—as well as to the processing and marketing of food—than recent censuses, because of definitional and other defects, have effectively recorded. For example, Deere (1977: 60) has shown that in the northern sierra department of Cajamarca, Peru, women make up about one-third of the permanent, salaried agricultural labor force, whereas the 1972 census shows only 3.8 percent of agricultural laborers to be female. It is commonly noted that in many world regions, rural development and agrarian reform projects provide land, training, credit, seeds, and fertilizer only to men, thus jeopardizing women, who as unpaid family workers traditionally grow much of the food and often participate in cash cropping as well. (For more information on Andean women.

see the special issue of *Estudios Andinos* [1976] edited by June Nash, particularly the article by Bourque and Warren: 77-97.)

In many places, women have limited opportunities to earn cash. Yet their need to supplement family income or to support themselves and their children if there is no adult male present may be critical. As more and more men migrate to mines, oil fields, plantations, or cities in search of jobs, the women who stay behind in the rural areas become de facto heads of households. Yet control often is entrusted to male relatives who do not migrate.

Women who themselves go to the cities—in most Latin American countries more women than men leave the countryside and have done so over the past two decades—are often not much better off. They tend to cluster at the lowest levels of the traditional labor market, typically domestic service or street selling. Studies show that women from the countryside have less job mobility than male migrants (Chaney 1977; Suárez 1975). Often they are women alone, the principal providers for dependent children, whom they must also set to work at odd jobs. (For a recent analysis of the female-based household, see Buvenić and Youssef 1978. Recent studies of migrant women in the metropoli of Latin America include Arizpe, Mexico City, 1975 and 1976; Boserup, Asian and African cities, 1970; Bunster and Chaney, Lima, 1978 and 1977; Ducci et al., Santiago, 1974; Hewett, Bogotá, 1976; Lomnitz, Mexico City, 1975; and Safa, San Juan, Puerto Rico, 1974. A good overview of women in the labor market in Latin America is Chang and Ducci 1977.)

So far as women in Peru and Chile are concerned (and there is evidence that the situation may be general for women in less-developed countries everywhere), their position in employment actually has *worsened* as the industrial process has gone forward. In both Peru and Chile, the proportions of women in the paid labor force have decreased. In Peru, for example, for women fifteen years of age and older, their overall labor force participation declined from 22.4 percent of all women in 1961 to 15.1 in 1972, with the reductions heaviest in agriculture, manufacturing, and commerce, all occupations with a significant number of women. In Chile, women in the labor force declined from 25.0 percent of all women in 1952 to 23.0 in 1970 (Villalobos 1975: II-19 and Ducci et al. 1974: 4). As a percentage of all workers, women represented 20.7 percent in Peru in 1972 and 23 percent in Chile in 1970 (Peru: Censo Nacional de Población 1972; Chile: Taboraga 1978: 51).

In the first great period of "economic development," when post-medieval man began to acquire knowledge that he could apply in a practical way to his activities, woman had no part at all; later she began to contribute her labor but only as a "hand" in the lowest-paid factory jobs. But as Ester Boserup (1970, chapter 8) has shown, as the industrialization process goes forward, the participation of women in the secondary sector declines. Industrialization typically begins in textiles, food processing, and leather goods, all at first requiring much handwork. Women, universally considered dextrous (and willing to work for lower wages than men), are preferred in employment. But when machines become more sophisticated, there is prejudice against giving women the more highly skilled and highly paid jobs.

Other obstacles may prevent women from ever finding opportunity in the industrial manufacturing sector. Sometimes women do not make the step from home industries to the factories in any great numbers because of social restrictions on women's remunerative work outside the home. In other cases, as Boserup also has noted (1970: 110-111), those countries industrializing now, if they have the capital, may invest in such advanced technology that women never leave the home industry phase for the factory. They simply have no part in the process at all, since late developers may skip entirely the labor-intensive stages of industrialization in which women of former times found opportunity. (Many of the implications of the industrial process regarding women's position are explored in Chaney and Schmink 1974 and in Schmink 1974. See also Elizaga 1974: 527-534; Safa 1976; and ECLA 1975.)

Maternity leaves, childcare provisions, and protective legislation (such as prohibitions against overtime and night work for women), often enforced in the manufacturing sector, ironically appear to work against incorporation of women in developing economies rather than in their favor. In Peru, for example, women are entitled by law to two months' maternity leave from the factory at 60 percent of their salaries. When the new mothers return to work, they may leave their new babies in the factory's day nursery. And they may take up to one hour off each day to nurse their children. But such laws make women more expensive to hire than men, and more troublesome, since their jobs must be covered somehow in their absence. David Chaplin (1967: 187-195), a sociologist who has studied the Peruvian textile industry, found that many factories had not hired a single new woman worker since the "enlightened" legislation was put into effect in 1956.

Boserup is not inclined to accept this explanation at face value, but rather points to the fact that childbirth is a much more frequent occurrence in the underdeveloped world than in Europe and North America, and hence the absence of women workers and the necessity to fill in with temporary workers, since the women's jobs must be held for them, might make women less desirable in the eyes of employers. As she remarks (1970: 113-114), the expenses of maternity leave and daycare at places of employment can be (and sometimes have been) passed on by the employer to the government—through the taxing of all employers, for example, and not just those who hire women. Moreover, as Boserup and other analysts have lately observed, there is some evidence that male-dominated governments and labor unions may connive in demanding both equal pay for equal work *and* special benefits for women, knowing that this will influence employers to favor men for the best jobs in industry. In the absence of any equivalent to "affirmative action" and in the abundantly supplied labor markets of Latin America, such policies may have been the determining factors in the declines of women in industrial manufacturing since the heydey of import-substitution industrialization in the 1950s and early 1960s. (Some reversal recently has been noted in the "runaway" shops or *maquiladoras* (assembly plants) along the Mexican border, as well as in off-shore U.S. industries in electronics, textiles, and pharmaceuticals located in Central America and the Caribbean. All of these employ, almost exclusively, young women between sixteen and twenty-five years of age. No studies yet exist on what may turn out to be a temporary phenomenon [but see papers from a panel chaired by June Nash and Patricia Fernández Kelly, "Women, Men and the International Division of Labor," Latin American Studies Association, 1979]).

Indeed, not only do women find less and less opportunity in the industrial sector as development advances, but they are also deprived by the industrial revolution of many of their economically valuable if anonymous tasks, which for many centuries made them contributing, useful members of the family unit. Until the middle of the nineteenth century—and much later in many parts of the world—most economic activity centered in the home, with women participating to the full. Then industry took over most of this activity from the home; the education of the children also was removed from the home, and the home lost its function as recreational and health care center. Only in peasant societies, where both men and women perform essential tasks (and the woman does not depend completely on the male, but manages at least the equivalent of "butter and egg" money) have women retained a rough equality.

Today, when development plans stress industrialization on capital-intensive models, and when the need to provide employment to the increasing numbers of both men and women entering the labor force each year is only beginning to be recongnized, not much hope can be held out that industrialization will solve the problems of the Latin American woman. Women in much of the Third World will not find any opportunity at all in the secondary sector, but will go directly from agriculture (as urbanization increases, and peasants migrate to the cities) to the tertiary sector. They will compete, however, not for the well-paid service jobs that affluent societies can offer, but for poorly paid and demeaning work in street vending, clerking, and prostitution—or in the virtual serfdom of domestic service.

There is one group of Latin American women, still very small in number in relation to the total of the economically-active, and miniscule in relation to the total female population, that escaped the adverse effects of the modernization process on women. These were the women who grew up in families that could afford to educate their children and who somehow had enough motivation to convince their parents that they should study for a profession. Because it is largely from this group that the first women active in politics and government have come, a detailed analysis of the middle-class professional woman forms part of the next chapter on old and new feminists in Latin America.

4. Old and New Feminists: Women's Rights in Latin America

Why have Latin American women made so little concerted effort until now to demand their rights? Most Latin American countries granted women the right to vote in national elections only after World War II (dates are given in Appendix I). Since then, frequent suspensions of electoral politics have afforded women few opportunities to use their franchise—but in most countries the "democratic" interludes have lasted long enough to demonstrate that woman suffrage by itself does not remove discrimination against women in education, employment, and political life. Today, as women in the United States and some Western European nations mount demonstrations and actions for women's liberation, may we look for parallel activity in Latin America? Will Latin American women insist that their interests be represented in some form, even in military regimes? Will they become militant feminists?

A partial answer may be found by exploring women's movements in the past. It is true that feminism on the British-North American model of the late nineteenth and early twentieth centuries found little resonance among the women of Latin America. Nevertheless, the suffrage movement, such as it was, is interesting because it was the first time that women worked together across ideological lines and, in a few cases (notably in Chile), across class divisions.

Indeed, the term "feminist" probably should be avoided in relation to Latin American women. Peru and Chile between them have produced only one woman dedicated exclusively to the cause of woman's emancipation who at the same time was capable of attracting a substantial following—María de la Cruz. An admirer of Juan Perón and a superb orator, she used some of the Argentine leader's ideas and techniques in founding the Partido Femenino Chileno (1946) and in building a woman's movement that contributed substantially toward the sweeping victory of Carlos Ibáñez in the presidential elections of 1952. The life of the party was short, however, ending in an

acrimonious division even before the presidential campaign was over. Two
"Partidos Femeninos" expelled each other's boards of directors, to the vast
amusement of male journalists and public figures (Klimpel Alvarado 1962:
127-136).

Of the several other Peruvians and Chileans who tried through the years to
found feminist movements, none succeeded except, in limited degree, Amanda
Labarca Hubertson in Chile. She managed to organize women's groups into a
"Chilean Federation of Women's Organizations" (FECHIF) to work for suffrage, but after 1949, when the vote was obtained, the movement fell apart.
The women's groups divided along political lines and were further split by
intense personal rivalries; women never succeeded again in generating a com-
parable degree of support for any cause. In similar fashion, Blachman (1973:
15) characterizes the efforts of the Brazilian feminist organization, the
Brazilian Federation for the Progress of Women, as "limited and sporadic."

Women themselves were not always enthusiastic about extending universal
suffrage to all their sisters. What was the foremost revolutionary party of its
time, the Alianza Popular Revolucionaria Americana (APRA) of Víctor Raúl
Haya de la Torre, took an official stand against woman suffrage because of
fears that the women who would qualify as electors would come from the
most conservative strata of society. Magda Portal, leader of the women's
forces in APRA, wrote in 1933:

> What class of woman would be likely to receive the right to vote? The
> cultural level of the Peruvian woman, her prejudices, her undoubted
> dependence on masculine and, many times, clerical influence, would
> make of the female vote a means of pushing forward conservative ideas
> rather than revolutionary ones (p. 16).

She concludes with the curious suggestion that "only the woman who works,
studies, and thinks" should be given the vote.

There is strong evidence that male politicians in many Latin American
countries were motivated to support female suffrage more to appear "modern"
in the eyes of the world than because they believed giving the vote to women
would be inherently progressive. In Peru, for example, women were handed
the vote in the hope that they would help elect a conservative successor to
General Manuel Odría. In Mexico the government leaders delayed extending
universal suffrage to women until 1953—more than forty years after the
revolution!—because they believed women opposed the secularization of the
Mexican state. Although the issue of women's greater political conservatism
must be explored with care (as also the question of their lesser activism), it
still is true that throughout recent Latin American political history women in

the electorate *as a group* have almost always proved to be a conservatizing element. (See the section in chapter 5 on "Women and the Vote" for a discussion on why women may be less conservative and more active politically than the stereotypes lead us to believe. What is important here is that men *believed* women to be less progressive in their views, inclined to passivity, and subject to manipulation.)

In Chile, as in some other Latin American countries, the votes-for-women issue captured fervent support among middle- and many upper-class women— but only in the last five years of a movement inaugurated thirty years earlier. Blachman (1974) documents a parallel development in Brazil, where middle-class women mounted an extensive campaign and were granted the right to vote by the Constitution of 1934. In Colombia, granting women the vote (exercised for the first time only in 1957) was tied to the National Front political goals aimed at ending the decade of violence between Liberals and Conservatives, and was not the result of any feminist campaign (Harkess and Pinzón de Lewin 1975: 441). Without any notable agitation for suffrage on their part, Peruvian women were given the vote in 1955. The broader issues of women's legal rights in education and employment never inspired mass political movements in any of these countries, although individual women from time to time set themselves to work for wider emancipation. Today women in Latin America still live under civil codes, based on Roman law, that tend to treat women, children, and imbeciles alike as legal minors. Women's position in the legal codes of Peru and Chile is sketched briefly in Appendix II. (For a discussion of some important changes in married women's legal rights in Brazil, see Blachman 1973: 6-7.)

Winning the Vote in Peru

The movement for women's suffrage began in both Peru and Chile just before World War I. In the latter country, as will be detailed below, the campaign in its final stages attracted many followers. In Peru, one extraordinary woman, María Jesús Alvarado Rivera, carried on a lonely battle for fourteen years before she was banished to Argentina in 1925. Her story is told in detail here because it was she, working almost alone, who was most responsible for launching the suffrage movement. Her story also illustrates the dangers to women who refused to stay within the boundaries of proper womanly behavior.

María Alvarado's life as a young schoolteacher and self-styled "sociologist" includes episodes that give it the character of a novel: underground activity against the dictator Augusto B. Leguía on behalf of workers and students; championship of justice for the Indians; imprisonment and exile. Not simply a feminist, and strikingly beautiful into the bargain, María Alvarado with her advanced social ideas alienated many of the more cautious women of Lima, who might have been willing to work simply for the vote.

Only in 1969 would María Alvarado be acknowledged as the first modern champion of women's rights in Peru by her country's National Council of Women, which itself grew out of the organization she founded in 1914 under the name "Evolución Femenina" (Feminine Evolution). Typically she refused to attend the ceremony at which she was to receive a medal. "The idea of women pinning large decorations on each other," she told me in an interview, "seems to me an utter waste of time." (Except where noted, the material on María Alvarado's life comes from several personal interviews and from material shared with me from her library and clipping files.)

María Alvarado was largely self-taught. After finishing her primary education (as class valedictorian she startled her teachers and fellow students with a precocious talk entitled "A Cry for the Broad, Efficient, and Professional Education of Women"), she never returned to school on a regular basis. She tried high school but did not like it. In the girls' *liceo* directed by the famous pedagogue Elvira García y García, as Castorino (1962: 16) relates, she found, to her disillusionment and sorrow, that the articles published by the director on pedagogy and new methods of teaching were not put into practice, but that the teaching system continued in the same archaic and routine manner as always.

Abandoning high school, María embarked on a voracious reading program that laid the basis for her advanced ideas on such problems as vocational education, nutrition and health, control of venereal disease and the necessity for a prenuptial medical examination, and the use of film in education, as well as for her social agitation on behalf of women, children, the Indian, and the working class. Using her small inheritance, she opened a free school for the daughters of workers in which she tried to put into practice some of her ideas on the need to reform education—to make it more dynamic, without abstractions and memorization—and to link education to life. At the same time, through the society "Pro Indígena" she regularly received delegations of Indians from the sierra who had learned that she was willing to intercede for them before the Congress and the various government ministries in reclamation of their rights.

During these years, a North American educational mission nominated María as its candidate to study in the United States. But when she went to be interviewed by the President of the Republic, Leguía denied her the necessary permission to leave: "It wouldn't be a good idea for you to go abroad because we would lose you that way. You are much too pretty for the *gringos* to let you return. You would marry there." Thus, through what María Jesús called the "eternal *tenorio* [Don Juan] complex that affects even Presidents in spite of their high office," she lost the chance to become the first Peruvian woman sent abroad by the government for higher study.

María Alvarado launched public discussion on the "woman question" in Peru in 1911 with a talk before the Geographic Society of Lima, a meeting presided over by the famous author and folklorist Ricardo Palma (*La Prensa:* 1911). Her presentation received a mixed reaction from the audience and in the press. The daughters of Palma, Angélica and Augusta—who thirty years earlier as young women had heard similar ideas from Clorinda Matto and Mercedes Cabello—were enthusiastic: "Finally the woman has appeared who will liberate us from the oppressive subordination in which we live" (Castorino 1962: 22).

But others were not convinced, and María Alvarado had to labor another four years before she succeeded in founding Peru's first women's organization, "Feminine Evolution." A small group of women consented to inscribe their names on the membership rolls, but there was much talk that the new organization would "provoke a war between the sexes and take women out of the home, which would cause anarchy and dissolution of the family" (Castorino 1962: 22). At one point, the organization was accused of being "Protestant," and María Alvarado—who by that time had become an undeclared agnostic—had to defend her Catholic members against what was for the times a terrible indictment (*La Patria:* 1915). As late as 1924, *La Crónica* of Lima carried a photograph of women in attendance at a talk given by María on the social condition of women; many of those present had removed their hats in order to shield their faces behind them from the photographer.

In 1922, Evolución Femenina succeeded in a nine-year campaign for passage of a bill to allow women to act as directors of the "Public Welfare Societies" (Sociedades de Beneficencia Pública), which, until then, had been run exclusively by men (Castorino 1962: 67-69). With vast properties at their disposal (often taken over from the church in epochs when church-state relations worsened), the agencies rented out or sold the lands and allocated the proceeds to hospitals, orphanages, and other social works. Thus, a seat on the directing committee of such a society often meant more political power than a seat in Congress or on a departmental or municipal council. A landowner could make advantageous land deals for himself and his friends and console himself for any irregularities with the thought that the proceeds would go to charity. The law permitting women to serve was significant because until then women were excluded even from charitable enterprises whenever these involved large sums of money or political power.

By 1923, a few other women's groups had joined with Evolución Femenina in the fight for women's enfranchisement. The crown of María Alvarado's labors came in that same year when the leading North American suffragist, Carrie Chapman Catt, arrived in Lima in her capacity as president of the International Women's Suffrage Association. Mrs. Catt wanted to group all women's organizations in Peru into an affiliate of her organization, but on condition that María would agree to serve as secretary. The president, Mrs. Catt remarked, should be a prominent woman with social status, but "the secretary is the soul and arm of the institution. Thus you will be the secretary" (Castorino 1962: 39).

But the organization, which was constituted the next year as the National Council of Women in Peru, immediately began to suffer from internal rivalries. Not all the members agreed that women ought to work for any rights beyond the vote; when María Alvarado asked the council, on behalf of Evolución Femenina, if she might present a project to reform the civil code and give women, especially the married, equality before the law, there was an uproar in the newspapers and among some of the council's affiliates. The delegate of the Unión Católica, a group of conservative Catholic women, declared that civil rights for women would be incompatible with the principles of her institution (*La Prensa:* 1924a). There was some discussion among the women as to whether the council had been misrepresented by *La Prensa* because the newspaper had inserted headings that made it seem as if the council had decided to back María's project, when it only had agreed to debate it. As one member put it, the men, who "generally don't read the news very well, but only the paragraph headings, are going to believe that the council is about to ask for the equality of women before the law!" (*La Prensa:* 1924b).

The men apparently decided that María had inflamed their women enough. Shortly before Christmas of 1924 she was taken to the Santo Tomás jail as a political prisoner; she remained there in solitary confinement for three months before being deported to a twelve-year exile in Argentina. Not only had she offended "by the passion with which she defended the most advanced feminist doctrines," as one newspaper editorial put it (*La Crónica:* 1925), but she had also printed one pamphlet too many on the small press in her school. When no print shop would accept them, María had edited and printed for workers and students their manifestos on

the eight-hour day; on fascism; . . . one critical of the "Vial" law which obliges all Peruvians to work *gratis* on the public roads every six months for six days. But in reality the law applies only to the Indians, victims of the most vicious exploitation.

Others denounced and accused President Leguía of bloody assassinations, of arbitrary actions and misconduct of every kind. We didn't put any identification of the press on the folders, but one day they found out the truth and I was imprisoned. [*Tribuna Nacional de Buenos Aires:* 1925]

The same newspaper editorial cited above demonstrates the combination of masculine superiority and gallantry with which Peruvian men of that day viewed woman's political activity. María Alvarado ought to be punished, but not to excess:

> When women meddle in men's affairs they expose themselves to the necessity of suffering the consequences of their masculine acts. But even though this may be true . . . it also is appropriate to recall the duty of *caballerosidad* [gentlemanly behavior] and of considering the condition of woman. Those who unfortunately must mete out punishment against her ought to do so with a bit of benevolence and respect. [*La Crónica:* 1925]

Women never succeeded in building a movement in Peru, and the 200-odd organizations that today constitute the National Council of Women have no record of effective action in the broader field of women's rights, although individual women's groups in Peru did engage sporadically in work for women's enfranchisement. Through the years a few women also wrote and agitated for issues going beyond suffrage, among them Peru's most distinguished women educators, Elvira García y García and Teresa González de Fanning; María Alvarado's contemporaries, Luisa G. de Llona, Susana Solano, Zoila A. Cáceres, Virginia de Izaguirre, and Beatriz Cisneros; at a later period, women like Irene Silva de Santolalla, Matilde Pérez Palacio, María Luisa Montori, and Marta Pajuelo Eduardo.

Still, as has been mentioned, the conferring of the vote on women by General Odría in 1955 caught most women by surprise; it came as a gift for which they had not expended any large amounts of energy. Indeed, the general disinterest in the question was so great that, as María Alvarado pointed out to me, neither *El Comercio* nor *La Prensa,* Lima's leading dailies, bothered to carry any stories about the pro forma debate on General Odría's bill in the Congress.

Woman and the Vote in Chile

Woman's emancipation in Chile was, from its beginnings, an activity that involved many women. There is, however, one woman who holds the undisputed place as the leader of feminism in Chile, and the movement for women's suffrage properly begins in 1915 when Amanda Labarca Hubertson founded a Círculo de Lectura (Women's Reading Circle) at which women met to study literary and philosophical works. The circle was not only the first club of its kind for women but also the first women's group to be organized through lay initiative and not under clerical sponsorship (Labarca 1967a: 79).

Women of the upper class immediately decided that they also wanted to organize, and at the end of the same year they formed a Club de Señoras presided over by Delia Matte de Izquierdo; the two clubs began a more or less cordial collaboration and some women joined both groups (Labarca 1967b).

The French writer Marcelle Auclair, who lived as a young woman in Santiago, recalls how the Círculo de Lectura "let a breath of fresh air into a closed, colonial Chile, with the best of thought, science, and literature" (*Ercilla* 1968: 60). Juan de Soiza Reilly (1924 [?]: 84) notes particularly the "anxiety felt by women of the higher class when they were confronted with the intellectual superiority of the 'little teachers' like Amanda Labarca." He quotes one of the founders of the Club de Señoras, Inés Echeverría de Larraín, who under the name "Iris" was to become the unofficial scribe of the emancipation movement: "To our great surprise, there appeared in Chile a middle class, and we had no idea how it came to be born . . . with the most perfectly educated women who had professional and teaching degrees, while we upper class women hardly knew the mysteries of the rosary."

As Amanda Labarca points out (1967a: 79), the foundation of these clubs owed nothing to men and everything "to the leadership of the women themselves." Such groups, which also began to appear in pre-World War I Peru, thus had no connection with the salons of other epochs. Women from this time on met for intellectual and political discussion almost always with members of their own sex, as they do to this day. Even the political parties, with their sex-segregated women's sections, have not brought men and women together again to exchange ideas on political and social issues.

The salon had, of course, admitted only a small group of truly gifted and outstanding women, whereas the founders of women's groups after 1915 wanted to reach many more women and to awaken them to a more active intellectual and cultural (and later social and political) life. Perhaps for this reason, such women's groups were strongly opposed not only by men—particularly the clergy—but by the more conservative women. Says Amanda Labarca, recalling the pioneer years of the Reading Circle, which inevitably was attacked as "Masonic" and was identified with the secularizing principles of the Radical party to which she and her husband belonged: "A simple Reading Circle was for the social and political bigots the incarnation of the devil, because without a doubt we would read books 'against morality and convention' whose very acquaintance would break down the family traditions so honorably preserved from colonial times" (quoted in Mayoraga 1968: 43).

If discussion of social and political ideas by women was not acceptable to Catholic conservative circles, the vote for women was anathema. When woman suffrage began to be discussed—and in 1917 when the youth section of the Conservative Party actually proposed that a bill be introduced to give women political emancipation—women who advocated such a measure were threatened with excommunication (Mayoraga 1968: 44; Labarca 1934: 125 ff.).

In 1919, members of the Reading Circle and the Women's Club joined forces to found the National Council of Women, which became the principal agitator for the feminist movement during the 1920s (Labarca 1967a: 79). Many other groups were formed between 1920 and 1940 specifically to work for women's rights, including associations of university women, leagues for civic action, and study groups. But most of these women's organizations had a limited life; moreover, as Klimpel Alvarado (1962: 93) notes, it was the same women leaders who would appear over and over again to found new organizations, and these then would attract the same clientele as before without, however, "capturing the sympathy of the great masses of women."

Amanda Labarca recounts how president after president, once in office, went back on promises to sponsor bills for women's emancipation because "they had no confidence in how women would use the vote" (*Ercilla* 1964: 6). Even Pedro Aguirre Cerda, a member of Amanda Labarca's own Radical Party, who became president in 1938 as the candidate of the leftist Popular Front,* went back on his word to promote national woman suffrage. She reports how the president made clear

> in our many conversations with him his doubt that the woman, having acquired the vote, would continue along the same line that had brought him to the Presidency of the Republic. That is, he didn't believe in the continuing leftism of the woman.
>
> In this, as a matter of fact, there was a basis in fact. The men—secularists, Masons, leftists, and even Socialists—simply didn't bother to orient their womenfolk toward their own political ideas. [Quoted in Mayoraga 1968: 44]

Only in 1944, when the first National Congress of Women was held, did the movement for women's rights begin to awaken mass support. The Federation of Women's Organizations was formed as a result of this conference, with Amanda Labarca as its head. Despite the dissolution of the Popular Front in electoral politics, the women created a board of directors that incorporated leaders of all political ideologies from the extreme right to the extreme left,

*The Popular Front, the first alliance of leftist parties in Chile, and a predecessor to Salvador Allende's Popular Unity coalition, was formed in preparation for the presidential election of 1938 and patterned after the Popular Fronts of Europe (Gil 1966: 67).

including María Marchant (whose mother had earned her livelihood selling vege-
tables in the Vega, the central market of Santiago) and Julieta Campusano,
both of whom were active in the Communist party until the 1973 coup; María
Aguirre, leader of the Presbyterian Women's Association of South America;
and the elegant and aristocratic María Correa Morandé, then a Liberal and later
a leader in the National Party (Labarca 1967b).

Five years later, after much patient work on the part of a small group, particularly Amanda Labarca, Elena Cafferena, and Ana Figueroa (the latter two
women were prominent Communists), women received the vote (*Ercilla* 1964:
6). Once suffrage was obtained, however, the women's movement fell apart
exactly as it had thirty years earlier in the United States, and to this day
Chilean women never have achieved the degree of organization they attained
during the heyday of the federation. Feminists in the United States had
structured their movement around the limited aim of obtaining national
suffrage; learning nothing from the experience, Chilean women also neglected
to plan for any action beyond winning the right to vote.

Prospects for Women's Liberation Today

There was a strong belief among Peruvian and Chilean women (as also was
the case in the United States) that the women's vote would purify the political
process and, at the same time, automatically gain for women their other rights—
better opportunities in education and employment and removal of legal disabilities. The women of Latin America were slow to realize that the vote
would mean little without changes in the traditions and institutions of society.
They now acknowledge that early feminism brought them limited benefits,
but they have so far shown few signs of organizing "new feminist" movements
to take up the battle for full feminine equality.

The situation no doubt was made more difficult in the case of Chilean
women by fierce party and class divisions; as Amanda Labarca (1967b) notes,
once the Popular Front fell, the women found great difficulty in working
together. But the failure of these movements to go beyond suffrage has deeper
causes; to cite women's apathy in continuing the fight for their rights is to
point to a symptom, not a cause. The old feminists failed to attract any large
or lasting following; new feminists, if they should appear, probably will not
be any more successful, because the *image* of woman's proper role has not
undergone any fundamental change in Latin America. The suffrage movement fostered rather than challenged the feminine stereotype by emphasizing
how the women's vote would infuse society with the womanly virtues. Indeed,
as was the case in Peru, other rights issues sometimes were soft-pedaled in
order to keep the tenuous collaboration of more conservative women in

winning the vote.

At first, these assertions seem paradoxical. Are not women in the more advanced Latin American countries entering the universities, the professions, and the work force in large numbers? Evidently they are, as the preceding chapter demonstrates, but they do so without affecting their inferior position as women. What must be noted is the extreme degree to which most professional women of Latin America are relegated to a feminine world where few men are present. Girls attend *liceos* and *colegios* staffed entirely (by law in Chile) by women teachers and directors unless, for certain courses, a woman teacher is not available. If they continue, they most often study for feminine professions in schools and institutes staffed and administered by women where their fellow students are, in the main, women. From these "feminine faculties," women go on to careers or public service posts in which their supervisors and colleagues are largely women; their clients also are primarily females and juveniles. Women simply do not develop "colleague relationships" with men, nor do they have much opportunity for regular collaboration with them in their work.

Much of the interchange between men and women thus takes place on a social plane. Perhaps because women's occupational and political roles most often have mirrored their wife-mother vocation, relations between men and women in Latin America lack almost entirely any sense of overt competition. Moreover, the depreciation of women in Latin American society is counterbalanced by the tradition of gallantry and *caballerosidad*. Admittedly, "playing the gentleman" is a ritual, but often, too, the caballero conveys a genuine appreciation and respect. For these reasons, male/female conflict in Latin America never has been (and perhaps never will become) as acute in these societies as elsewhere.

Indeed, the caballero tradition, in the view of some observers, explains why Latin American women have never been feminists. A strong feminist reaction, they say, is provoked only by extreme masculine depreciation of women's position, as in some of the Arab countries (see Chombart de Lauwe 1962: 273; Mattelarts 1968: 18). In the lower classes, where women sometimes still walk behind the male bearing the burdens, a more explosive reaction might perhaps some day be expected.

The caballero role and the attitude of *coquetería* it evokes from the woman have an insidious side seldom perceived by Latin American women who are proud of their men's polite behavior. Discussion of ideas or issues is not encouraged by rituals of teasing, flirting, and compliments. Not since the days of the *tertulia* have men and women met together on an institutionalized basis to examine national problems. If men and women do not even talk to each other seriously, how can they envision working together as equals?

The situation is even more complex. The very fact of their margination to designated feminine fields gives Latin Americans an advantage that North American women largely have lost: the opportunity to rise to the top in certain professions. In North America since World War II, men have moved into primary and secondary teaching, paramedical fields, social work, and library services; they also have moved rapidly upward to "masculinize" the administration of these fields. In Latin America such professions still are feminine-stereotyped not only because of the supermadre syndrome (the belief that women are better at these tasks) but also because of machismo, the virile male's attitude that does not permit him to do "female" work. If they respect the proper boundaries, women may achieve a certain status in "their" fields, if not great power. This fact may account for the lack of militancy among Latin American women; far less oppressed on this score than their North American sisters, Latin Americans may have less apparent reason to revolt.

Yet it is important to stress again that such opportunities are by no means open to all women. Professional and political activity has until now been the province of middle- and upper-middle-class women; not only are they the only ones who qualify in terms of education and preparation, but most privileged women enjoy their freedom to exercise a career at the expense of the lower-class women they employ as maids. Two in five of all economically active women in Latin America work as domestic servants. It is ironic that the political activity even of radical women depends on a servant class. A Communist official in a workers' district of Santiago, whose own origins are lower class, told me she could not function without the two servants she employs!

Most lower-class women are, of course, subject to a double burden if they work in paid employment; after a full day outside their own homes, they face all the household tasks, in which their men rarely share unless, as one working wife put it, "the woman is mortally ill or dying." Yet there is lack of concern for the less favorably situated women of the lower classes, even among those women in careers nominally dedicated to the amelioration of social ills, a lack noted time and again by the Mattelarts. Privileged women have an obvious stake in maintaining the status quo and feel great anxiety at any prospect of losing their servants. Even among fairly enlightened middle-class women, one encounters definite opposition to public or private initiatives to upgrade the education and training of domestics—unless the training courses are directly geared to improving performance in the home.

In my own study, only women of the left and some of the Christian Democrats distinguished between the legal freedom that now exists for women to study and work and the fact that only a privileged few have any real education and career options. Very few ask, "Who shall be the servants of the servants?" which is, of course, the revolutionary question of "How shall we restructure society to give more options and opportunities to all women?" No one except leftist women questions the structures themselves or talks about such innovations as day-care centers for working women and scholarship assistance for girls of the working class.

The deepest reasons for the lack of feminist movements in Latin America may lie here. To succeed, feminism demands a sense of unity and common purpose among women of many backgrounds and social origins. Most Latin American women of the left place working-class solidarity above identification with "women's issues" as a matter of principle, whereas many women of the upper and middle classes stereotype the lower-class woman as "sad, lazy, poor, always expecting things to be given to her and not to work" (Mattelarts 1968: 45). Neither has collaboration among women of different backgrounds been possible, because of what Mota (1974: 2-3) aptly describes as fear of "the despotism of the masculine left." As she notes, this leads to a reluctance to theorize about women's oppression and inhibits the creation of feminist movements. Conservative women have other reasons for avoiding the label "feminist"—it is associated with the "unfeminine" qualities of the old feminism and the radicalism of the new. Klimpel Alvarado (1962: 114) cites yet another reason why even women of similar educational and social background cannot work together:

> . . . [individualism] is the consequence of the fight the professional has had to reach success, generally a lonely battle with neither support nor help from others. Her disinterest in uniting with other professionals comes from a deep conviction that whatever the particular goal, it will be accomplished better through individual rather than collective effort. As for her insensibility in worrying herself with the problems of her less fortunate . . . sisters, the majority of professional women prefer to ignore them. To be bothered with such things is to go back to that hated time from which she herself has been freed.

Predictions are risky, but a new era of feminist activity in Latin America does not appear likely under present conditions. Women may rally around special issues such as legal divorce (which does not exist in many Latin American countries), but full-scale feminist movements probably will not develop for many years. In other parts of the world, women today seek a much broader equality, going far beyond the traditional women's rights issues that still provide the agenda for most women's groups in Latin America. Militant, vocal groups of women in North America and Europe today are talking about women's liberation in terms of the freedom to develop their human potential as *persons*. This goal includes such measures as full access to birth control for the unmarried as well as the married woman, the legalization of abortion, the establishment of day-care centers to free women from total absorption in their traditional role, and the like. Such an emphasis introduces issues that challenge Latin American traditions even more drastically than do voting and legal rights. If movements built around the last-named issues enjoyed little success in Latin America, it is extremely doubtful that a more nearly total women's revolution will make any headway there.

The most potent barrier probably remains the pervasive belief that man and woman each has a "proper sphere" in professions and public service; neither men nor women wish women to overstep these boundaries. Women may very well be content to continue their marginal existence, dedicating themselves to their feminine tasks far from the seats of power. Certainly the fact that over 80 percent of the women students in Peru and Chile are preparing for "feminine" careers—about the same proportion as their mothers' generation—would not predict any sudden shifts into male career strongholds.

Paradoxically, the reluctance of women to challenge the division of labor in society and polity eventually may work to their long-run advantage, as will be suggested in the final chapter. Certainly the work in society designated "feminine" is not unimportant, even if males do not value it. As one of my conclusions, I suggest that women in Latin America, more in control of certain professions and tasks than their North American sisters, might first work to transform their "own" fields, then use them as a power base to move out to the mainstream of social and political life. Because of the macho tradition, there may be less risk that Latin American males will take over these professions as they are modernized and upgraded.

In an ideal world, men and women would qualify for professional and political assignments solely on the basis of capacity and training; in Latin America, however, the image of what is proper to men and women prevents any approximation of the ideal even though few legal barriers now prevent Latin American women from assuming whatever political posts or professional tasks they wish. Feminist activity to achieve the ideal is difficult to envision because there is no history of confrontation between men and women in Latin America. The Chilean case is exceptional; women certainly did not "win" the right to vote and in most cases were simply handed that right by conservative male leaders. Women were considered to be a conservatizing force in the electorate, or at least it was believed their vote would prove no threat to the status quo. Male leaders so far have been proved quite correct in that expectation.

For all these reasons Latin American women probably will not confront men directly over questions concerning their full emancipation because they feel feminist militancy is completely foreign to their tradition. Many women told me they have an almost pathological fear of being laughed at by men; a few recent, tentative efforts to organize for women's rights have been ridiculed to death in the male-dominated press. Many women want to get ahead in their professions and in public life, but they do not plan to do so by "waving banners over our heads," as one put it. Rather, they want to advance by excelling in their professions and by remaining as feminine as possible. (These two ideas were expressed over and over again by my interviewees and by many other women.)

Small pockets of feminist activity exist today in almost every large Latin American city, but the activists are isolated and beleaguered. Such initiatives probably will not become broad movements. On the other hand, Latin American women leaders may have the possibility of exploiting their separate spheres for their own benefit and that of other women. Support for the continued separation of women and men may be the form that feminism—not called by that name—takes in some Latin American countries. Although their sphere has less power, women already are working with and for other women in it. They can rise to the top in certain professions within it; they can maintain an identity. And in the end, as I have already suggested, "their" issues may move to the center of the policy arena.

Winning the vote focused women's attention on politics, and some immediately moved to take advantage of the fact that they could now not only vote but also compete for political office. The next chapter recounts their first ventures into public life.

5. Women in Politics and Government

Woman and the Vote

Everywhere today people are asking whether the mere act of voting in elections, no matter how many citizens exercise it, can be considered a genuine index of the popular will. Many believe that political participation is meaningless if it does not go beyond choosing among candidates who most often represent privileged minorities; they believe decision-making must extend to areas over which the average citizen now has no direct control, including responsibility for the organization of work and the distribution of profits and for educational, cultural, and social welfare institutions.

Whether or not voting is meaningful, winning the right to vote served an important function for women. It focused women's attention for the first time on the political process. Many of my interviewees mentioned that they only began to read about and discuss political issues when women were given the right to vote in national elections.

(In the following discussion of women and political participation, I am incorporating data from several studies completed concurrently with or after my own: Blachman [1973] on Brazil; Harkess and Pinzón de Lewin [1975] and Schmidt [1975] on Colombia; Mota [1974] on the Dominican Republic; Lewis [1971] on Argentina. See also Jaquette 1974 and 1976.)

For Chilean women, enfranchisement came in 1949, with their first opportunity to exercise their new right in a special senatorial election the next year, when a woman ran for the first time for national political office. Candidate of the Partido Femenino Chileno, María de la Cruz won many more votes than had been expected, although she did not win office until the next elections (Klimpel Alvarado 1962: 132-134). Peru did not enfranchise women until 1955, and thus was one of the last three American republics to do so, being followed only by Colombia (1957) and Paraguay (1961). Dates of woman suffrage in the Americas are given as Appendix I.

Chile provides a unique electoral laboratory for anyone interested in study-ing male-female voting patterns. Women had been qualified to vote for *regidor* or *regidora* (male and female council members) in local elections throughout Chile since 1934. When the franchise was extended to national elections, it was more convenient for women to continue registering on the separate rolls that had been maintained for them for municipal elections. For practical reasons, this forced the establishment of separate polling places and separate tallying of election results, thus providing (down to the *comuna* or precinct level) what few other countries in the world can boast; national election statistics by sex.

The relationship between interest in politics and the right to vote in national elections is clearly underscored by rates of women's political participation in Chile. Only when suffrage was extended to national elections did women begin to vote in significant numbers *even in local* elections. For the municipal elections of 1944, the fourth time women had voted, they formed only 19 percent of the electorate. By the municipal elections of 1967, as table 1 shows, they numbered almost half the registered voters of Chile. Both men and women voters increased in numbers, but there was a greater increase in participation by the latter. (Blachman [1973: 13] shows the same trend for some states of Brazil; Harkess and Pinzón de Lewin [1975: 442] document a fluctuating pattern for Colombian women.) It should be clear that high rates of *activism* in politics are not necessarily linked to either radical or conservative political *attitudes*. See the end of this section and the final chapter for a dis-cussion on possible relationships of political activism to political ideology.

Before the suspension of elections by the military junta in Peru, registra-tion and voting were required by law of all literate citizens. Women never-theless formed a lower proportion of the electorate in Peru (37 percent), not only because women in Chile have voted in more elections for national leaders (nine elections in contrast to three for Peru) but also because of the higher level of literacy among Chilean women. In Peru a survey in 1973 revealed that 32 percent of women had never had any schooling (Villalobos 1975: 1–4), whereas in Chile in 1970 only 5.25 percent had never been to school (Barbieri 1975: 51). Moreover, the fact that purely legal measures do not go very far toward changing institutions and attitudes has been demonstrated nowhere more clearly than in the slowness of women all over the world to exercise their right to vote. (In the table, data are given for the mid-1960s for comparison of the two countries.)

The situation was further complicated in Peru, however, because the *libreta electoral* (voting registration card) served as an essential identification card required in order to obtain any employment covered by minimum wage and hour laws and social security (including domestic service), and to marry, open

TABLE 1
REGISTERED VOTERS, PERU AND CHILE (MID-1960s)

| | Men | Women | Totals as % of Voting Age Population | | |
			Men	Women	Total
Peru	1,470,607 (63%)	867,713 (37%)	57	33	46
Chile	1,625,837 (54%)	1,420,309 (46%)	78	61	69

Sources: República del Perú, Registro Electoral del Perú 1966, typewritten.
Totals of voting age population calculated from population figures
for 1965 given in República del Perú, SERH 1966: 7. These percentages do not take into account the fact that the married could
vote in Peru at 18 and that voting (and registration) are not compulsory after 60. Percentages also include men and women of age
20 (1 year too young to vote) since a less inclusive breakdown is not
available. Also República de Chile, Ministerio del Interior 1967.
Percentages for voting age population calculated from population
figures for 1966 given in República de Chile, Dirección de Estadística
y Censos 1966: 47. These figures include men and women of age 20
(1 year too young to vote) since a less inclusive breakdown is not
available.

a bank account, receive registered mail, register in a university and receive a
degree, exercise a profession, sign a contract, obtain a passport—in short, to
perform any civic act (Patrón Faura 1972: 12-13). Those who do not know
how to read and write receive a document that serves as an identity card but
does not permit them to vote.

Despite the high rate of illiteracy among women, this would seem to forecast a much higher inscription of women in the electoral registry—including
many who would register for purposes more important to them than voting—
than was actually the case. But numbers were kept down (perhaps intention-
ally, or so it was asserted by several women lawyers who handle cases of
women attempting to secure their voting cards) by making registration highly
complicated for women, especially those in and from the rural areas. They
had not only to demonstrate literacy but also to prove their birthdate and
present their marriage certificate (often difficult in a country where rural
records are incomplete and inaccurate, and where many women live in con-
sensual unions). If birth, baptismal, and marriage records were not available,
establishing the date of birth involved a lawyer to prepare the papers and a

journey to the province of birth for a court hearing (Valdez de del Busto 1965). The procedure was much simpler for men who already were registered for army service; their service identification was the only document needed to obtain their voting card (Patrón Faura 1955: unnumbered page facing title page).

In Peru, too, a substantial fine equal to several days' pay, levied to revalidate a card after failure to vote in an election, certainly reduced the significance of voting statistics as an index of genuine interest in politics. Such a sum was substantial for a working-class woman, and she might well have voted solely to escape the fine. Among those registered to vote, over-all abstention rates were low in Peru, only 5.62 percent for the last presidential election in 1963.

In Chile, voting was nominally compulsory, but there were no such complicated procedures and penalties clouding the relation between voter registration and interest in politics. Moreover, Chile's civic tradition, the church-linked appeal of the Christian Democrats, and the fact that politics always has been a respected activity would lead us to expect a high rate of political participation for Chilean women. We are on safer ground, therefore, in concluding that the high participation rates for women do, in fact, indicate a high degree of feminine interest in politics, at least so far as voting is concerned.

Chile's over-all abstention rates were higher than Peru's, ranging from 25 percent for municipal elections to almost 17 percent in the presidential election of 1970. It is significant, however, that abstention rates for *women* were consistently lower in Chile than for men, sometimes by as much as five or six percentage points, a fact that challenges stereotypes about women's lesser political activism. Paul H. Lewis (1971: 428-430) found similar patterns in Argentina, where turnout rates for women in at least one election (1965 congressional, the only election for which statistics are available) were higher than for men in fourteen of seventeen provinces, in several cases by over four percentage points. Nor was higher turnout an artifact of low sex ratios, since there were provinces with higher female turnout rates where women of voting age were not in a majority.

Other Latin American countries reflect varying rates of voter turnout for men and women, making it clear that it is incorrect to generalize that Latin American women vote less than men. In Colombia, less than one-third of the eligible female population votes (Harkess and Pinzón de Lewin 1975: 440); in Brazil in 1970, 48 percent of the eligible electorate were women, and they made up 42 percent of those registered (Blachman 1973: 13). In fact, there are low, intermediate, and high participation rates for women among the twenty-one American republics, probably correlated to general standard-of-living and educational indices among countries, and whether or not elections are regarded as meaningful.

Within countries, studies of political participation in Western Europe and the United States—participation being defined as reading and talking about politics, distributing literature, attending political rallies, as well as voting—have shown that rates of political activism are higher for women of middle and upper-middle socio-economic status groups (with a decline for upper-class women). Low socio-economic status seems to affect men's participation rates less than women's; women's rates fluctuate as noted above among status brackets, but men's rates remain more or less the same (Lane 1959: 209-216). Brunilda Vélez confirmed these tendencies among men and women in the Chilean electorate (1964: 42-43, 58).

Robert E. Lane (1959: 214-215), while cautioning that the evidence is uncertain, summarizes research showing that in the United States women of Latin ethnic groups (Italians and Mexicans) and Jewish and Black women are less politically active than those of Scandinavian and Irish extraction (the women tend to participate less than the men in *each* ethnic group, but the gaps between women and men in the Latin ethnic groups are greater).

Other investigators have suggested higher educational and occupational status, mature age, marriage, and urban residence as well as higher socio-economic status as correlates of greater political interest and activism for both men and women (Lane 1959: 209-216; Lipset 1963: 187-188; Almond and Verba 1963: 387-400). Lipset points out that these patterns are "strikingly the same" for all countries for which we have data.

Discrepancies crop up in matching behavior to political attitudes. For example, in the Mattelarts study (1968: 146), significant percentages of women who declared that their sex should leave politics to their husbands nevertheless had voted in the last presidential and congressional elections. On the other hand, many men and women who declared in theory that women ought to take part in politics were opposed when confronted with a concrete option, that is, when asked if women ought to become members of political organizations. In the same study, in some social groups men were more likely than women to say that they were willing for women to engage in political activity, yet often balked at the idea of their own female relatives setting out to run for office or join a party. A revealing example: Jorge Alessandri, perennial candidate of the right, who owed his election as president of Chile in 1958 to the women's vote, admitted that he had cast his ballot under protest for his own niece when she ran for congress in 1969:

Alessandri: I did it against my will because I didn't want her to run for office.

Question: Do you like to see women in politics?
Alessandri: I reserve my opinion on that! [*Ercilla*, March 5-11, 1969:
              12]

What this lack of congruence between behavior and attitudes may demonstrate is that *voting* has become acceptable for women in many countries but that any further participation in the political process is still considered out of bounds. The Mattelarts (1968: 146) suggest that political activism for women is identified almost entirely with voting: "The wife of a small proprietor seems to give us the key to this attitude, which may be contradictory only in appearance: 'No woman ought to get mixed up in politics, only vote.'"

There is some strong evidence from surveys in other countries that the act of voting often is not considered strictly "political," but rather the civic duty of the ordinary citizen. In a study of the political role of women in France, the Institut Français d'Opinion Publique (Duverger 1955: 174, 167) discovered that 64 percent of the women respondents (N = 2,146) regarded the act of voting as the performance of a duty. Moreover, whereas nearly one-half of women and men respondents in the same survey regarded running even for municipal office as unsuitable for women, only 5 percent of the men and 4 percent of the women thought voting regularly was unsuitable behavior for women. Such activities as becoming a member of a party, putting up posters and selling newspapers for a party (rejected by 94 and 96 percent of the men and women responding), or speaking at an election meeting were judged unsuitable by substantial margins. Even permitting women to discuss politics at a friendly gathering was frowned upon by over 40 percent of both men and women questioned in the survey.

The role of Christian Democratic parties in Europe and Latin America in making voting "respectable" and even a duty for women has been noted; Duverger (1955: 103-105) points out that the French and German parties enroll more women than do the other parties in those countries, and Edward J. Williams (1967: 275-279) has shown the same tendencies wherever Christian Democratic parties were active in Latin America. Yet party politics and political offices for women still were circumscribed by many taboos in most of these countries, reflecting the strength of the tradition that reserves the command echelons to men. Blachman, for example (1973: 15), concludes that in Brazil "women are systematically excluded from [political office at all levels], and that their participation in the political institution is relegated to the more passive areas of activity such as voting."

Men may approve feminine political activity that does not go beyond voting because they believe they can easily enough influence how their womenfolk cast their ballots. There is some doubt, however, that women necessarily vote as their men instruct them. Susan Bourque and Jean Gross-holtz (1974: 229-236) have effectively challenged yet another prevalent stereotype, showing that, in fact, the few studies we have demonstrate *mutual* influence of husband and wife on each other's voting decisions. The wide discrepancies in voting patterns for men and women in Chile at every socio-economic level—from workers' districts to the fashionable *barrio alto* of Santiago—demonstrate with hard electoral data that women do not necessarily vote as their men instruct them to do. In his survey of women in Cali, Schmidt (1975: 481) also found that women did not necessarily give the same party label to themselves as they ascribed to their husbands.

In Peru, where only 33 percent of the female population of voting age was registered before the 1968 coup—in contrast to 61 percent for Chile—exercising their franchise had not become a legitimate political activity for women. There was a great deal of talk about *politiquería* in Chile—"politicking" in the negative sense—yet I rarely encountered among Chilean women the degree of depreciation for politics that many Peruvian women articulate. In an interview in 1967, Pedro Patrón Faura, then director of the National Electoral Registry for Peru, speculated that it would take Peruvian women forty years from enfranchisement to reach 50 percent of the electorate, that is, they would not form one-half the voting population until 1995. This is not as far-fetched as it sounds, since we may presume that almost all literate, urban women registered for the 1956 and the 1962 and 1963 presidential elections; increments after this initially large group would depend on increasing literacy rates, a slow process. So far as politics was concerned, Patrón Faura commented:

> You are dealing here with a very old Spanish tradition and with principles that have been held for centuries. There is practically no history of feminism in Peru. Politics simply doesn't interest women here; it is viewed as the business of men. There is a certain fear of it. Many women tell me, "Politics is a dirty business, and I don't want to get mixed up in it."

It remains to be seen if the postponement of elections (at this writing the military junta not only has declined to set a date for elections but also has refused to say when it might do so) will push the timetable forward to the next century.

Before leaving the question of women's participation, it may be well to explore briefly here the relationship between women's activism (or lack of it) and the direction of their political sympathies. Because this is a key issue in my conclusions, a detailed analysis is postponed to the final chapter. What should be clear is the necessity of separating political activism from any particular political *stance.* Women who took to the streets with their rosaries in Brazil to support the military takeover in 1964 (although there is some evidence many women were manipulated) were certainly highly activist, at least on that occasion! The militant women who organized "Poder Femenino" (Feminine Power) in Chile in mid-1972 with the object of "saving our homes and families from Communism" (preceded by the famous march of the empty pots of middle-class women) were no less active than those who, in the same months, were organizing women in the popular barrios and planning a world congress of women representing the socialist countries. In neither of these cases is there any evidence of manipulation; on the contrary, as Michèle Mattelart (1974) makes clear, it was the women who manipulated the men of the right, shaming them for their hesitancy in moving against Allende. (For an account of the highly efficient and effective women's organizations of the right, see Mattelart 1974; for an analysis of the relegation of leftist women's mobilization and issues to secondary priority in Allende's Chile, see Chaney 1974.)

If one does not probe beneath the surface, statements about women's greater political conservatism can be documented in country after country, especially when one is using gross national electoral statistics. But such assertions do not always hold up when one begins refining the data or asking questions in the survey situation. As was suggested above, both social status and age may be factors in the apparent propensity of the women's vote to pull politics to the right. Women who received the vote after World War II are now forty-five years of age or older; as Sullerot (1971: 231) suggests, it may be only the mass of older women who have a more conservative attitude than men of the same age. She points out (confirming what Bourque and Grossholtz demonstrate for the United States) that public opinion polls conducted before various national elections show that the political choices of women twenty-one to thirty-five years of age differ very little from those of their male contemporaries.

Women and the Political Party

Today there is no political party in Latin America that excludes women; perhaps this ought to be considered a significant development. Yet as I visited the women's headquarters and talked to leaders of the feminine sections, it was evident that at this point in their history all suffered from a kind of schizophrenia. The women party leaders were ironic and resentful about being segregated in their party activity and thus virtually excluded from policy making. Yet they were diffident, unconvinced that women were capable of assuming equal responsibilities with men either in party affairs or in elected office. One party official summed up these conflicting attitudes:

> There is a great change from ten years ago—when we women used to joke that we were nothing more than the "sandwichero" called in when the men needed refreshments for their meetings. Now we count for more than this, especially since the women's vote is important. The party men really court us around election time, to be sure!

This same party official pointed out that many women at the normal age for selection to leadership roles were not prepared for high posts. "I know so many women thirty to forty-five years of age," she said, "who now wish they had studied. But even ten years ago it wasn't evident that there would be so many opportunities for women, so we simply didn't bother."

Even if women do study, however, they most often prepare for feminine careers and thus exclude themselves from future party leadership, not only because their career preparation often does not qualify them for political posts but also because "feminine" faculties are isolated from student politics. Apparently student politics does provide a training-ground for large numbers of future politicians, as studies by Bakke (1964), Bonilla (1960), and Emmerson (1968), among others, have shown. Women miss out, by and large, on this crucial start toward a political career because they generally do not study in politicized faculties. In collecting data on student politics in nineteen countries, Emmerson (1968: 403) found evidence that students in the social sciences, law, and the humanities were more likely to be politicized and leftist than their colleagues in natural and applied sciences. He specifically cautions, however, that faculties of philosophy, letters, and other liberal arts with high proportions of female students often do not follow the general trend toward politicization.

An exception was the highly-politicized Instituto de Pedagogía at the University of Chile in Santiago, which in 1969 had nearly equal percentages of men and women students. We do not have data on the political behavior of women in the Instituto; however, women students in Chile rarely were prominent in student political actions. Most often it fell to the women to set up the support systems, for example, to supply food to the males who would assume the leading roles, make the policy, and occupy the buildings. An interesting research question on the participation of women in student politics awaits investigation.

It should be noted at the outset of this discussion that a very low percentage of registered voters of either sex belongs to parties in any Latin American country. General membership parties are a fairly recent phenomenon in Latin America; at the end of the past century, Mariano Nicolás Valcárcel

(quoted in Pike 1967: 183) observed that all members of any Peruvian political party could be fitted into one railroad boxcar. In the late 1960s in Peru,
probably 15 to 20 percent of all party members were female, while in Chile,
women in the various parties probably totaled about 20 percent. (It should
be noted here that these figures are estimates suggested by the women party
leaders interviewed for this study. No exact statistics on either total membership or proportions of women in the parties are available.)

Recruitment of women to parties in Peru and Chile reflects the political
realities of each epoch. The first political group to recruit women in Peru was
the Aprista party, which, from its foundation in 1930, had its *sección femenina,* or women's division. Both Magda Portal (1933 and 1946) and Rómulo
Meneses (1934) document the activities of the "thousands of compañeras"
who took part in the early days. However, because of the long years of
proscription, women were not able to participate openly in party activity and
did not hold their first national convention until 1946. At that time, a feminine training command was inaugurated as a transition measure to educate
politically a group of Aprista women. From this command, the women were
to be graduated to whatever party brigades could make use of their services.

This initiative soon fell by the wayside, and the women had no specialized
organization again until mid-1967, when Antonieta Zevallos de Prialé, wife
of a prominent party official, organized a new women's division. In 1967,
about 40 percent of the inscribed membership of the Partido Aprista Peruano
was female, and one party official estimated that about 70 percent of APRA's
electors were women (the Apristas gained 34.3 percent of the vote in 1963
in the last Peruvian elections held before the 1968 military coup). Probably
more women would have liked to become party members but hesitated
because of the years of persecution and danger.

The Christian Democrats in Peru were the next to enroll women. One of
the pioneer Christian Democratic women, of aristocratic origins, confessed
that she used to look all around in the street before ducking into party
headquarters because she was afraid some of her women friends would see
her:

> In those days the women never spoke up or said anything. The men were
> very nice and welcomed us, but they didn't know what to do with us.
> After a while, I went to the leaders and said, "What shall I do?" and they
> couldn't tell me. They said, "You make a plan and tell us." So I decided
> to work with the women, and I began to be less afraid, for I saw that the
> men didn't know very much about how to run a party either. Except for
> the Apristas, men haven't had much experience with political parties in
> Peru—what with one dictatorship after another. So they really didn't

know much more about it than the women—and after a while I discovered that!

Women made up about 30 percent of the Christian Democratic party membership in 1967 in Peru, and Acción Popular, the party of President Fernando Belaúnde Terry, had enrolled roughly the same percentage of women. (The Christian Democrats probably represented 4 to 5 percent of the voters in the 1960s; Belaúnde was elected in 1963 with 39 percent of the vote.) Women's activity was characterized as "sporadic" by a top woman party leader of Acción Popular. Men tend to look on women as "electoral capital," she said, and to call on them mainly in emergencies. Nevertheless, the Acción Populistas were the most active women in Peruvian politics before the military coup of 1968.

In proportion to total party membership, women probably were most numerous in the party formed by the former dictator, General Manuel Odría, who won 25.5 percent of the vote in the 1963 elections. One woman leader estimated that the party membership probably was about 60 percent female, because of the great sympathy among women for the general. She acknowledged that his following "really is not a party, it is a movement that gets active around election time—then the women get busy." Women's prominence in the movement might also be attributed to the fact that María Delgado de Odría was active in well-publicized works of charity during her husband's years in office and was herself a candidate for mayor of Lima in 1963 (she was defeated by Christian Democrat Luis Bedoya Reyes).

Aside from their participation in the major parties, there is some related activity among Peruvian women. In 1955 a small group of women formed the Movimiento Cívico Femenino, patterned in some respects after the League of Women Voters in the United States. The founders wanted the MCF to remain non-partisan and to educate women for civic responsibility. In reality, however, the membership tended to remain Catholic women, many of them "graduates" of Catholic Action movements. One member admitted that the group had been organized by Catholics to counteract the Aprista women and to give Catholic women "their" group.

In Chile, the Radical party was the first to open its doors to women; they entered the party as early as 1888, but did not have their own organization until 1934. (Much of my information on early participation of women in political parties is based on Gallo Chinchilla 1945.) Most of the women members have been teachers or government bureaucrats. The Radicals long boasted two of Chile's outstanding political women on their central executive committee: Inés Enríquez Frödden, the first woman to win public office in Chile (see section immediately following), and Amanda Labarca, the distinguished educator and feminist whose activities were sketched in the last chapters. About 10 percent of the membership was female, and the party and its splinter group, Democracia Radical, won 12.1 percent of the vote in the 1971 municipal elections, the last elections held before the 1973 military coup.

The Conservative party created a woman's section in 1941 specifically to occupy itself with the *noblesse oblige* aim of "intensive work in social action among the poorer classes." The Liberals allowed their women's group, formed in 1939, to intervene only in municipal affairs during the first years in which women were admitted to the party. United in the National party, these upper-class women found their activity blocked for a time in the late 1960s, when their own party leaders asked certain prominent women of the aristocracy to work behind the scenes in a general effort to give the Conservative-Liberal coalition a new image. With the presidential candidacy of Jorge Alessandri, mounted in late 1969, these women became active again. The National party won 26.2 percent of the vote in the 1971 municipal elections.

Women marched with Emilio Recabarren, founder of the Communist party of Chile, from the beginnings in 1911, and this party was the only one that did not segregate women. The Socialists established a woman's section called "Acción de Mujeres Socialistas" in 1933 and continued to maintain a woman's division. Women were active in the Falange, predecessor of the Christian Democratic party, from its foundation in 1938; they probably made up some 20 to 30 percent of the membership in these three parties before the 1973 military intervention. In the 1971 Chilean municipal elections, the Communists won 17.4 percent of the vote, the Socialists 23.9, and the Christian Democrats 26.2.

As was mentioned in the introduction to this section, the fact that women's political activity was organized apart from the men's was much resented by most of the women leaders (I interviewed the top leaders of every political party in the two countries). But most still said separate organization was necessary, not only because they believed women needed to be educated politically to bring them up to the men's level but also because of custom and tradition. Declared one woman party leader in Peru: "Women feel closer to other women, they have problems in common. It is necessary to have a feminine section because here the woman isn't accustomed to take part in politics." Her husband, a major party leader, added that a feminine section was necessary because "women have their own special schedule; they can't go out alone at night as men can." Other officials concurred in this view. Said a national official of another party,

The men prefer that the women have their own party activities and their own night in the Centro. Otherwise, the husband thinks, the wife might hear something not nice for her ears. A man may let slip some expression in a moment of passion or heat. That's why so many more women participate in party activities in Miraflores or in San Isidro than in other districts—there they're more developed, everything is on a higher and more refined level.

The segregation of women tended to lessen the potential influence women might have had on party policy, although the executive committees of even the most conservative parties included at least one woman member. These women did not, however, have much voice in party policy, and this has been true from the beginning. Magda Portal (Boger 1965: 37-38) has characterized her own participation in the executive councils of the Aprista party as an elaborate charade. Portraying herself as the character María de la Luz in a novel written in 1946 (*La Trampa,* or The Trap), Portal describes her relationship to the Aprista high command:

[María de la Luz] holds an important post in the High Command. But meetings devoted to high policy always take place without her. How could one have confidence in feminine discretion? . . . María is not subservient. . . . She has intellectual prejudices. She doesn't get on with the leaders' wives because she thinks herself better than they. She doesn't get on with the party leaders because the presence of a woman among so many men shocks them. Moreover, she always sits in judgment. When she makes an appearance in the High Command, they only take up formal business. And when she disagrees, the majority of the Command refute her. She stands alone. Often she leaves the room as a sign of protest, and then all breathe easier.

Women in parties encountered difficulties not only from men but from other women. A woman running for office often could not count on her friends for support. One interviewee reports that her woman friends were incredulous when she decided to join a party and run for office in her municipality in 1963, although their attitude afterward mellowed to some extent: "They have a vision of political parties as 'dirty' organizations," she recounted. "To belong was a case of lowering one's social position. They said to me: 'What an awful thing!'"

Another interviewee lamented that, in spite of her long record of volunteer work and her wide acquaintance in her municipality, her women friends refused to circulate her nomination papers because they did not agree to her candidacy. "It was my milkman, my gardener, the Chinese in the corner grocery who collected my 3,000 signatures," she recalled.

Within the party, too, women were not always at ease with one another if they came from different social classes. One interviewee spoke of the bad

taste of a *pobladora* (woman from a marginal area or *población*) who had risen
in her party and bought a fur coat. A pobladora who had some leadership
training outside her población recounted how lower-class women in the
Chilean Christian Democratic party found the going difficult:

> We sense that there is a class difference; we are not the same, and we are
> made to feel it in little ways.
>
> In the Centros de Madres, the *asesores* [women who come in as advisers to
> the Mothers' Centers] often do not allow leadership to develop, or only
> to a certain level. They work in the manner of *patronas*. Sometimes the
> pobladoras just go along with this, are passive; sometimes they play up to
> the señoras as a way of getting—or so they think—more out of them.
>
> One thing we resent very much is the way these people who come in from
> outside "tutear" us [use the familiar form of "you"] from the very first,
> while we always must continue with "Señora" and "Señorita." Why
> should this be? Why should not a pobladora who has worked and fought
> for her children, who is respected by us and listened to, not also be
> respected by the *asesores* and called "Señora"?

Women's Power at the Polls

A review of women's voting and party activity would be incomplete without a discussion of women and the Chilean presidential elections—one of
the few electoral situations in which women have demonstrably exercised
power.

Contrary to a myth current even in Chile, women have not "decided" all
three presidential elections since they received the vote, but only the
Alessandri-Allende contest of 1958. They are nevertheless considered poten-
tially as the "hacedores de presidentes" (makers of presidents, as a popular
phrase has it) because thus far they have tended to vote more as a group and
to polarize more compactly around a particular candidate than do the men.

In 1952, the first time women voted for president, they cast 287,794
ballots (23 percent of the total); their votes did not affect the outcome, and
Carlos Ibáñez was elected by nearly 450,000 masculine votes.

In 1958, however, women's votes jumped to 35 percent of the total
1,250,000 cast and gave Jorge Alessandri a 33,000-vote plurality. If women
had not voted in that election, Salvador Allende would have won with the
18,000 majority the men gave him over Alessandri.

In the 1964 presidential election (with women casting 47.6 percent of
the ballots), Eduardo Frei won a plurality of both masculine and feminine
votes. The men gave him a close victory of only 59,000 votes over Allende,
who again was the Socialist candidate, whereas the women inundated Frei

with a 372,000 plurality. If women had voted for Frei in the same proportion as the men, the election would have been thrown to the Chilean congress, since no candidate would then have received a majority. Even at this early date, however, there was a marked class difference in the way women voted, as table 2 makes clear. Many more women voted for Allende in the popular barrios than in the well-to-do communities.

In the 1970 elections, Allende won with 36.2 percent of the vote, and Petras (1973: 16) shows that working-class women were one of the major factors in his victory. Petras combines all municipalities in greater Santiago that contain 40 percent or more industrial workers, and finds that Allende received 119 feminine votes for every 100 feminine votes for Alessandri and 147 for every 100 for Tomic. Indications are that working-class women voted in even greater proportions for Unidad Popular in the 1971 municipal elections (all voting statistics from República de Chile, Dirección del Registro Electoral, various dates).

Women in Public Life: The National Governments

Women in Latin America generally received the right to hold office at the same time they received the franchise. In Chile, so that no one would have any doubts on the matter, Ley 9292 expressly states that Chilean women can "elect and be elected *even* President of the Republic" (Klimpel Alvarado 1962: 88—emphasis added). The decree is equally explicit in Peru (Patrón Faura 1972: 9).

Whatever their country, few Latin American women are found in the top echelons of the executive branch or, except in the case of Chile, in the national legislatures. (Most figures in this section are for 1967 and 1968, the years before many Latin American countries once again came under military rule. In most cases, this fact means that neither men nor women civilians remain in office.) Probably because the judiciary is less rewarding financially than private law practice, women make up nearly one-third of Chile's 514 judges and court officials; however, very few are found in the top levels of the judicial hierarchy and none at all on the supreme court (República de Chile, Corte Suprema de Justicia 1967: 5-13). Few Peruvian women become judges.

Before the respective *golpes*, Peru and Chile were governed by strong presidential systems with legislative powers accorded to bicameral congresses. Each president carried out his mandate with the assistance of a council of ministers, twelve in Peru and fifteen in Chile, plus a variety of semi-independent agencies, most of them reporting directly to the chief executive. In neither country was any of these posts occupied by a woman. In late 1969, only four women occupied cabinet-level posts in the Americas. Haydée Castillo served as minister of development in the Christian Democratic government of

TABLE 2
MALE/FEMALE VOTES CAST FOR ALLENDE, TOMIC, AND ALESSANDRI (1970) IN SELECTED BARRIOS

| | Allende | | | | Tomic | | | | Alessandri | | | |
| | Men | | Women | | Men | | Women | | Men | | Women | |
	No.	%	No.	%	No.	%	No.	%	No.	%	No.	%
Middle Class:												
Providencia (45,289)	3,217	(7.1)	3,427	(7.6)	3,901	(8.6)	6,520	(14.4)	10,410	(23.0)	17,814	(39.3)
Las Condes (47,861)	4,706	(9.8)	4,514	(9.4)	4,544	(9.5)	7,509	(15.7)	10,011	(20.9)	16,577	(34.6)
Popular:												
San Miguel (111,848)	28,403	(25.4)	23,325	(20.8)	11,930	(10.7)	15,591	(13.9)	13,686	(12.2)	18,913	(17.0)
Quinta Normal (64,383)	15,003	(23.3)	11,539	(17.9)	7,854	(12.2)	9,849	(15.3)	8,890	(13.8)	11,248	(17.5)
La Cisterna (59,914)	13,329	(22.3)	10,831	(18.1)	7,098	(11.8)	9,503	(15.8)	8,142	(13.6)	11,011	(18.4)

Source: Calculated from Dirección del Registro Electoral: Elección Presidencial 1970.

Venezuela; in the Dominican Republic and Puerto Rico, women held the labor ministry portfolios; and in Guatemala, a woman served in the cabinet level post of secretary of social welfare. Six more women held sub-cabinet-level posts throughout the Americas (OAS, Inter-American Commission of Women 1969). If we take twelve cabinet posts per country as the average, women occupy only 1.5 percent of them. (The United States is included in this calculation.)

Peru never had a woman in a cabinet level position; Chilean women held cabinet posts in the administrations of Gabriel González Videla and Carlos Ibáñez: Adriana Olguín de Baltra, lawyer and wife of a prominent political leader of the ruling Radical party, was minister of justice in Videla's cabinet, and María Teresa del Canto, a retired schoolteacher, served as minister of education for Ibáñez. The latter was proposed for the office by María de la Cruz as the candidate of the Partido Femenino Chileno. Neither held office for a long period.

The two highest administrative posts held by women in pre-coup Peru and Chile were both in education. Renée Viñas Joan, who was only thirty-two at the time, was appointed in 1967 as director of primary and teacher education in Chile, at the same time that Marta Pajuelo Eduardo held the equivalent teacher education post in Peru. Both women were reform-minded, experienced, and highly trained professionals.

In the United States, no woman has served at the cabinet level in the past three presidential administrations, although two did so prior to 1955: Frances Perkins, who served from 1933 to 1945 as secretary of labor, and Oveta Culp Hobby, who was secretary of health, education and welfare from 1953 to 1955. In the lower grades of the civil service, three-quarters of the workers are women. But in the "super" grades, the women dwindle to insignificant numbers. Of the 1,632 persons in grade 18 and above, for example, only 1.5 percent are women (U.S. Civil Service Commission 1969: 21).

Women serve in legislatures throughout the Americas, but their numbers are few. This follows the world-wide trend; by 1970, some 123 countries had extended women the right to hold office, but women had been elected to legislatures in only 69 (United Nations, Implementation of the Convention on Political Rights 1970). Before the recent flurry of coups, 55 women served in lower houses and 8 in senates of the 21 American republics. This is about 2 percent of the total. Appendix III shows where they were serving.

The 14 women in the Chilean congress in 1968 represented the largest feminine delegation ever to serve at one time in an American congress, including the congress of the United States, where, in 1968, 10 of 26 women candidates were elected to the house, and the *lone candidate* to the senate was defeated (*New York Times,* November 10, 1968). This contrasts sharply, however, with the large increases in the number of women candidates in U.S. congressional elections. It is worth noting that Chilean women parliamentarians also outnumbered, as a percentage of the total, women in the national legislatures of such advanced countries as Britain, France, West Germany, and India. Exact figures of participation (all, however, below 15 percent for most countries) are given in chapter 1, pages 24-25.

The only exceptions appear to be Yugoslavia, where women made up 19.6 percent of the federal assembly (Durić and Dragicević 1965: 17), Finland, 17 percent, and Sweden, 15 percent (Devaud 1968: 62-63). Perhaps the percentages are higher because in these other countries women won their rights sooner? Such an answer would seem to beg the question, i.e., *why* did women get voting rights in Latin countries at later dates than in the non-Latin? Moreover, Britain does not follow the pattern, for women made up only 3.9 percent of the House of Commons. (To maintain comparability with the time period in Latin America when women were still serving, all figures given on women in legislatures are for the mid-1960s.)

So far as the judiciary is concerned, Chile again has a large feminine representation among its members, as indicated above. For some twenty years, women have been entering the courts in increasing numbers. Most observers attribute this phenomenon not only to the fact that so many women—in comparison to those in other countries—study law (from 1898 to 1969, 843 women received law degrees in Chile, about 10 percent of the total [Colegio de Abogados, 1969], compared to 3 percent in the United States), but also because women often find it difficult, if they do not have male relatives with a law practice, to gain employment in a law firm. Probably another cause is the fact that, as Klimpel Alvarado (1962: 111) observes, "the entrance of women has been facilitated by the disinterest of male lawyers in exercising these functions because they are so grossly underpaid." She adds that in spite of their long record of efficient service, few women judges attain the highest levels. A look at their placement in the judicial hierarchy in 1967 confirms her contention (see table 3).

In Peru, there were only 11 women judges or court officials, or 1.1 percent of a total of nearly a thousand (República del Perú, ONRAP 1966: 197-205). In addition, Dra. Ella Dumbar Temple was the *fiscal suplente* of the superior court of Lima. Women's representation in the Colegio de Abogados (the bar association), where 210 women lawyers were represented among 3,680 men (5.7 percent), also is small. (Totals were counted from membership lists at the Colegio in 1967. The executive secretary of the Colegio calculated that there were some 60 additional women lawyers in Peru who were not members of the association.) As in Chile, many women lawyers make their careers in the government bureaucracy rather than in private practice; the bar association's executive secretary asserted that there was "absolutely no chance for women lawyers to practice: very few make a success of it, and very few try."

TABLE 3
MEN AND WOMEN IN THE CHILEAN JUDICIARY ACCORDING TO GRADE

	Men		Women		Total	
	No.	%	No.	%	No.	%
Grades I-IV	160	43	23*	16	183	36
Grades V-VIII	209	57	122	84	331	64
TOTALS	369	100	145	100	514	100

*Includes 20 women juvenile judges in grade III.

Source: Calculated from República de Chile, Corte Suprema de Justicia, 1967: 5-13.

In the United States, 300 of the 8,748 judges (or 3.4 percent) were women in the same years (Gruberg 1968: 190); this reflected the 7,000 women lawyers who made up 3 percent of the total number of lawyers in this country (U.S. Department of Labor, Women's Bureau 1968: 2).

Female bureaucrats have, however, made decided inroads into two fields not strictly sex-stereotyped—budget and personnel. Particularly in Chile, there is a wide-spread, often-articulated belief among both male and female bureaucrats that women ought to be assigned to positions involving the budgeting and disbursing of funds because they are more honest than men. It would seem that this bit of folklore (probably often true) is widely enough believed to have gained Chilean women a solid entrée into some fields ordinarily filled by men. Some 35 percent of women in the Chilean bureaucracy (in both "feminine" and "neutral" agencies) deal with budgetary, planning, finances, and personnel matters.

This experience of women in Chile might indicate the direction for women in other Latin American countries who want to break out of feminine-type assignments. Of course, the supermadre image plays a part here, too. Besides the belief that women are more honest, assignment of women to budgetary or personnel tasks is justified on the grounds that women have had experience in family budgeting or have a natural bent for human relations.

Perhaps the classic remark along these lines was made by one of the few women in the study who believes her sex capable of assuming the presidency of her country; what she apparently has in mind, however, is an image of the woman blown up to a kind of greatest supermadre of them all. "If a woman of capacity is capable of governing her home," this interviewee declares, "she is capable of doing the same in the nation."

In summary, few women yet serve in the top echelons of the executive, legislative, or judicial branches of government in Latin America. (To round out the picture sketched in this section, see Blachman [1973: 13-15] and Harkess and Pinzón de Lewin [1975: 443-445] for information on Brazil and Colombia.) Appendix VI shows how the survey group in Peru and Chile—where most of the women clustered at the lower levels of the bureaucracy and a few occupied "visible" positions in congress or political parties—confirms these tendencies. In chapters 6 and 7 many of these facts about women in government service will be further developed with data from the survey, and the final chapter will explore the implications for the future of women's special patterns of participation.

Women in Municipal Government

What about the much vaunted notion that even if women are absent from the upper levels of government, they are making great headway in municipal politics? In terms of relative numbers, the situation in Peru and Chile was not a great deal better at the local level of government before the military coups in each country, although several hundred women were serving on their local municipal councils. Now in both countries municipal officials are appointed, including some women—the only level at which women in government have survived.

In the 1960s there was a renewed emphasis on municipal government in both Peru and Chile. The decree restoring municipal elections was the first official act of the Belaúnde administration in 1963, and 87.7 percent of those registered to vote participated in the municipal elections that year (República del Perú, Registro Electoral 1967a). Chile also experienced what one author terms a "most significant" degree of interest in municipal elections. In 1956, only 10 percent of those registered to vote bothered to exercise their franchise in the local elections held that year; in 1967, 85 percent voted (López R. 1967: 18).

Because municipal elections were often turned into "plebiscites" for national political programs, some of these votes doubtless did not demonstrate a high interest in local affairs. Nevertheless, the new interest in local government appeared real, not only in municipal affairs but also in efforts to extend decision-making through the creation of entities even closer to the people, such as the *juntas de vecinos* (neighborhood councils) and *centros de madres* (mothers' centers) in Chile.

Women in Chile had been eligible to hold municipal office since 1934, but few had taken advantage of the fact, perhaps because local office was considered—there almost was a folklore about it—a necessary apprenticeship for political service at higher levels. Thus, as long as the road to congress or other higher office was closed (the right to hold national office came with suffrage in 1949), only the woman who saw municipal office as an end in itself would bother to enter politics. Only 29 served as *regidoras* in their communities in 1944, 10 years after they were granted the municipal franchise (*El Mercurio* 1967).

In 1953, however, women could for the first time consider municipal office as a step toward a political career. This, along with the newness of their expanded voting right, may account for the large number of women—106—elected to municipal office that year.

But in the next municipal elections, the "business as usual" phenomenon may have come into play, because the number of women elected in 1956 dropped by almost 36 percent, to 68 *regidoras*. And it took three more elections to bring the numbers above the 1953 high: 83 women were elected to municipal office in 1960, 95 in 1963, and, finally, 123 in the elections of 1967 (*El Mercurio* 1967).

Not all parties were equally interested in pushing women forward, and it was almost unthinkable for anyone to run without party backing. One woman was elected *concejal* in 1966 at the head of an independent slate she herself formed in the important district of San Isidro in Lima, but she was exceptional.

The situation was more complicated in Peru than in Chile, because all those who appeared on a party list in a municipal contest campaigned for the entire list. Whether one was elected or not depended on the percentage of the vote the party commanded in that district and one's place on the ticket. Candidate no. 7 of Acción Popular, for example, was almost certain to be elected in a district like San Isidro, a party stronghold, but even candidate no. 1 on a list of the left Frente de Liberación Nacional would not win (and indeed, the FLN did not bother to run a list) in San Isidro.

Thus, women sometimes connived in acting as window dressing for their parties, which apparently felt they needed a token woman on the ticket. As one woman told me, a bit ruefully, she had been elected in spite of herself: "First of all, I wasn't expecting even to be a candidate. Then they put me no. 6 on the list, which was rather risky, as it turned out, because all up to and including no. 8 were elected."

The municipal machinery and personnel is much larger in Peru than in

Chile, not only because of the greater population but because local government extends to more of the small communities than it does in the Chilean system. More local officials are involved, too, because municipal councils in Peru are larger. Many have fifteen members, while in Chile a council generally has only five. Exceptions are the provincial capitals, which have seven, nine, or (in the case of Santiago) fifteen members. The totals are given in table 4.

TABLE 4
WOMEN IN MUNICIPAL GOVERNMENT: PERU AND CHILE (LATE 1960s)

	Distritos	Provincias	Departamentos	Total Concejales	Total Women/%
Peru	1,583	145	23	9,226	438 (4.7)

	Comunas	Departamentos	Provincias	Total Regidores	Total Women/%
Chile	276	[ ]ᵃ	25	1,629	127 (7.8)

ᵃNot significant for local elections.

Source: República del Perú, Registro Electoral 1967b, and *El Mercurio* 1967.

In Chile, 22 percent of the *regidoras* were found in the *comunas* of Gran Santiago. In the department of Lima, however, women constituted exactly 5 percent of the *concejales,* only slightly above the national average, whereas in the northern departments, Aprista strongholds that had a long history of feminine political participation even before women received the vote (Ancash and La Libertad, for example), women reached nearly 10 percent of the total of council members. In contrast, in Indian regions such as Junín and Puno, women numbered scarcely 2 percent of the total elected to municipal council membership (República del Perú, Registro Electoral 1967b; República de Chile, Dirección del Registro Electoral 1968). In Chile, ten women were elected mayors of their *comunas,* while in Peru thirty-eight became mayors (República del Perú, Registro Electoral 1967b, and República de Chile, Contraloría General 1968).

Thus we see that women had made relatively little progress at the municipal level in either country. The fact that so many of the women elected had no intention of seeking another term in office demonstrates how tenuous was the position of women in municipal politics even before the military governments suspended the electoral process.

In the foregoing chapters, many barriers against the successful aspiration of women to high political office have been singled out—old regimes resistant to new political aspirants of either sex; the return to "business as usual" after extraordinary events, for example, in the aftermath of the world wars; the resumption of passive attitudes when the novelty of suffrage wears off; the reluctance of political parties to push women candidates. These are facts that explain women's disadvantaged position only in a limited way, however; the facts themselves pose further questions. Other obvious, straightforward barriers have been discussed, among them women's much greater involvement in bearing and rearing children, women's near monopoly of the "wrong" professions for political recruitment, or very simply the fact that (as many women party leaders pointed out to me) cultural and social prejudices have prevented women from forming a sufficiently large pool of capable potential political leaders to whom responsible positions might be offered.

For an intermediate explanation we may logically turn to all those prevailing images of woman existing in the minds of men and women in many cultures, but perhaps changing less in the Latin American *ambiente* than in any other society. We have noted already the dominant, aggressive masculine and the submissive female images that most Latin American societies regard as "ideal" because in the Latin view they are ordained by sacred natural law and confirmed by four centuries of history and convention. Sex-related differentiation between men and women is nowhere more starkly defined than in the sphere of politics, not only in Latin America but everywhere. In Duverger's view, the hostility to political activity for women is based on the same kind of primitive mentality that sees war as a "sport for men." There is a similar tendency, he says, to regard the club, the forum, debates, parliament, and political life in general as "typically masculine activities" (Duverger 1955: 10).

Probably no ultimate explanations are possible, but it would seem that the questions of political leadership and the policy-making process in general (as distinct from the less controversial act of voting, which often is not very important in a society) are crucial for women because it is *here* that they have made the least headway in the contemporary world. What should be borne in mind is the fact that the "political club" is the last male stronghold women have attempted to enter, not without some degree of reluctance and doubt on the part of the females as to the rightness of doing so. No final judgment can be made yet on whether woman will succeed in the long run, even in those professional and educational spheres where she has made much more progress (and where she has been present a much longer time). An important research project awaits scholars, that of looking at the role of women's political activity in newly independent countries to see whether the suggestive trends of initial enthusiasm/return to passivity hold everywhere and whether any signs of reverse trends are yet visible.

6. Women Leaders in Peru and Chile

The Survey and Its Object

This chapter and the following explore survey results from interviews with 167 women active in government in Peru and Chile in the late 1960s. The countries were chosen in order to study women in two contrasting political cultures that have, however, some similarities of language, history, and social attitudes.

Although events have overtaken most of these women, although they have been "retired" from government by the military coups in their respective countries, the analysis not only has historical interest but is also of value as the first systematic exploration of women in politics in Latin America. The results can, with caution, be extended to women leaders in countries where conditions are similar.

The study was designed as a small, pointed investigation of a crucial population rather than a more general survey of attitudes and activities involving a representative sample of a larger universe. Eighty-four of the interviewees were working in the national bureaucracy or serving as party leaders or legislators in Peru and Chile when this survey was carried out in 1967. The other eighty-three interviewees were active in municipal politics. During the months of the survey (February-August), Fernando Belaúnde Terry was in his last full year in office before the military coup of 1968 (after assuming the presidency in July 1963), and Eduardo Frei Montalva, elected in September 1964, was in the fourth year of a six-year term.

In addition to the 167 questionnaire interviews, I chose 12 women in each country willing to engage in four or five informal but directed conversations, totalling twelve to fifteen hours each, that provided an opportunity to discuss in depth many of the issues raised in the questionnaire. In most cases, I was allowed to spend a day observing these women officials at work. Appendices

IV, V, and VI show the positions occupied by the interviewees as well as the type and level of their offices. In 1972, some of those who participated in the original study were interviewed again.

Only women holding government or party posts (either elective or appointive) and candidates for the municipal councils were defined as political leaders for the purposes of this study. To be chosen, a potential interviewee also had to be involved in decision-making, even if only in a circumscribed area within her own ministry or agency, and she also had to have subordinates. The number of subordinates ranged from one or two assistants at one end of the scale to the more than five hundred employees of an agency presided over by a Chilean woman bureaucrat.

Limiting the interviewees to those holding official posts inevitably excluded many political influentials, for example, certain wives (or mistresses) of key government officials, as well as women business entrepreneurs, feminine leaders in trade unions and campesino organizations, and others who did not figure officially in government. It was necessary, however, to set an objective criterion for choosing the interviewees. Identifying non-officeholders as politically influential is difficult even for "insiders."

Although some women who figure officially may not, in fact, have exercised any political power, whereas some powerful women held no official position, still my official elite is bound to include many women members of the leadership hierarchy who were at the same time influentials. Or perhaps it would be more accurate to say they are women leaders who exercised power to the extent and degree (not very broad or very high, as the ensuing study demonstrates) that women can be said to influence the political process in Latin America.

My original goal was to seek out fifty women serving at the national level in each country and an equal number in local government. This figure was scaled down when it became evident that women officials in national government in Peru did not total that number. Except for the dozen or so notables among Peruvian women leaders, the construction of the interview group there demanded that the women be sought out agency by agency. The usual procedure was to approach the public relations or personnel director in each ministry or agency, explain the study, and request an introduction to one woman official. This first woman contacted invariably knew the few other women officials in her agency and, in turn, presented me to them. For Chile, a purposive sample was constructed from several public administration guides, with an attempt being made to include a number proportionate to the total number of women officials serving in each type of assignment: budget, personnel, planning, administration, and so forth.

Selection of the municipal officials and candidates was based on election lists published in the newspapers and on lists collected from the respective political parties. Here inclusion in the sample was based on a rough attempt to keep party representation in balance and at the same time to include representation of the various class groups of Gran Lima and Gran Santiago. Thirty-eight barrios and municipios are represented in the group.

Except for the ministries of education, women in the bureaucracy did not necessarily cluster only in those ministries or agencies that carry out tasks of health, education, and welfare; the survey group accurately reflects the proportion of women administrators in these agencies. Approximately 35 percent of all women executives in the government bureaucracy of Chile worked in agencies dealing with these traditionally feminine tasks, and 36 percent of the survey group also worked in such agencies.

Such a percentage, at first glance, would not seem to support the allegation made throughout this study that women in government are forced by the supermadre image into feminine-stereotyped tasks. However, women in ministries or agencies that society would view as not especially suitable for female bureaucrats often perform "female" roles, that is, they serve as social welfare chiefs in the labor ministry, public works, and agrarian reform agencies or direct *artesanía* (craftwork) for the industrial development agency. If we consider the women by the *type* of work they do, then nearly 70 percent of the survey group engage in "feminine" tasks.

Characteristics of the Survey Group

The survey is designed to be exploratory and descriptive rather than explanatory (although the results suggest some possible areas for future research on why women engage in politics and why they act and think as they do). For example, my study does not explain why Chilean women were so much more active in politics than the women of most other nations. Nor can it provide answers to the intriguing question of what factors "cause" some women to seek political or government office when so many others of similar background and education do not.

In the early stages of the study, an attempt was made to construct a control group of women who had *not* chosen a political vocation, matched as closely as possible to the age, marital status, educational level, and professional background of the interviewees. Much thought and discussion also was devoted to the idea of a control group of men in government, matched to the women by the offices held, although, as Eli Ginzberg has indicated in his study of professional women (1966), the life-styles of men and women may be too divergent for comparisons between the sexes to yield much information of value. Ginzberg originally intended to study men and women professionals along much the same lines, but found he could not do so. The professional goals, the demands of homemaking, and the discontinuities in the professional lives of women proved too different from male career patterns, and he ended up with two separate questionnaires, two studies, and two books. Lack of time and financial resources also prevented me from setting up any control groups.

Two limitations are thus set at the beginning: the data cannot be used to support generalizations implying that members of the leadership group are only extreme variants of typical, middle-class professional women in Peru or Chile, although other studies and aggregate data have been utilized in making such an assertion. Nor, on the contrary, can this study—restricted as it is to one sample—assume that the characteristics discovered are distinctive to this particular group; some of the findings may be generalized throughout the population of middle-class, female professionals.

An Indian proverb has it that whereas a man of silver will do, a woman must be made of gold. The personal experiences and testimony of the women interviewed in this survey suggest that women must be more outstanding than men to aspire to a government or political career. Distributions of women in the present study, so far as status, education, and other characteristics are concerned, confirm these observations to a high degree. These distributions by no means "explain" a political vocation, however, as many observers have pointed out. For one thing, persons of low status, rural origin, and little education have become political leaders. For another, many who possess all the opposite characteristics do *not* choose political careers.

The data presented below nevertheless suggest that almost always the "required" elite social background and demographic characteristics must be possessed if a woman is to achieve a political leadership position, at least in formal political structures. They are necessary conditions for a feminine political vocation, although not sufficient to explain why a woman chooses it. The study of *informal* leaders among women—until now almost completely unexplored with the exception of some pioneer work by Bunster (1974), Garrett (1977 [?]), Nash (1975b), and Videla de Plankey (1974) and in two valuable issues of *Latin American Perspectives* (1977)—may reveal other prerequisites for popular leadership in trade unions, neighborhood associations, and the like. But the "visible" women leaders even of the popular parties in Latin America—with the notable exception of the Communist party of Chile, which had genuine working-class women cadres—still with few exceptions come from the middle, or in some cases the upper, class.

The interviewees emerge as an extremely well-educated group; over one-half are university graduates. Only 16 women among the entire 167 interviewees are not high school graduates, these being found almost exclusively among the politicians representing the poorer barrios. There are marked differences, however, between Peruvians and Chileans in the type of secondary school attended. Private secondary education, even under lay auspices, often has a strong religious and "female education" orientation, and there may well be significance in the fact that so many more Peruvians than Chileans (65 percent to 32 percent) were educated in private schools, most run by religious orders of nuns.

It is not surprising that professionals are over-represented in the sample, making up 76 percent of the interviewees, whereas they are only 7.0 and 11.5 percent of women active in the Peruvian and Chilean labor forces in the same years (Organización de Estados Americanos 1967: 128, 132). Only 36 of the women had no work history; these either were engaged in local politics or (in three cases) were leaders of conservative party women's branches.

One-third of the Chileans interviewed are of non-Iberian extraction on the paternal side; only 16 percent of the Peruvians have non-Spanish fathers. Kinzer (1973: 163-164) found in her study of women professionals in Buenos Aires an over-representation of daughters of immigrants, and suggests that the immigrant father who has torn himself away from Europe's ghettoes also has cast aside the traditional concept of women's roles; Argentinean immigrants have a long-standing practice of educating daughters. The greater activism of Chilean women may in part be due to the greater representation of immigrants in their country's population—particularly among the capital city's professional men and entrepreneurs (Pike 1968: 217-219).

The fact that married women in the survey worked in far greater numbers in local politics may not appear very novel, for this is the situation of women everywhere. Yet they did so not because they lacked *time* for involvement in politics or a bureaucratic career at the national level—many of the married women got very immersed in their unpaid municipal posts, making them a full-time career, something a man rarely did. Middle-class women in Latin America have greater freedom from domestic tasks and child care than women in most other countries. Many times interviewees remarked that "in Latin America we are lucky, we have our servants." Some said that they thought this imposed more of an obligation to get involved in public affairs.

Yet the kinds of posts these married women occupied demonstrate that they were not fully using their freedom for public service involvement. The women themselves did not give lack of time as an excuse for their lesser involvement in national politics, and the difficulty very probably goes back to one of image. Local politics is seen as appropriate for a married woman; national politics or a bureaucratic post are not. One national party leader, whose wife was a member of the municipal council in the residential barrio where they live, voiced an opinion that is widespread:

The municipality can be run by women much better than by men. Like most men, I go to the center [Lima] all day—often I don't lunch at home or even come for supper because of party work.

It is the women who are here all day, go to the markets, note if the garbage is collected, the streets clean, observe what the needs of the children are.

More details on the background characteristics of the interview group are included as Appendices VII and VIII; rather than give fuller descriptions here, profiles of typical Peruvian and Chilean activists have been constructed.

Profiles of the Woman Leader in Peru and Chile

If you had been a woman active in politics and/or government in Peru just before the 1968 coup, chances are you would have grown up in Lima or Callao, would belong to the middle or upper-middle class, and more than likely would have attended a private secondary school (probably run by a religious order of nuns). You would be just over forty years of age and, if married (chances being one in two that you were married or had been married at one time), you could well belong to that group among married women leaders (nearly one-half the total) with large families of four or more children. You would probably confine your activities to municipal politics unless your children were grown.

As a typical woman leader in Peru, you would be completing your second year in your present post or political office, although you would have engaged in your first political activity or embarked on your first bureaucratic job five or six years earlier. Your office more than likely would be at such a low level that it would not give you much prominence; you would be "notorious" only in your own community or within a limited circle of acquaintances and co-workers in the bureaucracy.

As a Chilean activist, your "demographic profile" would vary somewhat from that of the Peruvian leader sketched here. Although your girlhood would have been spent in Santiago or another large city and you also would come from the middle class, chances are that you would be some five years older than your Peruvian counterpart. Both you and your Peruvian colleagues in government would be considerably older, as a group, than the general population of economically active women in your countries.

You would be twice as likely as a Chilean leader to have been educated at the secondary level in a public *liceo*. Your family pattern also would differ from your Peruvian sister's. Although your chances of ever having been married would be about the same, you would be less likely to have a large family; two-thirds of all Chilean married women leaders in the survey have three children or fewer. If your children were still young, however, you would be less inhibited than your Peruvian colleague in taking on a full-time, national-level job. On the whole, however, you and your colleagues in Peru are far more likely to be married than women from the general population who are economically active.

As a Chilean you also would be completing your second year in the post you now occupy, but your government or political career history would be longer than the average for Peruvian leaders in that you would typically have begun your initial activity in politics or the bureaucracy eight or ten years ago instead of only five or six. Your office would not be likely to make you any more prominent than your Peruvian counterpart, since your chances as a Chilean of serving at a higher level would be only slightly improved.

If you were a national leader in either country, you would almost certainly have prepared for your work at the university, although the profession for which you studied might well have been a career other than teaching, social work, or nursing/health work. There would be roughly a fifty-fifty chance that you had studied a "masculine" profession such as law, or a modern career like architecture or commercial engineering, and then had chosen to exercise it in the bureaucracy instead of attempting to establish yourself in private practice. This would contrast sharply with the distribution of your professional sisters in the general marketplace, where chances of being in a strictly feminine career would be four in five rather than one in two.

Political Socialization

What makes a woman seek a career in politics and/or government? Leaders apparently must possess certain social background characteristics to be in the running, but evidently something more decisive is at work in determining which women elect political careers.

Do certain types of people gravitate to public roles? Until now, the contradictory findings of psychological studies do not show that leaders are distinguished from the general population by any particular personality traits. Thus my survey did not attempt to discover any personality "types."

It has also been suggested that those who choose political vocations may have grown up in families with a higher level of political interest and activity (linked to a positive concept of politics) than the families of those who do not elect politics as a career. Or perhaps future political leaders were in contact with political personalities or were challenged to political action through participation in student movements or volunteer organizations.

Political socialization is the term generally used to denote the process through which a citizen acquires the information, social attitudes, and personality characteristics that affect his or her future political behavior. Such learning can be formal or informal and can take place in childhood or later in life. This point is important in considering the socialization of future women leaders. In most of Latin America, a leadership role became a possibility for the present generation of women only in the mid-1950s, when most of them had already reached adulthood. We might therefore expect to find a strong family influence predisposing a woman to enter on a political career, but we would also not be surprised to find later influences decisive in some cases. This is the situation with the women leaders involved in my survey. Responding to questions about the principal influences on their political vocation, sixty-one mention the family, whereas forty-five mention the ideals of a political party and/or a political leader. These influences and others are discussed in more detail below.

The Family and the Political Daughter

We turn first to the remote circumstances that served to awaken initial interest in the political process among the women interviewees. Two emerge from the data as particularly influential: an exposure to politics in the family circle that left a positive image, and an introduction to the ideals and program of a political party (and/or of a male political figure). Table 5 gives the totals on these and several other "historical" circumstances leading to the interviewees' initial involvement in politics as the women themselves recall them. At this point, we consider answers only from the 71 percent (119 interviewees) who define their activity as "political"; of these, 34 are singled out as "aspiring" politicians because they were the only ones who had ambitions to rise in the political hierarchy. The remainder of the interviewees (N = 48) perceived their posts as apolitical, although this patently was *not* true in some cases. (The 34 *superpolíticas* are discussed in greater detail in chapter 7, in the section "Women at the Top.")

The large number mentioning the family is not surprising in view of the universal finding that the family is a principal agent of political socialization. Of the 119 interviewees who view their posts as political, 51 percent report that their families played a decisive part in awakening them to their first awareness of the political process. When the women were asked specifically about the family members who played the most important role in awakening their interest in politics, many singled out their fathers in their recollections. The family as a whole runs a close second; mothers, however, very seldom are mentioned as the decisive influence in arousing initial interest. Table 6 shows these more specific recollections.

The lack of mothers' influence on daughters' political careers is not

TABLE 5

MAJOR INFLUENCES ON POLITICAL SOCIALIZATION AS REPORTED BY MUNICIPAL AND NATIONAL LEADERS[a]

	Total[b]		Peru				Chile			
	No.	%	Muni.	Nat.	Tot.	%	Muni.	Nat.	Tot.	%
My family; my father, mother	61	(51)	10	24	34	(52)	15	12	27	(50)
Ideals, leaders of a political party	45	(38)	23	8	31	(48)	9	5	14	(26)
Injustice, poverty observed as a girl	25	(21)	10	5	15	(23)	7	3	10	(19)
Husband; when I married	17	(14)	5	3	8	(12)	5	4	9	(17)
Activities in student movement or Catholic Action	15	(13)	1	2	3	(5)	3	9	12	(22)
Women's movement; when women received vote	5	(4)	1	1	2	(3)	3		3	(6)
Other influence	9	(8)	3		3	(5)	5	1	6	(11)

Source: Q. 8 of questionnaire survey (the questionnaire is available from the author on request).

[a]These questions were not asked of the "hard core" of apoliticals (16 Peruvians and 32 Chileans) who do not believe their jobs are political and indicate they have no interest in politics.

[b]Totals add up to more than 119 and 100 percent because some of the interviewees recalled more than one influence on their political awakening.

TABLE 6
RECOLLECTIONS BY "POLITICIAN" DAUGHTERS OF FAMILY INFLUENCE ON THEIR POLITICAL SOCIALIZATION

	Peru		Chile		Total	
	No.	%	No.	%	No.	%
Interviewee recalls as decisive influence:						
Father's	15	(23)	14	(26)	29	(24)
Family's	13	(20)	7	(13)	20	(17)
Mother's	2	(4)	2	(4)	4	(4)
	30	(47)	23	(43)	53[a]	(45)
Other decisive influence	35	(53)	31	(57)	66	(55)
TOTALS	65	(100)	54	(100)	119	(100)

Source: Q. 9 of the questionnaire survey.

[a]"Family influences" do not total 61 answers as in table 5 because in this case only the first-mentioned or most decisive influence was taken into account.

surprising. None of the interviewees had "political" mothers, and only two of the mothers had been interested in women's rights. One of these was "Peru's first feminist: the first woman to go out alone without a relative or servant and one of the first to work" [as a teacher in the 1920s]. Only 27 of the interviewees had mothers trained for professions—20 were teachers—but often they did not actually work. A Peruvian interviewee comments: "My mother had a teaching certificate, but it was 'decorative'—women didn't work in her epoch."

Lack of early influence does not necessarily mean that mothers *now* frown on a daughter's career. One official remarked that her mother—and, "very important, my mother-in-law"—like it. She adds: "Maybe they're impressed because it's an important position and I make a lot of money."

In contrast, the encouragement of the father often was direct and decisive in the interviewee's formative years. Says one woman, now a legislator, recalling her father's influence:

My father always helped me along and encouraged me. I was always very close to him, and he inspired me a great deal, and also supported me in my desire to study. My uncles—no. There I had a lot of opposition. They said to Papa—"What's all this? You're letting your daughter study and work!"

A Peruvian woman lawyer (who, however, never has worked for a salary) comments:

We were three sisters, now one is a chemical engineer, the other a bibliographer. My father didn't want his daughters only to be decorations because he believed that every person was sent into the world with the obligation to do something and not simply vegetate. Thus the three of us have a university education, not very usual for those days.

Other interviewees specifically pinpoint their political career as inherited, as do these two:

Probably it's a hereditary vocation because my father was in the congress and I was always reading the debates—in those days no women were allowed to enter and listen.

From my family—my father was quite a politician, a congressman at twenty-one years of age. In my family there are a lot of politicians on my father's side.

Family influence thus emerges as an extremely important factor in the political history of the interviewees, but evidently it is not a total explanation of the activist role since more than half the interviewees mention other influences as decisive, either in addition to or instead of the family (see table 5).

Families might influence daughters in ways other than simply talking about politics. Perhaps the political career of a father or mother—or a distinguished relative or ancestor in public life—provided the model. Since only 51 of the 167 fathers (and none of the mothers) of respondents had ever been in government or politics, a father in government apparently is not a prerequisite for a woman political leader. Moreover, fathers who were neither officeholders nor party members produced just as many of the 34 interviewees who have further political ambitions—the "superpolíticas"—as the fathers who were public or party officials.

Twenty-five Peruvian leaders and six Chileans claim distinguished relatives or ancestors in public life. But since most respondents had neither, we cannot look to this kind of familial influence as any explanation for a woman's choosing a political career. The fact that nearly one-third of the

Peruvians mention a famous relative might be significant, however, in legiti-
mizing public service for women in a culture that does not look with favor
on such activism. It seems unlikely that a random sample of professional
women would boast so many distinguished political relatives. However, in
the absence of data from a control group, we can only speculate that the
"famous relative factor" *may* be important for Peruvians, who doubtless
would have heard these personages discussed in the family circle (and in
some cases would have known them personally in their childhood).

Before leaving the question of political families as keys to the socialization
of women leaders, another interesting comparison can be made—of the party
affiliation of fathers and daughters.

If we look at how Aprista fathers socialized their daughters, we find that
nine men who were active in the Aprista party produced four Aprista
daughters, three daughters who affiliated with Belaúnde's Popular Action
party, and two who declare they have no interest in any party. The highest
congruence of fathers/daughters in party affiliation is found among the right
in Chile, where sixteen fathers who were members of either the Conservative
or Liberal parties account for nine daughters who are members of the Partido
Nacional (the fusion of these two traditional groups) and six who are Christian Democrats.

On the whole, daughters as a group moved somewhat to the left of their
fathers (table 7). Three-fifths of unaffiliated fathers in Peru and Chile produced daughters with center-left or left sympathies, whereas conservative
fathers (especially in Chile) produced more daughters with leftist sympathies
than daughters who followed their father's political tendencies! What is most
notable, perhaps, is the high number of fathers (N = 96) who are reported
not affiliated or not in sympathy with any political party, contrasted to the
low number of daughters (N = 23) who do not sympathize with a party. (In
some cases, fathers in the politically neutral bureaucracy or the armed forces
might well have aired strong party preferences in the family.)

Role of the Party in Political Socialization

If we study the *age* at which respondents were recruited to public service,
we find a probable confirmation that something else indeed intervened to
give additional impetus to a political career; in many cases, the agent is the
political party. The women in both countries enter the bureaucracy much
earlier than they embark on a political career, reflecting the fact that for
most women the bureaucracy represents a professional rather than a political option (there are very few female political appointees to bureaucratic
posts). The median age for entering on one's first political office is well over

TABLE 7

FATHERS AND DAUGHTERS BY LEFT/CENTER/RIGHT POLITICAL AFFILIATION

Daughters	Peruvian Fathers				Chilean Fathers				Total
	Left	Center	Right	None	Left	Center	Right	None	
Left	7		9	11	4		1	5	37
Center	4	3	7	17		1	14	25	71
Right			3	9			12	12	36
None	2		1	8			3	9	23
TOTALS	13	3	20	45	4	1	30	51	167

Source: Q. 10 and Q. 11, questionnaire survey.

NOTE: Care should be exercised in interpreting this chart, since the Aprista party has been classified as "Left." This would have been true for fathers, but by 1967 the party had moved considerably to the right. However, so many of the daughters still perceive the image of the party as revolutionary that it seems inaccurate to classify them as rightists.

Left (this table only) = FLN, MSP, PDC, and PAP for Peru; PS and PC for Chile; center = AP for Peru, PDC for Chile; right = UNO and MDP for Peru, RAD and PN for Chile.

Key to Abbreviations: *Peru:* FLN = Frente de Liberación Nacional; MSP = Movimiento Social Progresista; PDC/PPC = Partido Demócrata Cristiano and Partido Popular Cristiano (since the split was still occurring in 1967, members will be treated together; at the time of interviewing, 3 of the 13 had changed to the PPC); AP = Acción Popular; PAP = Partido Aprista Peruano; UNO = Unión Nacional Odriísta; MDP = Movimiento Democrático Peruano (Pradista). *Chile:* PS = Partido Socialista; PC = Partido Comunista; PDC = Partido Demócrata Cristiano; PR = Partido Radical; PN = Partido Nacional (Conservatives and Liberals).

thirty years—indicating that women must spend some time earning the right to political appointment. Table 8 shows the age distributions for respondents entering the bureaucracy and embarking on a first political office.

The political party looms large in the socialization of women political leaders. We are concerned here with the party as the mechanism that accounts for the first awakening to political awareness of more than one-fourth of the women respondents (see table 5 above). The political party proves even more influential in the subsequent political careers of this group, since the women mention the "ideals and programs of my party" as their primary motivation for a vocation in government service more times than any other reason for becoming a leader, and an even greater number name their political party as responsible for their recruitment to their post.

TABLE 8
MEDIAN RECRUITMENT AGES FOR BUREAUCRATIC AND POLITICAL POSTS

Median Age for Entering Bureaucracy		Median Age for Entering First Political Post[a]	
Peru	Chile	Peru	Chile
26.5	25	32.5	34

Source: Q. 1-d and 6-c of questionnaire survey.

[a]Usually a minor party post.

Confining our discussion here to the political party's influence in initial socialization, we find two significant periods: women got actively involved in the Aprista party in Peru in the early 1940s, and there was a second surge of interest in political parties in the mid-1950s at the time when women received the vote, coinciding with the rise of what was then called the democratic left—Popular Action in Peru and the Christian Democrats in both countries.

Many women in Peru became acquainted with the Aprista party in their childhood and vividly recall the impression made on them. Indeed, seven Peruvian respondents joined the Aprista party *before* women received the vote! Such early political activity did not characterize any other interviewees except for one Communist and one Radical in Chile.

For the young woman of an Aprista family, joining the party made sense even though women were not yet allowed to vote. The party offered a way of life, and the idealistic young girl found social action outlets, recreation, and friends all within the party milieu. Indeed, if her family was Aprista, it was difficult to avoid involvement at an early age in the party. One Aprista leader recalls:

I am an Aprista because I grew up in an Aprista family, and the seed of Aprismo is very strong. Every day of my life I've heard about Haya de la Torre, Manuel Seoane, Heysen—and when the police would come in the old days, it made a great impression on me.

Another interviewee mentions the unconscious socialization that took place in the atmosphere of an Aprista home:

When I was a little girl and nobody was paying any attention to me or realizing that I was around, I used to listen a lot, and I read and thought. My father was an Aprista militant and lesser party leader, and he also was a political prisoner. Haya himself often used to come to our house.

Fernando Belaúnde Terry and his Acción Popular in Peru, and Eduardo Frei and the Partido Demócrata Cristiano in Chile also played decisive roles at a later date. Sometimes those women who had been exposed to politics earlier did not take any steps to become active before this time. Says one:

I always moved in a political environment, but it was just a case of talking until 1956, when the Christian Democratic party [Peru] began—and I realized that I thought in just the same way.

More typical of this group is the woman who had no interest in politics until a particular personality caught her imagination:

I became interested first when Belaúnde entered on the scene. I read his whole program in *La Prensa,* and realized that there was a person different from all the other politicians, one who could fulfill my ideals. Before this, I had not the smallest desire to join a party.

Another in the same vein (among the fifteen who say the Acción Popular party was responsible for their initial interest, ten mention Belaúnde by name):

When the figure of Belaúnde Terry came forward it was more than enough to animate me. I thought that the country just had to go forward on a program of development for the sake of my children's future.

Those who attribute their initial interest in politics to Christian Democracy in Chile stress the party program more, the figure of Frei less. Says one woman who typifies the more intellectual approach evidenced by PDC women members (in comparison to the followers of Belaúnde):

I've always had a certain preoccupation with political affairs, but I thought that the majority of politicians did not act with the honor and the honesty that they ought to. What we needed was a force to give a new direction to politics, and when this new force turned out to be the Christian Democratic party I was very happy and wanted to participate.

When we examine what the women actually did in their first ventures outside their households, we note a high congruence between what the women say about the party as an important agent of political socialization and the reality. Nineteen Peruvians and twenty-three Chileans joined a political party as their first public involvement. Table 9 shows the activities the women first engaged in outside the home. Table 10 shows numbers of enrolled party members, party sympathizers, and independents among the respondents. (Only eleven Peruvians and twelve Chileans assert that they do not at least sympathize with one of the political parties, however inconsistent this may be with the fact that forty-eight of the respondents declare they are "apolitical.") Active sympathizers are counted together with members in arriving at these totals, since some declare themselves "simpatizantes" only because their bureaucratic posts preclude party membership—and they are, in reality, long-time party militants.

TABLE 9
FIRST ACTIVITY WOMEN ENGAGED IN OUTSIDE THE FAMILY CIRCLE

	Peru		Total		Chile		Total	
	Mun.	Nat.	No.	%	Mun.	Nat.	No.	%
Profession	8	15	23	(28)	8	16	24	(28)
Bureaucratic app't.	3	14	17	(21)	2	21	23	(27)
Party work	18	1	19	(23)	15	8	23	(27)
Non-professional job	10	3	13	(16)	9	2	11	(13)
Volunteer work	6	3	9	(12)	5	0	5	(5)
TOTALS	45	36	81	(100)	39	47	86	(100)

Source: Q. 1-d and 6-e, questionnaire survey.

TABLE 10

DISTRIBUTION OF INTERVIEWEES AMONG ENROLLED PARTY MEMBERS, SYMPATHIZERS, AND INDEPENDENTS

	Peru		Chile		Total	
	No.	%	No.	%	No.	%
Members	52	(62)	57	(64)	109	(65)
Sympathizers	19	(23)	17	(19)	35	(21)
Independents	10	(15)	12	(14)	23	(14)
TOTALS	81	(100)	86	(100)	167	(100)

Source: Q. 10, questionnaire survey.

There is fairly high agreement among the respondents (71 percent) that all women should become active party members; there is agreement, too, that women ought to be well prepared before joining a party (reminiscent of Portal's caveat that only the woman who "reads, studies, and thinks" should be accepted into the Aprista ranks), and that, when they do, they will bring something uniquely feminine into the political arena. Some typical comments:

It depends on the woman. If she's capable, she should definitely be active in a party. But others—ye gods!

I think that in politics, as in every human activity, man is not complete. Men have a very partial vision, and it is a question of correcting the focus. Politics needs the woman just as do all the other aspects of life.

Women should join parties, bringing their special knowledge and feminine outlook.

Other explanations sometimes mentioned as important in awakening interest in the political process do not appear to have influenced this particular group of women leaders. Referring once more to table 5, we note that only seventeen women mention their husband's influence when they talk of their initial interest in politics. Only four women leaders mention their involvement at the time of the study as in any way connected to their husbands (as will be noted below when women's motives for their political activism are explored)—contradicting the notion that women often become active to help along a husband's political career.

Women's organizations—and even the movement to gain the vote for women—are mentioned only five times as being responsible for the initial impetus to a respondent's political involvement. This reflects the historical situation documented in chapter 4; the small, weak women's rights movements in Peru and Chile had little success in attracting women to political activity beyond the vote. However, as was suggested in chapter 4, this does not mean that the women's suffrage movement is unconnected to women's later political activity. For one thing, the movement gained for women the legal right to hold office as well as the right to vote. For another, the movement legitimated at least to some extent women's entry into political roles and created a climate in which the pioneers whose activities are documented here could take the initial steps into government and public life.

Nor did involvement in student activities perform any very important role in the political socialization of the interviewees. As was discussed in chapter 5, student movements even today have little appeal for women students, who may at times join in demonstrations but rarely take on leadership roles. Only ten Chileans and one Peruvian in the survey trace their first interest in politics to student days.

When we match words to deeds and look once again (table 9) at what the women actually did in their first activity outside the home, we find that not one of the 167 women joined a women's rights organization as her first activity and only 14 did volunteer work as a first step toward political involvement. Since there is almost a folklore about the efficacy of volunteer activity in preparing women for civic and political participation, the minor part volunteer organizations played in awakening this particular group to political consciousness appears at first rather surprising.

Almond and Verba (1963: 388-389) found that American and British women active in community affairs also were likely to be politically informed, observant, and emotionally interested in politics, whereas Italian, German, and Mexican women scored low on both community participation and political interest. Indeed, they go so far as to attribute the British and North American woman's greater interest in politics to what they call the "open family" in the United States and England. However, the present survey group is one in which many more women prepared for professions than would be true in a sample of the general population. Quite logically, 111 of the 167 respondents went to work as their first activity outside the home, and it is therefore not so remarkable that few attribute their political activism to volunteer interests.

In sum, for women political activists, their family—and particularly their father's influence—together with early exposure to party politics were the strongest motivations for a later political career. Professional life also looms large as a factor predisposing women for political activity.

Election of a Political Career

Socialization most often is passive, something that "happens" to us. The remote historical circumstances that may serve to awaken initial interest in the political process are rarely under our control. In contrast, people are actively involved in choosing a political or government career. In this section, the more immediate motivations for entering the political arena are examined.

Turning first to what the women themselves say about why they have chosen a career in politics and/or a position in government, we find that the influence of the political party again predominates. In the survey, the women were asked open-ended questions requiring them to name both the proximate circumstances leading to their appointment or candidacy at the time of the survey and the deeper, more enduring motives for electing a vocation to government service in the first place. "The ideals of my party," "to help my party," "asked by my party" are the reasons given by one-half the respondents for involvement both in the past and at present.

Another major motive for involvement, given by nearly as many (and mentioned especially by Peruvians), is the desire to solve the problems facing their countries. Others want to work for the welfare and rights of women and children, and still others mention the desire to fight injustice. When we separate out all the answers that touch in any way on problems, injustice, poverty, and the rights of women and children and then compare these answers with the other concerns interviewees mention, we find that nearly one-half give idealistic, "feminine" reasons for pursuing a political or government career. (For a more specific description of what the interviewees mean by "fighting injustice" and "making reforms," see table 12 in the next chapter—responses to a probe in the questionnaire that asked them their three top priorities if they were to become President of the Republic.)

Only eight women (seven of them Chileans) say they are interested in the political process as such—politics as a fascinating activity in itself, as a "game" to be played for its own sake. Gaining political power as an end in itself, or even as the means of carrying out a program, is never mentioned by any of the interviewees as a motive for their political involvement. Only fourteen mention professional advancement as a reason for seeking a public post.

Moving to the proximate, immediate incentives for taking on a particular office or post, we find that either the party was the mechanism (through political appointment, nomination through party petition in her electoral district, or party election to a municipal slate) or the woman became involved through her own initiative. The party was more important for women of the left and the right in their decision to run or to accept a bureaucratic post than for women who were members of the big center parties—among the disciplined Socialist, Communist, and conservative parties, the selection of candidates rarely was left to personal initiative. In Chile, two wealthy, upper-class party leaders told me that they had been ordered to remain in the background while "new faces" were put forward in an attempt to change the plutocratic image of the Partido Nacional. Most of the Aprista women mentioned with pride the fact that Haya himself had asked them to run. "When 'el líder máximo' commands," the women remarked, "we obey."

Political Generations and Women Leaders

In order to further refine the analysis, the 167 interviewees were divided into cohort groups according to the epoch in which they entered government or became politically active. The division of the women into such groups reveals some variations in the demographic characteristics over time, as well as some subtle changes in political motivation. Table 11 shows the interviewees by epoch in which they were recruited and their party affiliation at the time of this study. In only ten cases had the women changed their party identification since their *initial* recruitment.

In Peru, there is a noticeable increase in participation of upper-middle-class and upper-class women in later times. Of the 27 members of these classes in the sample, three-quarters became active in 1956 or after. In Chile, the distributions are much more uniform over time for women of all classes. This probably reflects the fact that politics has always been a more respectable career in Chile, while it only became so in Peru (at least for women) when Belaúnde appeared on the political scene in 1956.

In both countries, the median age for the first venture into politics increased over time. In Peru, in the 1920-1948 epoch, the median age of entry was 18 (reflecting the young age at which Aprista women were recruited); then median age climbed to 29 in the Odría epoch, 35 in the Prado, and 36.5 in the Belaúnde. Chile experienced the same phenomenon. In the years 1920 to the end of the Radical period (1951), the median age for women's first political activity was 26. By the Ibáñez epoch, it had increased to 30.5, and it reached 36.5 for both the Alessandri and Frei periods.

What this phenomenon may tell us is that the same cohort, inspired initially to political activity in the improved atmosphere generated in the 1950s by the suffrage movement, continued to be the principal activists in government. Younger women were finding their opportunity instead in the private sector, particularly in "new" careers that are not sex-stereotyped, such as broadcast and television journalism, public relations, data processing and management, and advertising (in Chile, particularly, these fields were attracting large numbers of women in this period). A similar phenomenon is

TABLE 11

INTERVIEWEES BY PARTY PREFERENCE AND EPOCH IN WHICH THEY BECAME ACTIVE

	1920-1948	Odría 1948-55	Prado 1956-62	Belaúnde 1963-	Totals
PERU					
No party	1	1	5	4	11
FLN	1		1		2
MSP		2			2
PDC/PPC	2	2	6	3	13
AP	2	7	12	10	31
PAP	5	2	2	1	10
UNO	2		7	2	11
MDP		1			1
TOTALS	13	15	33	20	81

	1920-1937	Radical 1938-51	Ibañez 1952-57	Alessandri 1958-63	Frei 1964-	Totals
CHILE						
No party		5	5		1	11
PS		2	1	1		4
PC	1	3		1	1	6
PDC	2	12	9	10	7	40
PR	2	2	1	1	1	7
PN	2	3	3	2	7	17
Unknown[a]		1				1
TOTALS	7	28	19	15	17	86

[a]The lone "unknown" is a Chilean judge who answered all but the political questions and declined to give her party preference.

Key to party abbreviations in table 7.

---

just being noted in the U.S., where the initial cohort of leaders in the women's movement is growing older. A new generation of political activists has been slow to seek careers in political office or government service or to take over the women's movement itself. At the same time, many younger women are making gains in the private sector.

So far as the age for entering the bureaucracy is concerned, in Peru the median age for first post definitely increased, from 22 years in the 1920-1948 era to 30 in the Prado and 35 in the Belaúnde eras. This did not happen in Chile, where the median age for entering bureaucrats hovered at around 30 years until the Frei epoch brought it *down*—bureaucrats entering after 1964 had a median age of 24 years. This exception may be attributable to a policy at the beginning of the Frei administration of recruiting younger men and women to government service.

If we examine whether the motives for embarking on a political or government career have varied over time, we find that the reasons given by the Chilean leaders have not changed from era to era. Interest in a political party and concern for the problems of the country are mentioned in almost equal proportions whether the women got involved in the Radical, Ibáñez, Alessandri, or Frei periods. This fact probably reflects the strong left that existed in Chile for over thirty years, bringing an awareness of social problems, and also the long history of the Christian Democratic party in Chile, which recruited present women leaders steadily over the years (twelve becoming active in the Radical period, nine in the era of Ibáñez, ten in Alessandri's time, and eight in Frei's).

In Peru, on the contrary, the influence of the political party on the recruitment of women varied from era to era (reaching a high in the Prado period, when women first were attracted to the figure of Fernando Belaúnde and recruited to his Popular Action party), while the problems of Peru and social injustice increasingly became motivating forces for women's activism. In the era before 1948, social problems are mentioned by only five of thirteen women recruited to politics and government in that period. Nine of the fifteen women who entered public service during the Odría administration mention problems facing Peru as a chief motivating influence, and for those from the Prado and Belaúnde epochs, the numbers jump to fourteen of twenty-three and seventeen of twenty.

This increase in social awareness among Peruvians appears closely correlated to the first campaigns of Belaúnde in 1956-1957. The former Peruvian president was mentioned by name more than any other political leader by the interviewees. Even in 1967, when his influence and prestige were waning after three and one-half years in office (during which many observers felt that he had been a weak president who had not pushed very vigorously any part of his ambitious reform program), Belaúnde still had a large and loyal following among women.

No one has ever studied the political attitudes of Peruvian women in the general population, but it is likely that if such a study were carried out, the then dashing and appealing "Fernandito" Belaúnde and his program would emerge as the greatest single influence motivating women of the middle and upper classes to political action. In the survey, Popular Action women recruited during the Prado period and the early Belaúnde years emerge as the only distinct group of women in Peruvian politics with similar background, motives, aspirations, and political activities. It is true that Haya de la Torre and his party also had a tremendous appeal for women, especially in the earlier years of his influence, and he retains a loyal following among voters of the lower-middle and popular classes. However, Haya's popularity peaked when women could neither vote nor hold public office, whereas the rise of Belaúnde coincided with their attainment of both rights. In consequence, in some cases among the interviewees Belaúnde reaped where Haya sowed; women socialized in Aprista families became active Popular Actionists (but the reverse did not occur). One woman put it this way: "When I was a girl, I was very impressed by the struggles of the Aprista party. Then, when Acción Popular was born, I identified very much with the ideals of this party, and I decided to participate." In the following chapter, we look at what women have done in the positions to which they were recruited.

7. The Supermadre in Government

Marta: Portrait of a Bureaucrat

Marta del Valle had just completed her first year in a new post at the national level in Peru when she participated in a series of interviews for this study, going well beyond the initial questionnaire. (Twelve women in each country were selected for intensive follow-up interviews, and with each one I spent a day observing her at her work.) But Marta was not new to public service; she had spent ten years working at the local level before being offered a post that also dealt with housing and services in the "new towns," as the barriadas or slums have been renamed.

Marta's immediate predecessor was an engineer, "muy brusco"—very brusque—and with "little sense for making relationships with people," Marta told me. She stressed the abrasiveness of this male official several times, perhaps indicating her own insecurity in taking over the job of a technically-prepared professional when her own background is social work. In our conversations, Marta often talked about the qualities she felt equipped a woman for a government post in which one must deal with people all day long—"the ability to listen, to tactfully suggest alternatives, to educate, all of which a woman does very naturally."

Marta often lamented how greatly the needs exceeded the slim resources and the limited personnel assigned to her agency. Many times she simply had no alternative, she said, but to send people on to other sections of her own ministry or even to other agencies; then she felt that she was doing "little more than giving them a typical bureaucratic runaround." Because the masses in Latin America have few intermediate structures or organized pressure groups, not only representatives of the municipal and labor union organizations but also persons who could not find help at a lower level often made their way to her office. A weeping woman evicted from her home in a barriada was not an unusual sight in Marta's waiting room.

Marta's bureaucratic style had a certain directness designed to cut through as much red tape as possible. For example, she would not write memos when she could avoid it.

> Instead of starting a new file, I drop in to see the officials involved or I talk to them on the internal telephone and try to settle things then and there—to avoid multiplying papers. In the afternoons I make the rounds of the other offices here and try to solve in person the problems that have come up.
>
> At first, when I came here, the man who is my assistant—who has worked here twenty-eight years—wrote the memoranda. They were models of bureaucratic art: "We thank you and acknowledge receipt of your memorandum that dealt with the question of _____"—and then the memo would repeat exactly what the person had said in *his* memo, with perhaps one word added. I watched this for awhile—and then I decided the whole procedure was ridiculous. But of course you can't go completely against the current, or you will find yourself out in the street.

Toward the end of our conversations, Marta revealed that she found the ministry a very strange and inhospitable environment. Often, she said, she wondered why she was there "in a world of men, doing work that is very, very demanding for a woman." She especially disliked the competition and jockeying for position within the agency. On her first vacation from her post, she nearly decided not to go back; during her weeks away from the ministry, she took extra vacation time to think about the future. But in the end she returned, although she was uncertain if she would stay more than the two years she initially set herself as a "trial period" on assuming her new position.

Marta del Valle's attitudes and reactions to her work reflect the experiences of many women in public posts in Latin America and elsewhere. The survey provides evidence of many similarities in the ways women in government are influenced by the feminine stereotype or, as I have chosen to call it, the image of the supermadre, and how they struggle to work out their public role within its constricting boundaries. Certain themes recur, whatever the specific questions the interviewees may be answering. First of all, many are beset by deep doubts about the "fitness" of public or political office for women (in these cases, the supermadre image is often employed defensively to justify their presence). A second, closely related theme is the subtle opposition of men to women in posts of public responsibility and the consequent belief that women must greatly excel in order to stay in the running, particularly if their posts are not obviously "female" terrain.

A third similarity is almost universal discouragement at the magnitude of the problems and the scarcity of resources available for their solution. The women generally do not put up any false fronts and pretend to command more than the meagre power they actually possess. Women are impatient, moreover, not only with their inability to solve problems but also with what they view as male *politiquería*—the excessive internal politicking that goes on and, to their mind, further reduces the effectiveness of their particular agencies. The women often picture themselves as "above politics," uniquely capable of cleansing a dismal and corrupt political arena through purer motives, lesser ambition, greater honesty, and, above all, women's willingness to compromise less and to work harder. This last is a universal belief: women not only must, but out of a unique form of *honradez* actually do, work harder at their jobs than men, often much harder.

Finally, rounding out the portrait of the woman official is the lack of aspiration already reported on at several points. Like Marta, most women in my study did not intend even to continue in public service, much less attempt to rise in the political or bureaucratic hierarchy. Many were in full retreat to private life, even before the militaries of the two countries "retired" them.

The Work the Women Do

A short introduction to the survey at the beginning of chapter 6 commented briefly on the fact that women in government throughout Latin America—as everywhere in the world—are overwhelmingly engaged in feminine-stereotyped tasks related to education, social welfare, health, and cultural fields. Moreover, even when they are assigned to "neutral" bureaucracies, most perform "female" tasks. Of the 167 women interviewed for this study, nearly 70 percent either did feminine work and/or held appointments in agencies carrying out tasks thought to be of special concern to women. Appendix IV shows where the women in the survey worked, and Appendix V classifies their assignments as "feminine" or "neutral," i.e., as posts to which a woman almost invariably is assigned or as posts which either a man or woman might fill.

Marta del Valle's new position entailed work for which she felt her social service training had not adequately prepared her. This is true for many of those women in the survey who studied for traditional feminine careers. Many felt their early training was greatly deficient. Strong doubts assailed many women leaders about the worth of a traditional profession and its relevance for equipping a person to deal with modern problems. Many acquired a second, more "modern" competence—typical are the lawyer in Chile who became an expert statistician and headed a division on legal statistics in a government agency or the former social worker who studied labor economics and became a labor expert.

Understandably, an official's educational background strongly influences whether she will work in tasks considered to be "feminine" or will move into a more neutral post to which a man might as easily be appointed. Seventy-five percent of all those in the survey who were trained in traditional professions worked in education, social welfare, or health fields in government, whereas only 30 percent of those trained in modern professions—in public administration, engineering and architecture, economics, sociology, and psychology—did so.

These results would seem to indicate that unless women enroll in larger numbers in the "modern" faculties, they will not easily break out of the feminine stereotype in public service. Indeed, they will not be recruited to key policy-making positions in *any* large numbers, at least so long as feminine concerns are defined as of lesser political priority (the conditions under which feminine issues might become more relevant politically are discussed in the last chapter). As I have suggested at several points in this study, recruitment to key positions in the more innovative agencies dealing with changes in social and economic structures is much less likely among persons trained in traditional feminine careers. Women in these professions cluster in the old-line ministries and agencies, and they have less chance to enter government or politics in any case; women in masculine traditional or modern professions are heavily overrepresented in public service.

There is evidence that governments and political parties in Latin America have difficulty in recruiting women to political posts, even when they are disposed to do so; the blame for women's absence from policy making cannot be placed entirely on male party leaders and officials. Several Christian Democratic interviewees in high posts in Chile commented on this situation in almost identical language. Said one:

> There frankly just are not *enough* professionals prepared in appropriate fields from which government and political careerists are drawn—economists, for example, and other kinds of *técnicos*. Fifteen years ago the number of women in the universities was very small, and this reason alone is enough to explain why the pool of talent among women is small.

Distribution of women students among the various university faculties (Appendix IX) does not, however, lead us to forecast any great changes in the new generation. Women in Chile were studying what their mothers had studied: 80 percent in traditional feminine careers, only 11 percent in law, medicine, and journalism, and barely 9 percent in what I have called modern careers. (A check with the latest available enrollment statistics in the mid-1970s indicates that these trends have not changed appreciably, with the exception that some 30 percent of medical students in Chile were women—but again in what are defined as "feminine" specialities: obstetrics and gynecology.)

There was almost universal agreement among interviewees that women ought to participate more and that, if they are well prepared, the women bring something "extra" to the political process that up to this time has been lacking: "I think that politics is like every other activity—the male is not complete, he has a very partial vision. It is a question of correcting the focus. Politics needs women just as do all the other activities in life." However, such a contribution was most often viewed in moral terms; only a small number of the interviewees failed to mention in one context or another women's obligation to counter what is viewed as almost universal male dishonesty and corruption. Closely linked is the often-expressed idea that politics is a suspect activity and that women in public life would do well to avoid it. One high official in Chile injected a humorous note into her complaint:

> One advantage of being a woman in public service is that we really are left out of a lot of the *politiquería* that goes on. Whenever you telephone a man who holds a public post, he is sure to be away from his desk: of course he's out in a corridor somewhere talking politics with the other men.

> A woman, on the contrary, feels out of place doing this. I would never inject myself into one of these discussions. The woman official prefers to go to her office, sit at her desk and do her work.

Women at the "Top"

When the positions women held in government are ranked, in neither Peru nor Chile had women progressed very far up the ladder, and few could be described as powerful or even very influential. Only eighteen women in the survey occupied national legislative positions or headed large agencies of sufficient prestige to give them "visibility" in the country at large. These eighteen leaders represent 11 percent of the survey group, but women in public service actually held only perhaps 2 or 3 percent of the posts at such a level, indicating that women in "top" leadership positions are overrepresented in the survey in relation to men in such positions as well as to totals of women in politics and government. There were no women in the highest governmental positions in either Peru or Chile—at the ministerial, subministerial, or ambassadorial level or on the supreme courts (see Appendix VI for ranking of the positions in which the women served).

Under what conditions *do* women rise to posts of power and influence? Do we find that the "top eighteen" leaders possessed any similar characteristics that might indicate why they were so successful in their careers, at least relative to other women? Those in the top positions did not owe their rise to length of service, since their recruitment was distributed over every epoch. Nor do we find any one profession with a monopoly on the top positions—the group includes professors, lawyers, two of the medical doctors, an engineer, and one woman with no professional training.

All of the eighteen except the one non-professional had a university education. Not surprisingly, university attendance is associated with high-level leadership—the higher the level of position, the greater the proportion of the university-educated. At the middle level, where 52 of the 167 women officials served, 73 percent had a university education; at the lower levels, only 30 percent did.

So far as background characteristics are concerned, occupying a top leadership position also appears to be highly associated with class—the upper class status of these eighteen women probably also explaining the better educational opportunities they have enjoyed. Two-thirds of the women in the top eighteen are of the upper-middle or upper class; only one is of the lower-middle class. At the middle level of posts, on the contrary, more women are middle class than either upper-middle or upper. Twenty-four of the twenty-six lower-middle-class women represented in the survey are, however, found in lower level posts. This last item is interesting in view of the fact that the whole sample is nearly three-quarters middle class or higher; to rise to the higher levels in government, "extra" class status would seem to be essential.

Did the top eighteen also have an assist from their powerful relatives—were they part of the "old boys' network"? This is hard to determine. About one-half the eighteen have family names of at least some renown. Yet all of these appeared to be performing well in their posts; indeed, the only two among the eighteen who appeared not to be entirely competent did not have aristocratic names.

Three others were wives and two were sisters of men prominent in their respective parties; yet it would be difficult to argue that any of the five was not qualified in her own right; an urban planner with a U.S. degree and two lawyers were among them. Six others were single women universally recognized as extremely competent, and none of these had a recognizable family name or connection (but of course, I might well have missed an obscure linkage through marriage of a relative into the power network).

All the women in the top eighteen were thirty years of age or older, with representatives of this group distributed evenly in each age group older than thirty. There is only one interviewee under thirty years of age who had achieved even a middle-level post. Success in public life comes late—the age level is, on the whole, older for women in government than for those active in non-political careers.

Two-thirds of the top eighteen were single or widows; only six were married at the time. At the other levels, the ratio of married to single is 6:4. Thus, being single apparently gives one more freedom to advance to the higher posts, even in countries where servants are available. The influence of the family situation is confirmed by the fact that of the women with children in the top level group, *none* had more than three. At the middle level, only 13 percent of the women had more than three children; at the other levels, 32 percent had four children or more.

Thirteen of the women (70 percent) in the highest-level posts were aspiring politicians—the highest percentage at any level. At the lower levels, on the contrary, only 35 percent of the women wanted to rise. Success apparently feeds aspiration and ambition; the small number of the highly successful could, however, have a dampening effect on the ambition of those at the lower levels.

It is appropriate here to remind the reader of the extreme "tentativeness" in commitment to politics characteristic of the survey group. Of the 167 interviewees, 104 disclaimed any interest in a political office in the future; only 34 had political ambitions that involved a higher office. The tentative nature of women's commitment to politics and government service is also revealed in the fact that 112 (67 percent) of the 167 women had never held any other position. Of these, 69 (or 41 percent of the total 167) were among those who did not want to continue in government. These figures reveal the high number who try public service and become disillusioned with only one experience.

An insight into the reasons for the lack of political ambition is given by the career history of a Chilean interviewee—an upper-middle-class housewife who lives in a big, comfortable house full of children—who was particularly objective and honest about her motivations:

> My involvement goes back a long time, to my student days when I was active in the young women's section of Catholic Action. I've always been a militant in the Christian Democrats, since my husband was one of the first members of the party. I remember when party meetings would fill only one room.

> Let me be honest with you about my feelings. I go to meetings when the party needs numbers, but not often otherwise because meetings seem to me a waste of time. I stood as a candidate because the party wanted my name—but I don't have any ambitions. I find this one experience very entertaining, and I'm satisfied for now even though I was against becoming active for such a long time. But this will be it. I've chosen family life, and the moment my job stands in the way, I'll leave it overnight.

This woman is not atypical.

Another Chilean, much more of an activist (she chaired the women's section of a major party for many years) than the interviewee quoted above, said:

> We certainly are, in Chile, a culture in which women serve the men. To be frank, I like it that way. If my husband were still alive, and if he wanted to be active politically, I would withdraw in his favor. It is the way I am made. I think women were born to serve men in this way.
>
> I know of any number of doctors, dentists, social workers who either have ceased to practice their careers or who carry on at a very reduced level, devoting their main efforts to their homes. If it comes to that, they will sacrifice their careers—for example, not advancing as far or as fast as they might because of family considerations, or leaving their professions or the public service altogether—if these interfere too much with family life.

When the women were questioned about their "dream occupation," an even smaller number professed interest in a political future—only seven Chileans and three Peruvians. Forty-two said they would like to be involved in some sort of communal or neighborhood work or to work with women and children. Seventeen wanted to return to the private practice of their professions. Seven would have liked to be doctors, and twelve said they would study public relations if they could. (This is a profession much in vogue in the two countries.) Twenty-four Peruvians and 18 Chileans professed themselves happy with what they were doing and had no "dream" ambitions.

Life Chances of Women: Emancipation, Professions, Marriage

We find clues that reveal why more women do not aspire to political careers when we look at the pessimism that characterizes this generation of women leaders. The pessimism is reflected in their opinions on both the extent of women's emancipation in their countries and the possibility of combining a public career with marriage. The first generation of women in politics is not confident that they can successfully do both.

Only one Peruvian in the survey ventured to assert that "all" the women of her country were emancipated, and only thirteen Chileans thought so. Many more Chileans than Peruvians, however (80 percent in contrast to 50 percent), felt that at least some women were making progress in their country. Nearly one-half the Peruvians declared that only a few women in their country were emancipated.

Three questions on women's "life chances," that is, their opportunities to work and study, as well as the professional's chance to marry, were combined to give an "index of confidence in women's life chances" (see Appendix X, A).

On this scale, Chileans again come out more confident than Peruvians, probably reflecting the real situation in the two countries. Chilean women *are* more emancipated than Peruvian women, do have more chance to combine profession and married life, and are freer to enter professions. Twenty-two percent of the Chileans register "high confidence" on the scale, whereas only 7 percent of Peruvians do so. On the low end, 71 percent of the Peruvians are dubious about women's life chances, contrasted to 35 percent of the Chileans. The remaining women register "moderate confidence."

It is interesting to note how the negative opinions about women's life chances vary with the position of the interviewee's political party. Women of the left are far less certain than those of either the center or the right whether any except a small elite really are free to enter whatever profession they wish. The Socialists, the Communists, and several of the pobladoras (residents of the marginal districts) of the Christian Democratic Party in Chile qualified their answers: Yes, *legally* free to enter a profession, but the reality is something else again:

> Providing they have the preparation. But given our underdeveloped state, many times they don't have the economic means to matriculate. [Member of the National Liberation Front, Peru]

> In the universities nobody gets in except those with big names and the economic means, especially at the Catholic University. [Christian Democratic pobladora, Chile]

> Daughters of workers have to be put to work in a factory or workshop, and they don't really have much opportunity to develop themselves. When they don't have enough to eat, good health, work, then how can one talk about a girl's truly having freedom to emancipate herself? [Communist party member, Chile]

On the question of the professional's chances to marry, 52 percent of the Peruvians felt she has less opportunity, whereas only 23 percent of the Chileans did. (However, fully 70 percent of the married professionals in the survey married either during or shortly after their university days, a circumstance that undoubtedly would parallel the experience of most women professionals— as would the fairly high incidence of divorce and separation.) Many of the Peruvians voiced the opinion that men do not like "educated," "independent," or "competitive" women. They echoed Margaret Mead (1949: 234), who noted that, in many cultures, "the more successful a man is in his job, the more certain everyone is that he will make a desirable husband; the more successful a woman is, the more people are afraid she may not be a successful wife."

Male views on the professional wife were not all perceived to be negative. Many Chileans remarked that men's ideas had changed on the score of working wives: inflation and the high cost of living made men much less likely to "dispute the right of women to work if they wish, even welcoming it in cases where the wife earns enough so her employment is not anti-economic" (in the sense of the costs of her clothing, hairdos, and help in the home). Some admitted, however, that their husbands were not so delighted with their political activism. One gets the impression of silent sufferance from such remarks as "He doesn't like it much, but he refrains from giving his opinion," or "He doesn't forbid me, but it doesn't make him very happy." Driving me home from my interview with his wife, who had reported him "completely in agreement" with her political career, one husband said: "I don't oppose it actively, but I definitely do not approve. Women should participate as social workers, teachers, not in government. There is enough for them to do there."

The respondents also agreed that censure comes if the professional does not manage well in her role as housewife. A high woman official in Chile, who also presided over a large home and family, declared that women have won the right to go out and work without "having established any rights to more of a partnership in the home":

> The working wife's husband, his friends, her friends—and often she her-self—still expect her to be a model homemaker. And she will get no help from her husband on this. He leaves it all to her, and on top of this he is apt to be very demanding.

> The men do not see that bringing in an extra salary gives the wife any special rights to relief from or help with the home duties. This is pre-eminently women's work, and the changing structures that have per-mitted women to go out to the university and to enter the labor force have not yet changed sufficiently to challenge the traditional division between "men's work" and "women's work."

Another respondent, with a touch of irony, echoed what a number of respondents told me: many men are apt, she said, "to look with a great deal of sympathy on women in political careers—always supposing their own wives are not involved." In this case, she added, a woman would be faced with the dilemma of choosing between the satisfaction of participation and "the generous renunciation of all this so that they will not compromise the har-mony of their home."

Another large group of women in both countries (37 percent) believed that a career is necessarily all-absorbing and does not allow marriage.

Moreover, many believed that a professional is generally more exacting in the choice of a partner. One of my interviewees, who held a very high position in the Chilean bureaucracy—and, incidentally, was an extremely attractive and charming person—indicated that both these reasons entered into her own decision not to marry:

> About marriage? I have doubts about whether marriage and a job like this go together. For my own part, I don't think I have sufficient talent to make a go of this and also have a home. Because I'm a perfectionist, and I'd want the home to be run at the best possible level—and I've just decided I'm not capable of doing both things. So I've decided not to marry.

> Also the difficulty is, at my age and at my level of post, there just aren't that many men around. Several professional women I know have married men technically "beneath" them. "If one wants to marry and have a home," they tell me, "one just has to compromise." Well, I can't compromise on the man. So I imagine I'll stay single.

Women's Political Competence

A woman's success in a government or political career will be affected not only by the objective situation, that is, by how emancipated and qualified women really are in her culture, but also by whether she believes strongly that women ought to be active in government and by her feelings of competence in fulfilling her own particular task.

An attempt to measure these two facets of women's attitudes showed that many women leaders in Peru and Chile were themselves unable to envision women acting in government outside the supermadre image. At the same time, many were doubtful of their own abilities to be successful in a government career.

An index constructed to test the women's own images and stereotypes regarding the appropriateness of women in government (see Appendix X, B) reveals that only 13 percent had a completely unstereotyped view—a belief that women may occupy any post in government for which they qualify and that no areas of public service ought to be fenced off as "feminine." Half the women in the survey think that there are some government posts for which women officials would be preferable and, conversely, that there are some posts for which women would be unsuitable. The remainder of the 167 interviewees register an ambivalence on one question or the other; contrary to the general pattern of responses, Peruvians and Chileans do not differ substantially in their views in this instance.

Probing behind "yes" and "no" answers reveals the extent to which these women are addicted to the supermadre image. Government posts for which women are considered preferable include education and health posts, and offices dealing with women and children, singled out by virtually all the women in the stereotyped or ambivalent categories. "Women have more understanding, more sensitivity regarding human problems," many said. "Women can deal better with problems of women and children." "Some posts simply are against the nature of woman," others asserted. "It would be too much against our traditions." One woman put her motive for answering negatively this way: "I wouldn't be crazy about seeing a woman president or women mayors, but that is because I'm influenced by traditional thinking. I have no reason for saying this." Others articulated reasons like the following:

> I just don't think women would be appropriate for posts like the presidency, ministers of defense, foreign relations, interior, and the like because they carry so much responsibility, and for the woman the fundamental role in life is her home and family. These are posts for men. A woman in such a post would be really strange, completely outside our experience.

> Posts related to labor laws or labor relations, or posts in which a woman would have to make pacts with labor unions, would not be appropriate. Women have just not succeeded in reaching the level where people will accept that they give orders or make demands.

There are very few high scorers on the "index of personal political competence" constructed for this study (Appendix X, C). High scorers (only 12 percent) believe that training, hard work, and talent are more important for getting ahead in life than dependence on God's help, knowing important people, or good luck. In addition, they think that, in order to succeed in public life, women need work only as hard as men, and that professionals are considered by men to be just as feminine as non-professionals. The high scorers also tend to see barriers against women in public posts as stemming from women's own lack of confidence rather than from society's traditional institutions and/or male prejudices. Low scorers—who believe the opposite on all these questions—total 60 percent of the survey group; the remaining 28 percent score in a middle position on these questions. One-half the Chileans and 70 percent of the Peruvians are among the low scorers— those who feel little political competence.

The women who say that their sex must work harder than men in the same post if they are to be successful think that "women are on trial, they must demonstrate their capacity to handle a government post." Others believe men simply do not want women competitors and deliberately set out to obstruct their success in politics or the bureaucracy.

One woman, asked to name the three major barriers to the complete emancipation of woman, was very emphatic: "First, second, and third, men!" Two other women who held high bureaucratic posts put it this way:

> I think many men are very open to the idea of seeing women come into the bureaucracy, but others certainly made a veritable war over my appointment because a lot of them wanted this post. For a woman to get ahead costs much, much sacrifice in Peru. There is a great deal of rivalry with the men. [Medical doctor in health agency]

> I was the first woman in the _____; now there are three others. The fight with the men is something! All of us feel the weight of being women, we feel we are held back deliberately by the men. Ohhhhh they are something, let me tell you, and the women around here have got to make a tremendous effort. I have five *cartelones* [higher degrees] and even so, it's difficult! [Official in Ministry of Foreign Relations]

Another official commented on the "little things, unimportant things" that the men use to show their sentiments. For example, in meetings with the minister—she was the only woman—the minister almost always called on the men to speak first. A Chilean mentioned that whenever a woman bureaucrat submits a written report, "it is scrutinized and commented on" much more than would be the case with a report submitted by a man. This situation appears to be general in the Americas. In a United Nations survey (1974: 13) on the participation of women in public life, the representatives concluded in their official report:

> There is a tendency, supported by age-old tradition, to look upon man as a superior being, and the emancipation of women is still too recent to break it down. A woman about to exercise leadership or to take up a post in government is surrounded by a general air of expectancy. As there is nothing unusual in a man being in government, all that is expected of him is the normal performance of his duties. As it is uncommon for a woman to be in government, her work is expected to be outstanding.

So far as "de-feminization" of the professional woman is concerned, 40 percent of all respondents believe that women in government or a profession appear "less feminine" to men than non-professionals. This is partly because, they say, some professional women have become masculinized, particularly among the older generation of bureaucrats. Women leaders also appear "less feminine," the women say, simply because men aren't used to seeing women in public offices—"The man here continues thinking that woman equals home, so the homebody thus appears more feminine to him that the woman with a profession." One respondent explained the difficulty in a comment that sums up the situation in a Latin country very well:

> Unfortunately, the woman who has other things on her mind simply can't think that much about her appearance. You will have noted that to be in fashion here is very complicated and takes a lot of time. But men like to see women very well dressed and all fixed up.

One final comment on the question of femininity, this one from a respondent who pointed out that part of the difficulty lies in the fact that the image of woman is itself a mistaken one:

> Men, at least in this country, have an idea about woman and femininity that is not very correct. They think about woman in terms of the beauty, the toy, the doll, and of course a creature like that could never pretend to "equality." Now men are jealous and insecure because they don't know what to make of the new type of woman.

The tensions involved in going against traditional male ideas about women's image and proper activity actually contributed to one legislator's decision not to seek re-election:

> Men still are not at all used to the idea of women participating in public life. To men, women still are inferior beings. In my own days in congress, there were all kinds of pressures and, indeed, all kinds of chaffing and even crude joking. "How does Sr. _____ like having a legislator in his house?" "What does he think of your coming home so late?" [The congress meets in the evenings, and sometimes the sessions go on all night.] "How does Sr. _____ like sleeping alone?"

Women Leaders and Development

Women in the survey were told to imagine that they had been elected President of the Republic. Because of limited resources, it would be necessary to set priorities; they were asked to consider what the three main goals of their administration would be.

As table 12 shows, the women would certainly not entirely neglect socioeconomic change. Yet several aspects of the chart call for comment. The small number of responses mentioning changes in structures (only 29 percent of the total), in comparison to "housewifely" or legal-formal adjustments, does not argue that the respondents really understood development priorities. Only one respondent mentioned any of the issues related to neo-colonialism and dependency (the failure of import-substituting industrialization; the perennial balance of payments and exchange rates crises; the fluctuating prices in international markets for primary products and the like) as requiring priority attention, even though in these years theorists like Julio Cotler and Aníbal Quijano in Peru and Theotonio dos Santos, then resident in Chile, were in the forefront of those Latin Americans defining the relationship between stagnating internal development and external dependency.

Because they often are not equipped to appreciate the priorities governments must set to effect structural change, women in government sometimes increase the almost irresistible pressure to divert scarce resources from projects (social and educational as well as economic) that are developmental to those which have little potential for economic or social return. Governments of developing nations often are forced to placate their diverse clienteles by diverting disproportionate amounts of money to short-range, non-reproductive projects that are attractive because of their immediate payoff in votes and political support. Men, of course, also lack vision—or make promises from motives of political opportunism. One does not get the impression that women officials are, by and large, either insincere or cynical—simply inexperienced and uninformed.

For example, it was difficult to justify investing nearly 25 percent of the national budget in agriculture (as the Planning Institute of Peru [1966: 241] suggested for 1967-1970) when thousands lived without electricity, water, and sewage disposal facilities in the marginal areas around the cities—a favorite target of women in politics. In the long run, however, more social as well as economic benefit may derive from policies making it possible for rural areas to retain their populations and to grow food and products for domestic consumption and export than from policies that may tend to swell the streams of migrants to the urban areas.

Table 12 also reveals the relatively small numbers (14 percent) who believe that political reform should have priority. But this lack of interest is understandable when attitudes toward government are explored; the women apparently do not have sufficient faith in the governmental and political processes to believe reforms in this area are important (see the next section below).

Population control is another issue hardly mentioned by this group of women leaders. If not the most pressing problem of all, certainly the high birth rate is of immense concern in the developing areas where yearly population increases match and sometimes outstrip hard-won increases in per capita output of goods and services (population growth is a more serious problem in Peru than in Chile, which has registered some declines since 1960).

Moreover, in Roman Catholic countries where other means of birth control are not available, abortion has become an increasingly seriuos problem. Some

TABLE 12

PRIORITIES INTERVIEWEES WOULD SET "IF I WERE PRESIDENT OF THE REPUBLIC"

	Peru		Chile		Total	
	No.	%	No.	%	No.	%
1. Legal-Moral	15	(8)	42	(20)	57	(14)
Change people's mentality	3		16		19	
Encourage hard work	3		8		11	
Make officials set good example	1		7		8	
Give people more religion	5		2		7	
Enact better laws	2		3		5	
Reform constitution			4		4	
Other	1		2		3	
2. "Housewifely" Adjustments[a]	53	(28)	32	(15)	85	(22)
Better housing	12		12		24	
More jobs	11		9		20	
Electricity, water in the barriadas	12		5		17	
More, cheaper food	14		2		16	
More social security	3		2		5	
Other	1		2		3	
3. Education and Training	48	(26)	33	(16)	81	(20)
4. Socio-Economic Change[b]	53	(28)	63	(30)	116	(29)
Industrialization	13		17		30	
Tax, budget reforms	13		9		22	
Public health programs	7		5		12	
Population control	3				3	
Socio-economic reforms[c]	16		25		41	
Other	1		7		8	
5. Political Reform	19	(10)	38	(18)	57	(14)
Planning	6		12		18	
Change of regime			4		4	
Reform of bureaucracy	4		3		7	
Community organization	8		6		14	
Structural changes in polity[c]			4		4	
Other	1		9		10	
TOTALS[d]	188	(100)	208	(100)	396	(100)

Source: Q. 33 of questionnaire survey.

[a]When changes were suggested without reference to any social or economic reforms needed to bring them about, they were put in category 2, as the type

of little "mejoras" housewives suggest. "More food for the people" is considered a "housewifely" answer. On the contrary, "Reform in the economic structures" or "Better income distribution so people can have more food" is considered an economic development answer and is classified in category 4.

[b]The answer "Agrarian reform" was eliminated because probing proved that it had become a slogan and many of the women could not define what they meant. For the same reason, "Build roads" (suggested by thirteen Peruvians and no Chileans, probably because the famous Marginal Highway of the Selva, Belaúnde's pet project, was so much discussed at the time) was also eliminated from this section.

[c]Structural changes suggested without further specification.

[d]Numbers do not add up to 3 x 167 because suggestions given fewer than three times were not recorded. Percentages are for *total* answers given by country and grand total (last column).

---

estimates put the abortion rate in Latin America as one for every two live births (Requeña B., 1966). Yet, in this delicate area where the women public officials could do a great deal (and perhaps are the only ones who could), the problem goes unrecognized, or at least unnamed among this set of leaders. This is puzzling in view of the fact that in Chile, particularly after the Planned Parenthood World Federation held its World Congress in Santiago in 1967, family planning became a "respectable" topic that could be discussed in public forums and in the press—something that was not possible before that time. Moreover, the Chilean government under Frei inaugurated a public program through the national health service to distribute information and contraceptives. In Peru, governmental policies were not defined at the time of the survey, although since then a pro-natalist stance has been adopted, precluding, at least at this writing, all programs, discussion, and research dealing with this problem.

One reason for the silence may be the fact that many in the interview group feel they must appear at least formally committed to what the Catholic Church teaches. The church itself followed such a policy in relation to Rome, tacitly agreeing not to oppose the official population control program yet not saying any public word in favor of it. Moreover, even though Chilean women have the reputation of being the most "secular" of all Latin American women, neither my results nor those of the Mattelarts on two related questions would appear to support such a contention (Mattelarts 1968: 87). On the question of whether the influence of the church and religion ought to increase, continue the same, or diminish, 66 percent of my respondents chose the first possibility, although some qualified their answers to make clear they were not talking about the traditional church. Replies of Chileans differed little from those of the Peruvian respondents, reputed to be among the most religious in Latin America. See table 13.

TABLE 13

"INFLUENCE OF RELIGION" IN PERU AND CHILE: OPINIONS OF INTERVIEWEES

	Peru		Chile		Total	
	No.	%	No.	%	No.	%
Q. 31. The influence of religion on the people should:						
Increase	43	(53)	44	(51)	87	(52)
Increase—but[a]	14	(17)	6	(7)	20	(12)
Remain same	19	(24)	20	(23)	39	(23)
Diminish	4	(5)	13	(15)	17	(10)
Don't know	1	(1)	3	(4)	4	(2)
TOTALS	81	(100)	86	(100)	167	(100)

[a]Qualified answers: "Increase if you mean church of Vatican II"; "Increase if we are talking about interest in problems of the people"; "Increase, but not the old style where the priest told everyone what to do."

In order to give a more accurate picture of where women leaders in the survey stand on the question of structural changes in society (which a chart summing up total answers cannot do), a scale was constructed placing the respondents in three categories: "housewives," "reformists," and "revolutionaries." Housewives are those who do not, in their three opportunities in Q. 33, mention even one structural change and who, in answer to Q. 1-b, describe literally the tasks they perform in carrying out their responsibilities in their political post or government bureau. Reformists mention at least one structural change in answer to Q. 33 and describe their own responsibilities in broader terms—as a contribution either toward improving the standards of their profession or toward bringing about change in the country.

Revolutionaries include at least two structural changes—social, economic, or political—in their answers to Q. 33 and describe their own task as one in which they hope to contribute toward deep change in their field or in the country. For example, here is a job description that puts the interviewee in the revolutionary category:

> My reason for joining the _____ was not only the possibility of applying a new method of social service but also the possibility of motivating a group of very influential people who, in turn, have the possibility of influencing the masses. This post, directly and indirectly, gives me the opportunity to influence many.

The results of the scaling appear as table 14.

TABLE 14
INTERVIEWEES AS HOUSEWIVES, REFORMISTS, AND REVOLUTIONARIES, BY COUNTRY

	Peru		Chile		Total	
	No.	%	No.	%	No.	%
"Housewives"	30	(37)	28	(33)	58	(35)
Reformists	45	(56)	51	(59)	96	(58)
Revolutionaries	6	(7)	7	(8)	13	(7)
TOTALS	81	(100)	86	(100)	167	(100)

As the table shows, there is a strong "housewifely" strain in the replies the women gave on priorities they would set in government, and a substantial number (35 percent) of pure "housewife" types were found among the interviewees. Among the national leaders, twenty-one were "housewives" (nine Peruvians and twelve Chileans), sixty-eight were reformists (twenty-four Peruvians and thirty-four Chileans), and only five were revolutionaries (four of these in Peru). A leader of the women's section of a major party in Chile sketched in almost classic form the "microsocial" approach to change that characterizes the supermadre's attitude:

> If I were president I would, in the manner of a good *dueña de casa* (housewife), do my best to budget so that everything essential would be covered.

The housewife must feed her family and house them; she has to see to their education and to their health. These things are, to my mind, the most urgent facing Chile at the present moment: better nutrition, housing, and education.

Commenting on the reasons why so few women are able to think in terms of structural change, another Chilean woman party leader said:

I think it is because women are not used to thinking in terms of economics—neither their education nor their later experience has prepared them to think other than in a short-range way. ... A very short time ago, most women were completely dependent on men: first on their fathers, for everything, then on their husbands. They were not included in discussions on problems of finance or planning, and therefore it is quite natural that their horizons should be limited.

This has been true even as women have entered politics. Men simply have not wanted (and do not yet want, I think) to give into the hands of women those aspects of the political world that traditionally have been the sphere of males. When women begin to be taken more seriously by men, when they are treated as persons, then they will begin to think in a larger way.

Attitudes of Women: Confidence in Government/Faith in People

Two sets of questions probe the interviewees' attitudes toward the governmental process and toward other people with whom the interviewees must interact as leaders in politics.

As many analysts have observed, among the orientations required for the successful functioning of a participant political system are both the belief that human beings are capable of governing themselves in a responsible fashion (called here "confidence in government") and an underlying faith in human nature, that is, in the capacity of people to be generous, open, and reliable in their dealings with one another (Rosenberg 1956).

To turn first to the question of the women's confidence in the governmental process, many of the interviewees score fairly high. This may reflect the optimism with which women in Peru viewed the Belaúnde regime in 1967, when the Peruvian leader still was riding the crest of his popularity, and the fact that in Chile disillusion with the Frei government had not yet set in, at least among Frei's own supporters, who are represented in large numbers.

Among the questions that explore the degree of confidence the women place in the government and political process are inquiries on how the interviewees assess the performance of officials in the three branches of government and how they assess the progress of development in their country.

On both sets of questions, Peruvians are more likely to be optimistic; Chileans temper their enthusiasm by taking the middle position. The only exception to this trend is the fact that more Peruvians than Chileans feel that "very few" government officials are truly concerned over the problems facing their country. Perhaps this relates to the perception of many Peruvians that politics is a dirty business and not an altogether honorable occupation. Table 15 shows the distribution of the replies to the first question; table 16 gives the opinions on the second.

When, however, the direct question is put to the women about whether they, and women like themselves, have any possibility of helping to solve the problems facing their country, one-quarter of the respondents feel that women have little or nothing to contribute to government, and only 35 percent are found among the high scorers who think there is "much" that women can do. The remaining 40 percent feel they can do "something." This puts the women in the position of having much more confidence in the government "out there" than in their own capacity to participate in leadership roles. Perhaps this contradiction in attitudes partially explains the "withdrawal" phenomenon noted throughout this study: there is a degree of confidence in the government process, as such, but not in the ability and qualifications of the woman to take part. Table 17 shows the distribution of answers; again, the Peruvians are decidedly more optimistic, perhaps reflecting—as has been suggested several times—their lesser experience in government and consequently less time in which to become disillusioned.

Perhaps a partial explanation of women's lack of confidence in themselves as capable of helping to effect change and solve the problems of their countries is the fact that they lack faith in others human beings. Morris Rosenberg (1956) designed a scale that attempts to measure attitudes indicating "faith in people." He found that high scorers on his scale also scored high on questions related to democratic values and attitudes (his populations consisted of college students in the United States). Almond and Verba used Rosenberg's scale in measuring attitudes in their five-nation study *The Civic Culture* (1963: 266-273); their findings also show that faith in people relates to faith in democratic values and that high scorers on the "Faith in People" scale were more apt to be found in the countries that exhibit an open, participant style of political participation.

In my own study, four of the Rosenberg questions and an additional one from the Cornell-Peru study (from a questionnaire made available by the Instituto de Estudios Peruanos, Lima) were combined in a "Faith in People Index." (My scoring method, differing both from Rosenberg and from Almond and Verba, is explained in Appendix X, D.) Table 18 shows the results, first giving the distribution of answers to the five questions, then the

TABLE 15

OPINION OF INTERVIEWEES ON PERFORMANCE OF GOVERNMENT OFFICIALS, PERU AND CHILE

Question: How many officials of each government branch are seriously concerned with solving the problems facing the people?

	Peruvians		Chileans		Total	
	No.	%	No.	%	No.	%
Officials of National Government						
"Many"	36	(44)	27	(31)	63	(38)
"Some"	19	(23)	38	(43)	57	(34)
"Very few"	24	(30)	16	(19)	40	(24)
DK or NR	2	(3)	5	(7)	7	(4)
	81	(100)	86	(100)	167	(100)
Officials of Municipal Government						
"Many"	32	(39)	21	(24)	53	(32)
"Some"	28	(35)	39	(45)	67	(40)
"Very few"	18	(22)	14	(17)	32	(19)
DK or NR	3	(4)	12	(14)	15	(9)
	81	(100)	86	(100)	167	(100)
Congress						
"Many"	28	(35)	25	(29)	53	(32)
"Some"	26	(32)	40	(46)	66	(40)
"Very few"	23	(28)	16	(19)	39	(23)
DK or NR	4	(5)	5	(6)	9	(5)
	81	(100)	86	(100)	167	(100)

Source: Q. 26, questionnaire survey.

combined score using the index. On this index, it is interesting to note that more Chileans score on the positive side in contrast to their propensity to score lower than Peruvians on most of the other confidence/competence scales constructed for this study. Thus the tendency of those who belong to more

TABLE 16

OPINION OF INTERVIEWEES ON PROGRESS OF DEVELOPMENT IN PERU AND CHILE

	Peruvians		Chileans		Total	
	No.	%	No.	%	No.	%
Development is proceeding						
Rapidly	47	(58)	24	(28)	71	(42)
So-so[a]	16	(20)	27	(31)	43	(26)
Slowly	10	(12)	27	(31)	37	(22)
Not at all	4	(5)	6	(7)	10	(6)
DK or NR	4	(5)	2	(3)	6	(4)
	81	(100)	86	(100)	167	(100)

Source: Q. 32, questionnaire survey.

[a]The word in Spanish is "normalmente"—"as usual"—but the connotation is "nothing special," "nothing extraordinary."

TABLE 17

CONFIDENCE IN WOMEN'S CAPACITY TO CONTRIBUTE TO GOVERNMENT

	Peruvians		Chileans		Total	
	No.	%	No.	%	No.	%
Women can contribute:						
Much	34	(42)	24	(28)	58	(35)
Something	28	(34)	39	(45)	67	(40)
Little	12	(15)	17	(20)	29	(17)
Nothing or DK	7	(9)	6	(7)	13	(8)
	81	(100)	86	(100)	167	(100)

Source: Q. 36, questionnaire survey. The question asked specifically what possibility "you and women like you" have of contributing
(a) to the municipality, if the women were in local government, and
(b) to the country, if the women were in national government.

democratic, open, and participant political cultures to score on the positive end of this scale appears confirmed for the present study.

TABLE 18
"FAITH IN PEOPLE"

	Percent who give "trust" or positive answers:		
	Peruvians	Chileans	Total
Statements of Faith in People[a]			
Q. 38. When we're talking about a project that benefits the people, there is (a great deal, some, little or no) cooperation	77	72	74
Q. 39. Some people say that most people can be trusted. Others say you can't trust anyone else. How do you feel about it?	63	71	67
Q. 40. Would you say that most people are inclined to help others or more inclined to look out for themselves?	32	34	33
Statements of Distrust in People			
Q. 42. If you don't look out for yourself, people will take advantage of you (agree/disagree).	35	56	47
Q. 43. If you make a mess of things, nobody is going to care much (agree/disagree).	53	69	62
INDEX: FAITH IN PEOPLE			
High Trust	12	23	18
Moderate Trust	48	40	44
Low Trust	40	37	38

[a]Includes both "a great deal" and "some" answers.

With the analysis of the work the women do and their attitudes on the opportunities open to them, on government, and on social change, the presentation of data from the questionnaire survey is completed. In the final chapter, after a summation of the background material forming the context of this study and the situation of women leaders in Peru and Chile, some suggestions are offered for the future.

8. The Future of Women in Politics

The introduction and first chapter of this study posed a series of questions about women and development, revolving around the implications of women's virtual absence from the command echelons of society and polity. The key issue, so far as the future is concerned, is whether the participation of women at the decision levels may be expected to increase and whether their presence would make any difference. Telescoping these questions, the analysis addressed itself to four principal issues:

1. Why are so few women found in leadership positions? Does the sex status "female" explain more about women's absence from responsible participation in economy, society, and polity than such characteristics as class, age, marital status, race, religion, and other intervening variables that might affect behavior?

2. Should we be concerned that women today play so small a role in policy-making? If women *did* participate, would they contribute anything distinctive? Is there a feminine perspective to development and social change?

3. How might women begin to participate as policy-makers? Since increased indices of urbanization, industrialization, education, and economic activity do not appear to correlate with increased numbers of women in policy-making roles, what *would* produce more women leaders?

4. Could Third World societies develop without ever emancipating women to compete on an "equal" (in the sense of identical) basis in a masculine world? Particularly in traditional societies such as the Latin American, could women make a quantum jump from their oppressed status to a significant neo-feminine—and powerful—role in their societies?

Women in Government Today: A Summing-Up

Maurice Duverger (1955: 123), who studied women in government intensively in four countries (France, West Germany, Norway, and Yugoslavia) and used data from fifteen others, saw a "progressive decline in women's influence" everywhere as the higher levels of leadership were reached. He noted, too, that although differences in the proportions of men and women *voters* were lessening in some countries, women's representation at parliamentary and governmental levels tended to stabilize at very low levels after the first elections following suffrage. Duverger's study was published more than twenty years ago, but the trend has not changed; Sullerot (1971: 222-230) analyzes at length what she calls "women's decreasing political power" in many countries of the world and demonstrates that the phenomena noted by Duverger had not altered at least to the time of her writing.

As this study has shown, since the late 1950s women in Peru, Chile, and other Latin American countries also made a tentative entry into government and politics. Very few were active at the top levels, however, and only rarely are women found among the decision-makers involved in development and social change. This state of affairs continues in those countries still under civilian rule.

One factor explaining this situation appears to be the nearly universal tendency-regardless of class status, race, religion, or educational background—for women (and men) to define women's public activity as an extension of their traditional family role to the public arena. If society assigns to women only one honorable vocational option, then any deviance from the norm apparently must be justified in terms of the valued universal model. But the fields to which women gravitate in both their professional and their political careers are not the tasks to which developing countries assign first priority; many women who do achieve a political or government appointment are relegated to old-line ministries or agencies that stifle any attempts at innovation. Few are recruited to positions in newer entities (for example, those dealing with agrarian reform, industrial development, tax reform, and fiscal policy) that are created precisely to get around the intricacies and dead ends of the traditional bureaucracy. Their intervention—and the situation of Peruvian and Chilean women differs only in degree from that of women in most other countries—has been characterized by its tentativeness and its restriction to feminine tasks. In short, most women, even when they achieve governmental positions, operate far from the seats of power.

Nor do women show much inclination to struggle against this situation in any direct fashion. Moreover, because the depreciation of women in Latin American society is counterbalanced by the tradition of gallantry and *caballerosidad,* and machismo by *marianismo,* conflict between men and women probably will never reach the levels of confrontation that feminist movements have generated in the United States and Western Europe (see Stevens 1973b: 90-101).

This lack of aggressiveness toward men does not mean that all women are satisfied with their professional opportunities and life chances, as the survey results amply reveal. A substantial minority wants to get ahead in public life. But they do not plan to do so by "waving banners," not only because, on the left, feminism is considered a deviation from the general struggle against oppression, but also because Latin cultural traditions regulating female/male relations are so distinct. Most Latin American women reject conflict tactics as counter-productive, just as many Latin Americans object to the importation of development models from the industrialized countries, so we should not too hastily assume that they will necessarily replicate the style of women's liberation in the United States and Western Europe.

What, then, of the future? If Latin American women probably are not going to join together in militant campaigns to change their status, and if economic modernization does not automatically liberate women either in socialist or western political systems, what are the prospects of women *ever* achieving equality in professional life and policy-making?

So far as women generally are concerned, perhaps the most that can be achieved in the near future is a widening of options so that women can freely choose marriage/motherhood *or* an alternative, which could include a combination of both roles. The Mattelarts suggest that the "new Latin American society" may turn out to be different from other industrialized societies; because of the strength of tradition, the family role may continue to be put in first place. In their view, what depreciates the position of women so greatly is the fact that most women are locked into the role of wife and mother as their only option; liberation for Latin American women might be achieved not by downgrading the family but by offering alternatives to those who want them: "Once the principle of personal autonomy is recognized, it is evident that the roles of mother and wife may be reevaluated, since in this case one would not be dealing with an imposed role but with the deliberate acceptance of tasks that are not the only options" (Mattelarts 1968: 19).

So far as women in public life are concerned, a solution might be to center priorities on the most positive aspects of the stereotype—make the best possible use of it, as it were, in a less-than-ideal present. Working through women's traditional occupations and voluntary work, they would emphasize woman's role as guardian and expositor of the values that women (no assertion is being made that only women can be concerned with human relationships!) in western and some other societies have come to represent: care and reverence for the person; experimentation with new forms of family life (as Safa [1974: 127-128] points out, though men and women in Latin societies may be alienated in their work role, they have a domestic sphere to which they can retreat); fostering of interdependent relationships; the promotion of the life of culture and the life of the spirit. These are precisely the values and institutions that Latin American observers in the Ariel and Caliban tradition of Rodó have long extolled as the positive side of the Latin American ethos and have been fearful of losing as their countries took on the more impersonal, achievement-oriented values of industrial society (increasingly questioned even in the developed world). It is not suggested here that tasks and values are "masculine" or "feminine" in any essential sense; the blurring of masculine and feminine modes of being and ways of working is already going forward at a rapid rate in some parts of the world (although probably not as rapidly as some observers assert), but not in Latin America.

An objection could be interjected here: What if the development enterprise has been too narrowly conceived? Many today are questioning whether there is not too much emphasis on economic inputs and too little on the effects of development on people—in terms of equality and participation—and on the "unintended consequences," such as depletion of natural resources, pollution, deterioration of the quality of life, and the like. This is a legitimate observation, but for the moment I would like to pursue the question in terms of how most governments, until recently, have conceived of the development enterprise, with the emphasis mainly on economic growth.

A logical question now follows and must be dealt with here: Why accept the situation of woman? If women are not now participating in development (in a formal, technical sense) and are not trained to do so, why not set about remedying this state of affairs immediately? Especially if, as most observers now admit, there are no biological inferiorities or lack of native endowment to prevent women from succeeding in masculine-type endeavors?

There are several compelling reasons for counseling governments that they might be well advised to accept the present situation in relation to the educational and professional preferences of women. Indeed, from the other side, there might be positive advantages in encouraging women to view a distinctively feminine contribution as valuable and even indispensable to society rather than denigrating feminine activities.

For one thing, developing countries have very limited resources to devote to education; only a limited amount of these resources goes to the "modern" faculties—economics, sciences, agronomy, business, engineering—whose graduates will contribute most directly to economic modernization. Moreover, because of masculine prejudice women often are not allowed to progress very far, either in or out of government, in the career areas that relate to development. Even if they are well trained and perfectly capable, then, women need great tenacity and energy to rise to influential policy-making positions. Once there, however, if they have tracked themselves on a masculine pattern, will they have anything distinctive to contribute?

On the other hand, if university enrollment figures are accurate indicators, most women are not eager to enter "development" careers, at least as these are currently defined. This may be partly simple realism: though she may be perfectly free to enter a technical faculty, a woman knows that she will encounter many barriers in the actual exercise of a "masculine" profession. Thus, faculties in which women train for traditional feminine occupations still attract the bulk of women university students in Latin America. Women have not yet given any clear-cut indications that they *wish* to go in other directions, and one wonders if it would make any sense at all to launch massive campaigns to change the attitudes of both women and men in order to reverse these trends.

Certainly women in Latin America are not held back by legal restrictions in training for a profession or exercising it: most of these have disappeared. The basic problem is one of attitudes—those of women, those of society—and it is doubtful if even massive government intervention would have much effect. Women themselves would have to want to change their orientation. In the face of the strength of Latin traditions, they would have to want *desperately* to change before any change would come about. Now it would seem that both limited government resources and women's energies might be dedicated to more profitable ends than gigantic public-opinion campaigns to force women into new occupational tasks. A government that desires more energetic collaboration from women in roles unfamiliar to them will probably never win it unless, as Cuba did, it puts the whole society on an emergency mobilization basis to fight the battle of production or defend the homeland from an outside enemy.

Another compelling reason for accepting the present situation is the fact that women are far from representing an inert mass in society. Estimates are that women grow about 40 percent of the domestic food supply in Latin America, and they play the major role in rural areas in food processing, storage, and distribution. In the cities, more and more work in paid occupations outside the home, in the traditional labor market, and as clerks, secretaries, and accountants. As lower-level bureaucrats they participate in the development enterprise, even if they are not at the policy-making level. In their traditional feminine pursuits, they care for the sick and the old, administer what social welfare resources are available, teach the young, and carry on dozens of essential volunteer activities, among them an increasing participation in local government as municipal council members. Although one might quarrel with the widespread view that the *municipio* is just a big *casa,* still it can be argued that it is more logical for women to deal with "quality of life" issues such as local school problems, parks and community recreation, regulation of stores and markets, and problems of light, water, and sanitation than their menfolk, who most often leave their suburban communities or the "new towns" of the poor in the early morning and return from their work in the central city late in the afternoon.

If, then, we are considering a rational allocation of resources, why should anyone attempt to convince women—at least at the present time—to leave behind the productive and essential tasks they perform in society? Who would then perform them? Indeed, the very fields in which women today are principally engaged cry out for modernization and new approaches. Inventive and enterprising women would have scope and challenge enough in revolutionizing their "own" fields of health care, education, and social welfare. Men have not yet moved into these fields in great numbers, as they have in the United States, and Latin American women will encounter few barriers to creative and innovative experiment other than their own inertia and their own doubt that their contribution has value.

Moreover, it is precisely here that women, if they prepare themselves technically, might eventually make a significant contribution to the development enterprise. They cannot do so, however, if they persist in the super-madre approach, in which the medical professions, teaching, and social work are seen mainly as extensions of the mothering role. To transform the public health, welfare, and educational systems of Latin America will depend on women and men of vision, talent, competence, and adequate training who think in terms of transforming basic societal structures. Natural mothering instincts may give women a certain motivation for entering feminine careers, but they are no substitute for professional and technical competence when these women move to policy-making positions.

Apart from the controversy about priorities in development programs, there does seem to be agreement among scholars and observers today that the concept of development needs to be broadened. If this is so—if modernization demands both economic inputs and investment in human resources—then why could not women find their contribution to development precisely here: women of vision and technical competence on whom governments could call to lead in the modernization of education, social welfare, and para-medical fields? Such innovators also could do much toward improving women's performance and contribution in the home, and their direct collaboration is needed in the sensitive area of population control.

Finally, I want to argue that the approach sketched out here is not simply a surrender to the inevitable. Encouraging women to accept their feminine qualities and occupations may, paradoxically, also be *more* advanced in the long run than an attempt to force women into tasks more directly related to economic development. In this, and in other respects, Latin American development need not replicate our own history.

As most literature on the subject accurately asserts, women have not been very "successful" and have not emerged as equal partners with men in technological enterprises because only a few have adopted the necessary attitudes. Hardly anyone now denies that women *could* change their orientation if they wanted to do so. But as has been pointed out by more than one observer, we are on the threshold of a time when the sheer ability to produce goods and services in the most cost-effective manner will not be the only priority in development. Considerations on *how* we do so (with less damage to our fragile planet) and *for whom* we do so (with more equitable distribution to the world's poor majority) are entering into international discourse. Margaret Mead (1976-77: 156) points out that any arguments about the importance of women's inclusion or exclusion from agencies and administrations concerned with development and foreign affairs must also take into account their special contribution:

> In today's world, food, housing, population control, community planning, and the quality of life are all becoming subject to international negotiations. Food is often treated as a weapon in international trade agreements. Agreements to process raw materials in affluent countries and ship consumer goods, regardless of their suitability, back to countries that produce raw materials . . . are a continuing part of international negotiations.

> These affairs, which have traditionally been women's domain, are now being initiated, discussed and regulated in new fields of "unconventional diplomatic initiatives. ". . . These activities all have present-day models in women's roles in families, villages and neighborhoods. *When there are no women's voices heard in the international councils related to food or population control, the debate is one-sided,* limited to the traditionally or recently-preempted activities of men. *The people of the world therefore suffer* [emphasis added].

The crux of the question, if the premises of this study are correct, is certainly here: "women's issues" are moving to the center of the policy arena, and we must ask ourselves if it would not be absurd to abandon female values at this point. It is suggested that the major areas of work in coming periods will be education, the human care of human beings, and the creation of the good community, and that these activities will "demand empathy, intuition and cooperation, which appear to be predominantly female characteristics" (Theobald 1967: 14-15).

These insights are in accord with a view beginning to be expressed by many today within the feminist movement: that without the values for which women stand it may quite simply be impossible to preserve a viable society. Men generally have played, in western culture at least, the aggressive role of explorer, innovator, entrepreneur. Women play an affective, relational role; that is not necessarily good, if it leads to the supermadre approach alluded to many times in this study. Both roles are needed. Men's role has been overly emphasized, and to bring a needed balance into society, women must begin to play a part. To do so would require them to modernize their ways of working and to harmonize the traditional feminine values with attitudes of achievement and universalism.

Several observers have by now made similar suggestions (Bourque and Grossholtz 1973; González 1973; Jaquette 1976; Nash 1975b; Schmidt 1975; Sullerot 1971: 239-248) to the effect that women's approach to politics appears "conservative" in part according to how one perceives political reality. There is a concurrence among these analysts on the existence of a "feminine perspective" on politics, a perspective that directs women toward issues that are crucial to their lives. Such issues are, however, usually defined by the male power structure either as "non-political" ("male" issues revolve around questions of authority, power, war, arms, monopoly over resources, economic policy) or "conservative" ("female" issues tend to relate to the family, children and the old, food prices and inflation, peace, moral questions). As women gain more power, they may well have more of a say in defining what is "political," and "their" issues will enter more directly into the mainstream of politics, as, indeed, they already have begun to do. (Today, abortion, equal pay for equal work, daycare, even sharing the housework are issues at the center of the political arena in many countries. In Cuba, the new family code adopted in 1975 [see Center for Cuban Studies 1975 for a complete account] requires, among many other provisions designed to equalize the roles of men and women in society, that men shoulder 50 percent of the housework and childcare when women work.)

This question of the content of politics leads us back again full circle to the issue of women's political participation. As Bourque and Grossholtz (1974: 231) point out, women's lesser participation, where it exists, may not demonstrate female passivity or lack of interest but, in fact, could reflect women's shrewder assessment of political reality. They suggest that the male does not seem so aware that no one has much political power in any case; moreover, they ask, why *should* women invest time and effort in politics if they have so few stakes in the outcomes?

Schmidt (1975: 482-483) argues that women's participation will grow as they recognize the emergence of such issues as "food as politics." As has been noted often in this study, food and other "women's issues" today are moving to the center of world consciousness. What if women decide they finally *do* have a stake in the political process? Will they seek political power in increasing numbers as they become aware that their contribution is essential to the finding of solutions to the great problems perplexing humankind? From the other side, will women finally be admitted to the political arena as full-fledged power contenders, or will men simply co-opt women's issues and attempt to solve them on a masculine "power" basis (as they have largely done with population control, and as they appear to be doing in the quest for solutions to the problem of world hunger)?

Only a few analysts have addressed the central question of how women are to acquire political power. Schmidt (1975: 472-473) believes he sees evidence that as women become more active, even more of them feel they should participate. As women's participation grows, he says, "women themselves will begin to define society's values more and more."

I agree with the premise, but I am not sure the process will be so automatic as Schmidt assumes. Returning to a phenomenon documented throughout this study, we face once again women's propensity to withdraw. A cohort of women drawn into activism in a time of crisis may remain engaged for a relatively long time, but as the members of the particular cohort grow older (or simply tired) and withdraw, as a rule no new generation follows unless there is a new crisis. Women in Peru and Chile who entered public life in the late 1950s and early 1960s, when it became possible for women to aspire to political careers, were already beginning to withdraw at the time of my study. This phenomenon appears to be world-wide. It is true that each feminine cohort that enters the public arena when extraordinary events call women forth leaves behind a residue, but the isolated survivors—unless they are reenforced by new blood—can do no more than hold the ground gained (if, indeed, the process does not actually go backward).

A "political generation" is short—eight or ten years at the most. If new leaders do not appear in the first three or four years after the entry of an initial cohort, then the momentum gained at the outset obviously cannot be maintained. Perhaps the key to women's achieving power lies here. Women cannot wait for the appearance of a few great feminine leaders who will win power and hand it to the rest. Only if wave upon wave of women in successive cohorts keep coming forward at every level—local, national, international—and only if women are willing to put in the long years of political apprenticeship, together with a determination not to retire at the first signs of opposition, will there be any possiblity of solid gains.

This study began with the notion that women in Peru and Chile—and elsewhere—who became active politically in the 1950s and early 1960s defied the conventional image of women's proper role and were in this sense deviants. It was suggested that although women's very marginality discourages some, minority status may in other cases foster the determination to struggle—or so it has been with many of history's "out groups."

The key to women's winning a share of political power and exercising it on their own terms may lie here, along with the necessity of fostering a successor cohort with sufficient members so that there is a critical mass to continue the momentum toward change.

Elise Boulding (1977: 227) expresses this notion in her own work on women in the twentieth century:

Who will create the new images [of possible futures for the world]? It will be those who are marginal to the present society, who are excluded from the centers of power, who stand at the world's peripheries and see society with different eyes. . . . It happens that the category of human beings I have been writing about . . . fulfills the requirements of marginality, of exclusion from the centers of power, and of possession of practical everyday skills at the micro and intermediate levels of human activity—the family, the neighborhood, the town. Since they also represent approximately half the human race, their aggregate potential is incalculable. I am referring, of course, to women.

Appendices

APPENDIX I
NATIONAL WOMAN SUFFRAGE
IN THE 21 AMERICAN REPUBLICS

Country	Year in Which National Woman Suffrage was Recognized
United States	1920
Ecuador	1929
Brazil	1932
Uruguay	1932
Cuba	1934
El Salvador	1939
Dominican Republic	1942
Guatemala	1945
Panama	1945
Argentina	1947
Venezuela	1947
Chile	1949
Costa Rica	1949
Haiti	1950
Bolivia	1952
Mexico	1953
Honduras	1955
Nicaragua	1955
Peru	1955
Colombia	1957
Paraguay	1961

Source: Organización de los Estados Americanos, Comisión Inter-Americana
de Mujeres 1965: 17.

APPENDIX II
WOMAN'S POSITION IN THE LEGAL AND
CIVIL CODES OF PERU AND CHILE

Roman law, on which both the Chilean and the Peruvian civil codes are based, derives most of its provisions on women from canon law. In turn, canon law depends on St. Paul—anything but a liberal in his attitudes and pronouncements on the female sex—for its insights on the treatment of women. Both codes tend to treat women, children, and imbeciles alike as legal minors. In neither Peru nor Chile does the married woman yet enjoy equal rights with men before the law, although their single sisters suffer few legal disabilities. The famous "patria potestad," or patriarchal right of the father over wife and minor daughters, coming to America through Spanish law, is still spelled out in the civil codes of Peru and Chile. (Information on women in the civil code of Peru is based on Patrón Faura 1972; of Chile, on Klimpel Alvarado 1962.)

The present status of women in Chile is regulated by the civil code of 1855, the oldest still in force in Latin America and (being the work of don Andrés Bello) "untouchable, like the monuments" (Loyola Illanes 1969: 15). Most of the provisions dealing with women's legal rights in Peru are set forth in the civil code and constitution of 1933.

The relative incapacity of married women before the law is similar in both countries, although the situation of the Chilean wife is slightly better than that of the Peruvian. Inequality is especially evident in relation to property. In Peru, unless a legal separation of property is effected *before* marriage, the husband not only has the right to administer the income from his wife's goods (which are considered part of the goods they hold in common) but, if she does not contribute to the common household expenses, may also administer her property (Patrón Faura 1972: 20-22). In Chile, a similar provision was modified in 1934 to allow an agreement for separation of property to be entered into *after* marriage. But, as Klimpel points out, a woman most often will not make use of this right before marriage for sentimental reasons, and afterwards would only resort to such a measure when the husband had amply demonstrated his financial incapacity or bad will. In such a case, the major part of her property might well have disappeared (1962: 54).

Unless there has been a prior legal arrangement, the husband in Peru also acquires rights of administration and disposition over whatever the wife earns through her work or profession. Such earnings automatically become part of the common property. In principle, no wife may work without her husband's permission in either country, although such permission most often is tacitly assumed. Still, if he does not approve, a husband may take legal action to prevent his wife from working or to acquire control over her salary—and the law is on his side. In Chile, a husband now has no rights over his wife's earnings, but he, too, may resort to legal action to prevent her from taking a job in the first place. In Peru, civil divorce exists without the right to remarry, because civil divorce does not affect what is considered to be the indissolubility of religious marriage (Patrón Faura 1972: 28). In Chile, there is no civil divorce.

APPENDIX III

WOMEN SERVING IN NATIONAL LEGISLATURES
IN THE AMERICAS IN 1968

Country	Diputados	Senadores
Bolivia	1	
Brazil	7	
Colombia	7	4
Chile	12	2
Costa Rica	3	
Ecuador	1	
El Salvador	2	
Haiti	4	
Honduras	3	
Mexico	2	
Nicaragua	1	
Peru	2	
Uruguay		1
United States	10	1

Source: OAS, Inter-American Commission of Women, 1969.

APPENDIX IV
POSITIONS OCCUPIED BY WOMEN IN THE SURVEY

	Peru		Chile		Total	
	No.	%	No.	%	No.	%
Municipal Offices	44	(54)	39	(45)	83	(50)
Concejales or regidoras	30[a]		14		44	(26)
Candidates for concejal or regidora	14		25		39	(24)
National Offices	37	(46)	47	(55)	84	(50)
Senators, deputies	2		3		5⎫	
					⎬14	(8)
Party leaders	4		5[c]		9⎭	
Bureaucrats–ministries	22[b]		33		55⎫	
					⎬68	(41)
Bureaucrats–agencies	7		6		13⎭	
International representatives	2		0[d]		2	(1)
TOTALS	81	(100)[e]	86	(100)	167	(100)

[a]Because of the election dates and the timing of the interviews, there is a difference between the countries in the numbers of candidates vs. the numbers of councilwomen interviewed. Peruvians were interviewed after the elections of December, 1966, and therefore more who actually won a seat could be included. In contrast, many Chileans were interviewed before the elections of April, 1967.

[b]A former Peruvian congresswoman included here.

[c]One party leader is also a congresswoman; another is a former congresswoman.

[d]One Chilean congresswoman also acts here.

[e]Percentages do not always add up to 100 in this and subsequent tables due to rounding of numbers.

APPENDIX V
PERUVIANS AND CHILEANS
BY TYPE OF WORK ASSIGNMENT

	Peru		Chile		Total	
	No.	%	No.	%	No.	%
"Feminine" tasks	52	(64)	61	(70)	113	(68)
Social welfare (general)	15	(19)	30	(35)	45	(27)
Welfare and rights of women and children	13	(16)	21	(24)	34	(20)
Education	11	(14)	6	(7)	17	(10)
Art and culture	9	(11)	2	(2)	11	(7)
Health	4	(5)	2	(2)	6	(4)
"Neutral" tasks[a]	14	(17)	19	(22)	33	(20)
No special work assignment[b]	15	(19)	6	(7)	21	(13)
TOTALS	81	(100)	86	(100)	167	(100)

[a]Includes planning, personnel, budget and tax administration, census, statistics, employment, and economic development.

[b]In some cases, the interviewees work in so many tasks (all but four of these are at municipal level) that it was impossible to assign them to a specific type of work category; in other cases an interviewee had not yet received her assignment in the municipality.

APPENDIX VI
LEVELS OF GOVERNMENT
AT WHICH INTERVIEWEES SERVE

	Peru		Chile		Total	
	No.	**%**	**No.**	**%**	**No.**	**%**
Level I – Ministerial or subministerial						
Level II – *Dirección general* or equivalent	3	(4)	4	(5)	7	(4)
Level III – *Subdirección* or equivalent	3	(4)	8	(9)	11	(7)
Level IV – *Departamento nacional* or equivalent; important municipal offices	25	(31)	27	(31)	52	(31)
Levels V, VI – *Oficina nacional* or equivalent; remaining municipal offices	50	(62)	47	(55)	97	(58)
TOTALS	81	(100)	86	(100)	167	(100)

Officials have been classified on six levels as follows:

Level I – Ministers and assistant ministers; subsecretaries of ministries; ambassadors.

Level II – Officials heading a *dirección general* or equivalent (the major division within a ministry); senators; *diputados* if they also hold an important party office.

Level III – Officials heading a major *subdirección* (division within a *dirección*) or less important *dirección* within a ministry; subchiefs of *direcciones; diputados* without other offices; judges.

Level IV – Heads of *departamentos* within a ministry, often administrative or budgetary; municipal council members of Gran Lima and Gran Santiago; mayoresses of other districts; party leaders without other offices.

Level V – Heads of *oficinas* within *departamentos* in the ministries or equivalent; municipal council members in districts outside Gran Lima and Gran Santiago.

Level VI – Candidates for municipal office.

APPENDIX VII
PROFESSIONS OF INTERVIEWEES BY
COUNTRY AND LOCATION OF POST
(MUNICIPAL AND NATIONAL)

	Peru				Chile		
Rank	Profession	Mun.	Nat.	Tot.	Profession	Mun.	Nat.	Tot.
1	Teachers	7	9	16	Teachers	4	8	12
					Lawyers	0	12	12
2	Lawyers	0	8	8	Secretaries, accountants	8	2	10
3	Social workers	1	6	7	Public administrators	0	8	8
					Social workers	3	5	8
4	Secretaries, accountants	5	1	6	Economists, commercial engineers	0	6	6^a
5	Medical professions	2	3	5^b	Medical professions	3	2	5^b
	Engineers, architects	1	4	5				
6	Journalists	2	1	3	Entrepreneurs	1	1	2
	Public administrators	0	3	3				
7	Entrepreneurs	1	0	1	Engineers, architects	0	1	1
					Journalists	1	0	1
	Other	6	2	8^c	Other	4	0	4^c
	No training or experience	18	1	19	No training or experience	15	2	17
	TOTALS	43	38	81		39	47	86

[a]Commercial engineering is a career offered in the faculty of economics in Chile and prepares the student for public administration.

[b]5 doctors, 4 *matronas* (midwives), and 1 nurse.

[c]4 factory workers, a sociologist, a psychologist, a dancer, an artist, 2 vendors, and 2 unspecified.

APPENDIX VIII
INTERVIEWEES BY SOCIAL CLASS
(National Level Only)

	Peru		Chile		Total	
	No.	%	No.	%	No.	%
Lower middle class	3	(8)	1	(2)	4	(5)
"Middle" middle class	22	(60)	25	(53)	47	(56)
Upper middle class	9	(24)	15	(32)	24	(28)
Upper class	3	(8)	6	(13)	9	(11)
TOTALS	37	(100)	47	(100)	84	(100)

APPENDIX IX
UNIVERSITY FACULTY OF INTERVIEWEES AND
OF WOMEN GRADUATES FROM THE
UNIVERSITY OF CHILE, 1959-1968

Type of Faculty	Peru		Chile		Total		U. of Chile[d]	
	No.	%	No.	%	No.	%	No.	%
Feminine[a]	15	(36)	19	(43)	34	(39)	5968	(80.1)
Masculine								
Traditional[b]	18	(43)	17	(39)	35	(41)	825	(11.1)
Modern[c]	9	(21)	8	(18)	17	(20)	655	(8.8)
TOTALS	42	(100)	44	(100)	86	(100)	7448	(100.0)

[a]Pedagogy, fine arts, library science, social service, nursing, obstetrics (special four-year course for women), dentistry and pharmacy (both of which have become "feminine" careers, in that over one-half the graduates are women), medical technology and physical therapy (both of which are reserved for women students).

[b]Letters and philosophy, law, medicine, journalism.

[c]Natural sciences, engineering and architecture, social sciences, political science and administration, economics, and commercial engineering.

[d]Included here are total women graduates, 1959-1968, for campuses of the University of Chile (Santiago, Concepción, Antofagasta, La Serena, Talca, Temuco, Valparaíso, Osorno, Iquique, Nuble, and Arica) and the Catholic universities at Santiago and Valparaíso.

Source: Universidad de Chile, Sección Títulos y Grados 1969, typewritten. *Not* included in this document were figures for graduates in law, library science, obstetrics, and sociology. These were estimated by adding together all students in their final year in these faculties, 1959-1968 (figures from bulletins of the University of Chile), then subtracting 20 percent for attrition.

APPENDIX X
SCORING FOR INDEXES CONSTRUCTED FOR CHAPTER 7

A. Confidence in Women's Life Chances

Q. 15   In Peru [Chile], are the women in fact emancipated as they are from the legal point of view? (All, some, very few)

Q. 18   Are Peruvian [Chilean] women free to enter any profession at all, or are there special fields for women? (Free, specific fields, depends)

Q. 22   Would you say that the professional woman has (more, the same, less) opportunity to marry than other women?

Scoring: Q. 15: All = 2; some = 1
             Q. 18: Free = 1
             Q. 22: More = 2; same = 1

             Score of 0, 1, 2 – Low confidence
             Score of 3   – Moderate confidence
             Score of 4, 5   – High confidence

B. Feminine Stereotype Index

Q. 19   Do you think there are any government posts in which women officials would be preferable? (Yes, no)

Q. 20   Do you think there are government posts in which women officials would not be appropriate? (Yes, no)

Scoring: Two negative answers – Unstereotyped
             One negative answer   – Ambivalent
             Two positive answers   – Stereotyped

C. Index of Personal Political Competence

Q. 14   In your opinion, what are the three most important requirements for getting ahead in the world? (Professional training, God's help, hard work, knowing important people, luck, talent and capacity)

Q. 23   In the same public posts, would you say that women must work (more than, the same as, less than) men in order to be successful?

Q. 24   Would you say that professional women appear to men (more, neither more nor less, less) feminine than non-professionals?

Q. 25   Would you say that barriers against women in certain professions or public posts are due more to (masculine prejudices,
traditional institutions of society, women's own mentality)?

Scoring: Q. 14: Training, hard work, capacity = 1 each
Q. 23: Same = 1; less = 2
Q. 24: More = 2; same = 1
Q. 25: None = 2; women's mentality = 1

Score of 3 or less — Low competence
Score of 4   — Moderate competence
Score of 5 or more—High competence

D. Faith in People Index

Note: Questions 38, 39, 40, 42, and 43 used in the construction of
this scale are translated in their entirety in table 18 and thus
will not be repeated here.

Scoring: Q. 38: Great deal = 2; some = 1
Q. 39: Trust = 1
Q. 40: Inclined to help = 1
Q. 42: Disagree = 1
Q. 43: Disagree = 1

Score of 0, 1, 2   — Low trust
Score of 3, 4   — Moderate trust
Score of 5, 6   — High trust

Bibliography

Aguirre, Mirta
1948   *Influencia de la mujer en Ibero-América.* Havana: Servicio Feme-
nino para la Defensa Civil.
Alegría, Ciro
1967   "Clorinda Matto y su casa grande." *Expreso,* April 26.
Almond, Gabriel A., and Sidney Verba
1963   *The Civic Culture: Political Attitudes and Democracy in Five
Nations.* Princeton, N.J.: Princeton University Press.
Alpenfels, Ethel J.
1962   "Women in the Professional World." Pp. 73-89 in Beverly Brenner
Cassara, ed., *American Women: The Changing Image.* Boston:
Beacon Press.
Alvarado Rivera, María Jesús
1912   "El femenismo." Conferencia leída en la Sociedad Geográfica de
Lima el 28 de Octubre de 1911. Lima: Imprenta de la Escuela
de Ingenieros.
Aquinas, Thomas
n.d.   *Summa Theologica.* Paris: Vives, 1889. Translated by the Fathers
of the English Dominican Province. 2nd ed. London: Burns Oates
& Washbourne.
Arizpe, Lourdes S.
1975   *Indígenas en la ciudad de México. El caso de las "Marías."*
Mexico City: SEP/SETENTAS.
1976   "Women in the Informal Labor Sector: The Case of Mexico
City." Paper presented at the Conference on Women in Develop
ment, Wellesley College. Pp. 25-37 in *Signs* 3, no. 1 (Autumn
1977).
Aviel, JoAnn Scott
1974   "Changing the Political Role of Women: A Costa Rican Case
Study." Pp. 281-303 in Jane Jaquette, ed., *Women in Politics.*
New York: John Wiley & Sons.

*As is their own custom in their professional lives, Latin American women authors are
listed throughout under their family names (followed by de _____ if they are married).

Bakke, E. Wight
   1964   "Students on the March: The Case of Mexico and Colombia."
          Sociology of Education 37, no. 3 (Spring): 200-228.
Bambirra, Vania
   1971   "La mujer chilena en la transición al socialismo." *Punto Final* 133
          (June 22): suplemento, 1-8.
Barbieri, M. Teresita de
   1975   "La condición de la mujer en América Latina: Su participación
          social; antecedentes y situación actual." Pp. 46-131 in Comisión
          Económica para América Latina, *Mujeres en América Latina:
          Aportes para una discusión.* Mexico City: Fondo de Cultura
          Económica.
Bardwick, Judith M.
   1971   *Psychology of Women: A Study of Bio-Cultural Conflicts.* New
          York: Harper & Row.
Beauvoir, Simone de
   1953   *The Second Sex.* Trans. H. M. Parshley. New York: Alfred A.
          Knopf.
Benston, Margaret
   1969   "The Political Economy of Women's Liberation." *Monthly Review*
          21 (September): 13-27.
Bernard, Jessie
   1968   "The Status of Women in Modern Patterns of Culture." *The
          Annals of the American Academy* 375 (January): 3-14.
Blachman, Morris J.
   1973   *Eve in an Adamocracy: Women and Politics in Brazil.* New York:
          Ibero-American Language and Area Center, New York University.
          Occasional Paper No. 5.
   1974   "Selective Omission and Theoretical Distortion: Problems Encoun-
          tered in Researching the Organized Political Activity of Women
          in Brazil." Paper presented at the Conference on Feminine Per-
          spectives in Social Science Research in Latin America, Buenos
          Aires. Pp. 245-264 in June Nash and Helen Safa, eds., *Sex and
          Class in Latin America.* New York: Praeger, 1976.
Blumberg, Rae Lesser
   1976   "Kibbutz Women: From the Fields of Revolution to the Laundries
          of Discontent." Pp. 319-344 in Lynne Iglitzin and Ruth Ross,
          eds., *Women in the World: A Comparative Study.* Santa Barbara
          and Oxford: ABC Clio Press.
Boger, Sylvia
   1965   Untitled paper on Magda Portal prepared for the Peruvian Field
          Seminar, Ibero-American Studies Program, University of Wis-
          consin, Lima, Summer 1965. Typewritten.
Bonilla, Frank
   1960   "The Chilean Student Federation: Fifty Years of Political Action."

Journal of Inter-American Studies 2, no. 3 (July): 313-330.

Borgese, Elizabeth Mann
1963   *Ascent of Woman.* London: Macgibbon & Kee.

Boserup, Ester
1970   *Women's Role in Economic Development.* New York: St. Martin's Press.

Boulding, Elise
1977   *Women in the Twentieth Century World.* New York: John Wiley & Sons.

Bourque, Susan, and Jean Grossholtz
1974   "Politics an Unnatural Practice: Political Science Looks at Female Participation." *Politics and Society* 4, no. 2 (Winter): 225-266.
_____ , and Kay B. Warren
1976   "Campesinas y comuneras: Subordinación en la sierra peruana." *Estudios Andinos* 5, no. 1: 77-97.

Brenan, Gerald
1957   *The Literature of the Spanish People from Roman Times to the Present.* New York: Meridian Books.

Bunster, Ximena
1974   "The Birth of a Mapuche Leader." Paper presented at the Conference on Feminine Perspectives in Social Science Research in Latin America, Buenos Aires. Pp. 302-319 in June Nash and Helen Safa, eds., *Sex and Class in Latin America.* New York: Praeger, 1976. A Spanish version appears in María del Carmen de Leñero, *La mujer en América Latina,* vol. 3. Mexico City: SEP/SETENTAS, 1975.
1978   "Market Women in Lima: Source of Cheap Labor and Social Alienation." Paper presented at the Women and Poverty Workshop, International Center for Research on Women, Belmont Conference Center, Md.

Bussi de Allende, Hortensia
1971   "La mujer y la integración andina." *Plandes, Boletín Informativo de la Sociedad Chilena de Planificación y Desarrollo,* special issue: 147-155.

Buvenić, Mayra, and Nadia H. Youssef (with Barbara Von Elm)
1978   "Women-Headed Households: The Ignored Factor in Development Planning." Report submitted to the Office of Women in Development, Agency for International Development.

Castorino, María Sara L. de
1962   "Una mujer extraordinaria: María J. Alvarado Rivera." Pp. 7-64 in Dora Córdova C., ed., *Breve información sobre la cruzada por los derechos de la mujer.* Lima, mimeographed.

Castro, Américo
1954   *The Structure of Spanish History.* Princeton, New Jersey: Princeton University Press.

184   Bibliography

Castro, Fidel
    1966   "Women's Liberation: The Revolution within a Revolution." In
            Women and the Cuban Revolution. New York: Pathfinder Press.
Center for Cuban Studies
    1975   Cuban Family Code. Newsletter, Center for Cuban Studies 2, no.
            4 (May): 3-18. See also "Women in Transition," *Cuba Review* 4,
            no. 2 (September, 1974): entire issue.
Chaney, Elsa M.
    1971   "Women in Latin American Politics: The Case of Peru and Chile."
            Ph.D. dissertation, University of Wisconsin.
    1973   The Mobilization of Women in Three Societies." Paper presented
            at the IXth International Congress of Anthropological and Ethno-
            logical Sciences, Oshkosh and Chicago. Pp. 471-489 in Ruby
            Rohrlich-Leavitt, ed., *Women Cross-Culturally: Challenge and
            Change.* The Hague: Mouton.
    1974   "The Mobilization of Women in Allende's Chile." Pp. 267-280
            in Jane Jaquette, ed., *Women in Politics.* New York: John Wiley
            & Sons.
    1977   "Agripina, Domestic Service as Permanent Occupation: Implica-
            tions for Development." Paper presented at the Primer Simposio
            Mexicano-Centro-Americano sobre Investigación de la Mujer,
            Mexico City.
    _____ , and Marianne Schmink
    1974   "Going from Bad to Worse: Women and Modernization." Paper
            presented at the Conference on Feminine Perspectives in Social
            Science Research in Latin America, Buenos Aires. Pp. 160-182 in
            June Nash and Helen Safa, eds., *Sex and Class in Latin America.*
            New York: Praeger, 1976. A Spanish version ("Las mujeres y la
            modernización: Acceso a la tecnología") appears in María del
            Carmen Elu de Leñero, *La mujer en América Latina,* vol. 1.
            Mexico City: SEP/SETENTAS, 1975.
Chang, Ligia, and María Angélica Ducci
    1977   *Realidad del empleo y la formación profesional de la mujer en
            América Latina.* Montevideo: Centro Interamericano de Investiga-
            ción y Documentación sobre Formación Profesional (CINTERFOR).
Chaplin, David
    1976   *The Peruvian Industrial Labor Force.* Princeton, N.J.: Princeton
            University Press.
    1969   "Feminism and Economic Development." Occasional paper,
            typewritten.
Chombart de Lauwe, Paul H.
    1962   "Introduction." Pp. 7-25 in "Images of Woman in Society,"
            International Social Science Journal (UNESCO) 14, no. 1.
Colegio de Abogados, Chile
    1969   Consejo General. Personal communication.

Collier, Simon
    1967   *Ideas and Politics of Chilean Independence: 1808-1833.* Cambridge: The University Press.
Collins, Randall
    1971   "A Conflict Theory of Sexual Stratification." *Social Problems* 19, no. 1 (Summer): 5-21.
Collver, Andrew, and Eleanor Langlois
    1962   "The Female Labor Force in Metropolitan Areas: An International Comparison." *Economic Development and Cultural Change* 10, no. 4: 367–385.
Cruz, Levy
    1967   "Brazil." Pp. 209-225 in Raphael Patai, ed., *Women in the Modern World.* New York: The Free Press.
Cuadros E., Manuel E.
    1949   *Paisaje i obra . . . mujer e historia: Clorinda Matto de Turner.* Cuzco, Peru: Editorial H. G. Rozas Sucs.
Dalla Costa, Marirosa
    1972   "Women and the Subversion of the Community." Pp. 1-54 in Marirosa Dalla Costa and Selma James, *The Power of Women and the Subversion of the Community.* Bristol, England: The Falling Wall Press, Ltd.
Deere, Carmen Diana
    1977   "Changing Social Relations of Production and Peruvian Peasant Women's Work." *Latin American Perspectives* 4, nos. 1 and 2 (Winter and Spring): 48-69.
Dellepiane, Antonio
    1923   *Dos patricias ilustres.* Buenos Aires: Coni.
Devaud, Marcelle Stanislaus
    1968   "Political Participation of European Women." *The Annals of the American Academy* 375 (January): 61-66.
Diffie, Bailey W.
    1967   *Latin-American Civilization.* New York: Octagon Books.
Dodge, Norton T.
    1966   *Women in the Soviet Economy: Their Role in Economic, Scientific and Technical Development.* Baltimore: Johns Hopkins Press.
Ducci B., M. Angélica, Margarita Gili V., and Marta Illanes H.
    1974   "La mujer chilena y su incorporación al mercado laboral." Informe preliminar. Santiago: Instituto Laboral y de Desarrollo Social. Mimeographed.
Durić, Suzana, and Gordana Dragicević
    1965   *Women in Yugoslav Society and Economy.* Beograd: Medunarodna Politka.
Duverger, Maurice
    1955   *The Political Role of Women.* Paris: UNESCO.

Economic Commission for Latin America (ECLA)
  1975   "Participation of Women in Development in Latin America."
          United Nations, New York: ECLA. E/CONF.66/BP/8/Add. 1.
          May 13.
Elizaga, Juan C.
  1974   "The Participation of Women in the Labour Force of Latin
          America: Fertility and Other Factors." *International Labour
          Review* 109, nos. 5-6 (May-June): 519-538.
Elmendorf, Mary Lindsay
  1973   *La mujer maya y el cambio.* Mexico City: SEP/SETENTAS.
          Also published in English as *The Mayan Woman and Change.*
          Cuernavaca, Mexico: CIDOC.
Emmerson, Donald K.
  1968   *Students and Politics in Developing Nations.* New York: Praeger.
Encina, Francisco A.
  1954   *Resumen de la historia de Chile.* 3 vol. Santiago: Empresa Edito-
          ra Zig-Zag.
Ercilla
  1964   "Historia del voto con faldas: La pugna de los honorables." No.
          1528 (September 1): 6-7.
  1968   No. 1740 (October 3 through 29): 60.
  1969   No. 1759 (March 5 through 11): 12.
Faherty, William B., S. J.
  1950   *The Destiny of Modern Woman in the Light of Papal Teaching.*
          Westminster, Maryland: The Newman Press.
Festini, Nelly
  1968   "Women in Public Life in Peru." *The Annals of the American
          Academy* 375 (January): 58-60.
Flora, Cornelia Butler
  1973   "The Passive Female and Social Change: A Cross-Cultural Com-
          parison of Women's Magazine Fiction." Pp. 59-85 in Ann
          Pescatello, ed., *Female and Male in Latin America.* Pittsburgh:
          University of Pittsburgh Press.
Freyre, Gilberto
  1963   *The Mansions and the Shanties: The Making of Modern Brazil.*
          New York: Alfred A. Knopf.
Gallo Chinchilla, Margarita
  1945   "La mujer ante la legislación chilena." Memoria de Prueba (thesis),
          Universidad de Chile.
Garrett, Patricia
  1976   "Some Structural Constraints on the Agricultural Activities of
          Women: The Chilean Hacienda." Paper presented at the Confer-
          ence on Women and Development, Wellesley College. Madison:
          University of Wisconsin Land Tenure Center Research Paper No.70.

1977[?]   "The Organization of Working Class Women in Chile during the Popular Unity Government: Problems and Programs." Salt Lake City: University of Utah; mimeographed.

Gendell, Murray, and Guillermo Rossel
1967   *The Economic Activity of Women in Latin America.* Washington, D.C.: Pan American Union and the Inter-American Commission of Women.

Germain, Adrienne
1974   "Some Aspects of the Roles of Women in Population and Development." United Nations, New York: International Forum on the Role of Women in Population and Development. ESA/SDHA/AC.5/3/Add.1. February 13.

Gil, Federico
1966   *The Political System of Chile.* Boston: Houghton Mifflin Company.

Ginzberg, Eli
1966   *Life Styles of Educated Women.* New York: Columbia University Press.

Godoy Urzúa, Hernán
1971   *Séptimo año básico—Ciencias sociales. Tú y el mundo social.* Santiago: Editorial Universitaria, S.A.

González, Nancie L.
1973   "Women and the Jural Domain: An Evolutionary Perspective." Pp. 47-57 in Dorothy Gies McGuigan, ed., *A Sampler of Women's Studies.* Ann Arbor: University of Michigan, Center for the Continuing Education of Women.

Grez, Vicente
1966   *Las mujeres de la independencia.* Santiago: Empresa Editora Zig-Zag.

Gruberg, Martin
1968   *Women in American Politics: An Assessment and Sourcebook.* Oshkosh, Wis.: Academia Press.

Gutiérrez de Pineda, Virginia
1963   *La familia en Colombia.* Bogotá: Facultad de Sociología, Serie Latinoamericana.

Harkess, Shirley, and Patricia Pinzón de Lewin
1975   "Women, the Vote, and the Party in the Politics of the Colombian National Front." *Journal of Inter-American Studies and World Affairs* 17, no. 4 (November): 439-464.

Healy, Emma Thérèse
1956   *Woman According to Saint Bonaventure.* Erie, Penn.: Sisters of St. Joseph.

Hewett, Valerie
1976   "Rural Fieldwork in an Andean Community in Colombia: Preliminary Report." Bogotá: Corporación Centro Regional de Población;

mimeographed.

Houtart, François, and Emile Pin
1965   *The Church and the Latin American Revolution.* New York: Sheed & Ward.

Hunt, Chester L.
1965   "Female Occupational Roles and Urban Sex Relations in the United States, Japan and the Philippines." *Social Forces* 43, no. 3 (March): 407-417.

Jahan, Rounaq
1976   "Women in Politics in Bangladesh." Paper presented at the Conference on Women and Development, Wellesley College, June.

Jancar, Barbara
1972   "Women and Soviet Politics." Paper presented at the workshop on Politics and Social Change in the USSR, American Political Science Association Annual Meeting, Washington, D.C., September.

1978   *Women under Communism: A Cross-National Analysis of Women in Communist Societies.* Baltimore: Johns Hopkins Press.

Jaquette, Jane
1973   "Literary Archetypes and Female Role Alternatives: The Woman and the Novel in Latin America." Pp. 3-27 in Ann Pescatello, ed., *Female and Male in Latin America.* Pittsburgh: University of Pittsburgh Press.

1974   "Female Political Participation in Latin America: Some Observations in Search of a Model." Paper presented at the Conference on Feminine Perspectives in Social Science Research in Latin America, Buenos Aires, March. Pp. 221-244 in June Nash and Helen Safa, eds., *Sex and Class in Latin America.* New York: Praeger, 1976. A Spanish version appears in María del Carmen de Leñero, ed., *La mujer en América Latina,* vol. 1. Mexico City: SEP/SETENTAS, 1975.

Kinzer, Nora Scott
1973   "Women Professionals in Buenos Aires." Pp. 159-190 in Ann Pescatello, ed., *Female and Male in Latin America.* Pittsburgh: University of Pittsburgh Press.

1974   "Sexist Sociology." *The Center Magazine* 7, no. 3 (May-June): 48-59.

Klein, Viola
1965   *Britain's Married Women Workers.* London: Routledge & Kegan Paul.

Klimpel Alvarado, Felícitas
1962   *La mujer chilena: El aporte femenino al progreso de Chile.* Santiago: Editorial Andrés Bello.

Labarca Hubertson, Amanda
1934   *¿Adónde va la mujer?* Santiago: Ediciones Extra.

1947   *Femenismo contemporáneo.* Santiago: Editorial Zig-Zag.

1952   *Woman and Education in Chile.* Paris: UNESCO.

1967a   "La mujer chilena: ¿De dónde viene? ¿Y adónde va?" *Revista Paula* (December) : 78-81.

1967b   Interviews, spring 1967.

Lane, Robert E.

1959   *Political Life: Why and How People Get Involved in Politics.* New York: The Free Press.

Larguía, Isabel

1973   "The Economic Basis of Women's Status." Paper presented at the IXth International Congress of Anthropological and Ethnological Sciences, Oshkosh and Chicago. Pp. 281-295 in Ruby Rohrlich-Leavitt, ed., *Women Cross-Culturally: Challenge and Change.* The Hague: Mouton, 1975.

1975   "Aspects of the Condition of Women's Labor." NACLA's *Latin America & Empire Report* 9, no. 6 (September): 4-13. Spanish version in *Casa de las Américas* 15, no. 88 (January-February): 45-60.

Latin American Perspectives

1977   "Women and Class Struggle," 4, nos. 1 and 2 (Winter and Spring): 2-202; and "Population and Imperialism: Women in Revolution," 4, no. 4 (Fall): 2-136. Special issues.

Leacock, Eleanor Burke

1972   "Introduction." Pp. 7-67 in Frederick Engels, *The Origin of the Family, Private Property and the State.* New York: International Publishers.

Leader, Shelah

1973   "The Emancipation of Chinese Women." *World Politics* 26, no. 1 (October): 56-79.

Lenin, V. I.

1934   *The Emancipation of Women: From the Writings of V. I. Lenin.* New York: International Publishers.

Leonard, Irving A.

1964   *Books of the Brave.* New York: Gordian Press.

Lewis, Paul H.

1971   "The Female Vote in Argentina, 1958-1965." *Comparative Political Studies* 3, no. 4 (January): 425-441.

Lipset, Seymour Martin

1963   *Political Man: The Social Bases of Politics.* Garden City, N.Y.: Anchor Books.

Little, Cynthia Jeffress

1975   "Moral Reform and Feminism: A Case Study." *Journal of Inter-American Studies and World Affairs* 17, no. 4 (November): 386-397.

Lomnitz, Larissa Adler de
    1975   *Como sobreviven los marginados.* Mexico City: Siglo XXI Editores.
           English version, *Networks and Marginality: Life in a Mexican
           Shantytown,* trans. Cinna Lomnitz. New York: Academic Press,
           1977.
López R., Jorge
    1967   "Problemas administrativos y financieros de la municipalidad
           chilena." *Plandes, Boletín Informativo de la Sociedad Chilena de
           Planificación y Desarrollo* 23 (September-October): 18-22.
Loyola Illanes, Eliana
    1969   "Mujeres con oficina propia." *Ercilla* 1780 (July 30-August 5):
           72.
Mariátegui, José Carlos
    1955   *Siete ensayos de interpretación de la realidad peruana.* Santiago:
           Editorial Universitaria. English version, *Seven Interpretive Essays
           on Peruvian Reality,* trans. Marjory Urquidi. Austin: University of
           Texas Press, 1971.
Martínez Estrada, Ezequiel
    1961   *Radiografía de la pampa.* 5th ed. Buenos Aires: Losada. English
           version, *X-Ray of the Pampa,* trans. Alain Swietlicki. Austin:
           University of Texas Press, 1971.
Massell, Gregory J.
    1974   *The Surrogate Proletariat: Moslem Women and Revolutionary
           Strategies in Soviet Central Asia, 1919-1929.* Princeton, N.J.:
           Princeton University Press.
Mattelart, Armand, and Michèle Mattelart
    1968   *La mujer chilena en una nueva sociedad.* Santiago: Editorial del
           Pacífico.
    1970   *Juventud chilena: Rebeldía y conformismo.* Santiago: Editorial
           Universitaria.
Mattelart, Michèle
    1970   "El nivel mítico en la prensa pseudoamorosa." *Cuadernos de la
           Realidad Nacional* 1, no. 3 (March): 221-284.
    1974   "La mujer y la línea de masa de la burguesía: El caso de Chile."
           Paper presented at the Conference on Feminine Perspectives in
           Social Science Research in Latin America, Buenos Aires. English
           version pp. 279-301 in June Nash and Helen Safa, eds. *Sex and
           Class in Latin America.* New York: Praeger, 1976. The Spanish
           version appears in María del Carmen de Leñero, ed., *La mujer
           en América Latina,* vol. 2. Mexico City: SEP/SETENTAS, 1975.
Matto de Turner, Clorinda
    1889   *Aves sin nido: novela peruana.* Lima. Also published the same
           year in Buenos Aires: Imprenta del Universo de Carlos Prince. An
           English version appeared in 1968, *Birds without a Nest.* Notes by

Luis Mario Schneider. New York: Las Américas.

1902   *Boreales, miniaturas y porcelanas.* Buenos Aires: Imprenta Alsina.

Mayoraga, Wilfredo

1969   "La rebelión de las mujeres." *Ercilla* 1720 (June 5-11): 43-44.

Mead, Margaret

1949   *Male and Female: A Study of the Sexes in a Changing World.* New York: William Morrow.

1976-77 "Women in the International World." *Journal of International Affairs* 30, no. 2 (Fall/Winter): 151-160.

Meneses, Rómulo

1934   *Aprismo femenino peruano.* Lima: Editorial Atahualpa.

Mitchell, Juliet

1966   "Women: The Longest Revolution." *New Left Review* 40 (November-December): 11-37.

Moll, Willi

1967   *The Christian Image of Woman.* Notre Dame, Ind.: Fides Publishers.

Mota, Vivian M.

1974   "El femenismo y la política en la República Dominicana, 1931-45 and 1966-74." Paper presented at the Conference on Feminine Perspectives in Social Science Research in Latin America, Buenos Aires. English version, pp. 265-278 in June Nash and Helen Safa, eds., *Sex and Class in Latin America.* New York, Praeger, 1976. The Spanish version appears in María del Carmen de Leñero, *La mujer en América Latina,* vol. 2. Mexico City: SEP/SETENTAS, 1975.

Nash, June

1975a   "A Critique of Social Science Models of Contemporary Society: A Feminine Perspective." *Annals of the New York Academy of Science* 260.

1975b   "Resistance as Protest: Women in the Struggle of Bolivian Tin-Mining Communities." Pp. 261-271 in Ruby Rohrlich-Leavitt, ed., *Women Cross-Culturally: Challenge and Change.* The Hague: Mouton.

1976   "La mujer en los Andes," special issue of *Estudios Andinos* 5, no. 1: 1-171.

_____ , and Helen I. Safa, eds.

1976   *Sex and Class in Latin America.* New York: Praeger.

Organización de los Estados Americanos, Instituto Interamericano de Estadística

1971,   *América en Cifras, 1970 (and 1967): Situación Cultural y Situa-*
1967   *ción Social.* Washington, D.C.: Secretaría General.

_____ , Comisión Inter-Americana de Mujeres

1965   *Reseña historia sobre reconocimiento de los derechos políticos a* la mujer de América. Washington, D.C.: Pan American Union.

1967   *The Economic Activity of Women in Latin America,* by Murray Gendell and Guillermo Rossel. Washington, D.C.: Pan American Union.

1969   *Important Women in Public and Professional Life in Latin America.* Washington, D.C.: Pan American Union.

Ortner, Sherry B.

1974   "Is Female to Male as Nature Is to Culture?" Pp. 67-87 in Michelle Zimbalist Rosaldo and Louise Lamphere, eds., *Woman, Culture and Society.* Stanford, Calif.: Stanford University Press.

Pajuelo Eduardo, María Marta

1965   *Las bases de la educación peruana.* Lima: Talleres Gráficos Villanueva.

1968   Interview

Papanek, Hanna

1977   "Development Planning for Women." *Signs* 3, no. 1 (Autumn): 14-21.

Parsons, Talcott, and Robert F. Bales

1956   *Family, Socialization and Interaction Process.* Glencoe, Ill.: The Free Press.

Patrón Faura, Pedro

1955   *Legislación de la mujer peruana.* Lima: Editorial PGACE. Also Lima: Imprenta Colegio Militar Leoncio Prado, 1972.

Paul, Catherine Manny

1966   "Amanda Labarca H.: Educator to the Women of Chile." Ph.D. dissertation, School of Education, New York University.

Paz, Octavio

1961   *The Labyrinth of Solitude.* Trans. Lysander Kemp. New York: Grove Press.

Perón, Eva

1951   *La razón de mi vida.* Buenos Aires: Ediciones Peuser.

Petras, James

1977   "Political and Social Change in Chile," Pp. 9-40 in James Petras, ed., *Latin America from Dependence to Revolution.* New York: John Wiley & Sons.

Pike, Frederick B.

1967   *The Modern History of Peru.* New York: Praeger.

1968   "Aspects of Class Relations in Chile, 1850-1960." Pp. 202-219 in James Petras and Maurice Zeitlin, eds., *Latin America: Reform or Revolution?* Greenwich, Conn.: Fawcett Publications.

Plandes 71

1971   "Datos varios sobre la mujer." *Plandes, Boletín Informativo de la Sociedad Chilena de Planificación y Desarrollo,* special issue: 153-155.

Portal, Magda
   1933   *El aprismo y la mujer.* Lima: Editorial Atahualpa.
   1945   *Flora Tristán, la precursora.* Lima: Ediciones "Páginas Libres."
Purcell, Susan Kaufman
   1973   "Modernizing Women for a Modern Society: The Cuban Case."
           Pp. 257-271 in Ann Pescatello, ed., *Female and Male in Latin
           America.* Pittsburgh: University of Pittsburgh Press.
Puz, Amanda
   1972   *La mujer chilena.* Santiago: Editoria Nacional Quimantú.
República de Chile, Corporación de Fomento
   1967   *Geografía económica de Chile.* Santiago: CORFO.
_____, Corte Suprema de Justicia
   1967   "Escalafón del poder judicial, año 1967." Santiago: *Diario Oficial
           de la República de Chile,* June 7: 5-13.
_____, Dirección de Estadística y Censos
   1966   *Muestra nacional de hogares.* Santiago: Dirección de Estadística
           y Censos.
_____, Dirección del Registro Electoral
   1952   *Elección ordinaria de presidente de la república, 4 de septiembre
           de 1952.* Santiago: Imprenta y Litografía Universo.
   1961-   "Elección ordinaria de senadores—5 de marzo de 1961"; "Elección
   1973   ordinaria de diputados—5 de marzo de 1961"; "Elección regido-
           res 1963"; "Elección presidencial—4 de septiembre 1964";
           "Elección ordinaria de senadores varones y mujeres, 7 de marzo
           de 1965"; "Elección ordinaria de diputados varones y mujeres, 7
           de marzo de 1965"; "Elección presidencial—4 de septiembre de
           1970." All mimeographed. "Elección ordinaria de diputados y
           senadores, 4 de marzo de 1973—no oficial." *La Tercera de la
           Hora,* 6 March 1973: 21-48.
_____, Instituto de Investigaciones Estadísticas
   1959   *Desarrollo de la educación chilena desde 1940 a 1957.* 2nd. ed.
           by Erika Grassau S. and Egidio Orellano B. Santiago: Universidad
           de Chile.
   1962   "Supervivencia y pérdida del alumnado de la enseñanza superior
           en Chile." Santiago: Universidad de Chile, Informativo Estadístico
           No. 5.
   1970   "Alumnado de las universidades chilenas en 1969." Santiago: Uni-
           versidad de Chile. Informativo Estadístico No. 21, July.
_____, Sección de Títulos y Grados
   1969   "Profesionales titulados por la Universidad de Chile, 10 años
           (1959 hasta 1968)." Typewritten.
República del Perú, Consejo Nacional de la Universidad Peruana
   1970   "Población matriculada según universidades, ramas y especialida-
           des de estudio y sexo." Lima: CONUP. Boletín Estadístico No.
           4, April.

1972   "Universidad Peruana: postulantes a ingreso, año 1970 según procedencia y sexo." Lima: CONUP, Documento de Trabajo No. 6, May.

_____ , Instituto Nacional de Planificación

1966   *Desarrollo económico y social, recursos humanos y educación.* Lima: INP.

1967   *Plan de desarrollo económico y social, 1967-1970.* Lima: INP.

_____ , Oficina Nacional de Estadística y Censos

1973   *Censo Nacional de Población, 1972.*

_____ , Oficina Nacional de Racionalización y Capacitación de la Administración Pública

1966   *Guía del gobierno peruano.* Lima: ONRAP.

1967a   *Estudio sobre el gobierno municipal del Perú,* by Allen Austin. Lima: ONRAP.

1967b   *Guía de la administración pública.* Lima, ONRAP offices, September.

_____ , Registro Electoral del Perú

1966   "Inscripciones por sexos al 31 de diciembre de 1966, por departamentos." Lima, 31 December. Typewritten.

1967a   "Cuadro comparativo de electores y ciudadanos que no sufragen en las elecciones generales y municipales de los años 1963 y 1966 con porcentaje departamental." Lima, n.d. Typewritten.

1967b   "Miembros de los concejos municipales elegidos el mes de noviembre de 1966, clasificados por sexos, por departamentos." Lima, 22 September. Typewritten.

_____ , Servicio de Empleo y Recursos Humanos.

1966   *Diagnóstico de la situación de los recursos humanos.* Lima: Ministerio de Trabajo.

1970   *Informe sobre la situación occupacional del Perú, 1970.* Lima: Ministerio de Trabajo.

Requeña B., Mario, M. D.

1966   *Chilean Program of Abortion Control and Fertility Planning, Present Situation and Forecast for the Next Decade.* Santiago: Centro Latinoamericano de Demografía.

Ridley, Jeanne Claire

1968   "Demographic Change and the Roles and Status of Women." *The Annals of the American Academy* 375 (January): 15-25.

Rosaldo, Michelle Zimbalist

1974   "Woman, Culture and Society: A Theoretical Overview." Pp. 17-42 in Michelle Zimbalist Rosaldo and Louise Lamphere, eds., *Women, Culture and Society.* Stanford, Calif.: Stanford University Press.

Rose, Juan Gonzalo

1968   "Visión cultural." Pp. 119-149 in *Perú en síntesis.* Lima: Editorial Sanmartí, S.A.

Rosenberg, Morris
1956   "Misanthropy and Political Ideology." *American Sociological Review* 16, no. 6 (December): 690-695.
Rossi, Alice S.
1965   "Who Wants Women in the Scientific Professions? Barriers to the Career Choice of Engineering, Medicine or Science among American Women." Pp. 51-127 in Jacquelyn A. Mattfeld and Carol G. Van Aken, eds., *Women and the Scientific Professions.* Cambridge, Mass.: M.I.T. Press.
Safa, Helen Icken
1974a   "Class Consciousness among Working Class Women in Latin America: A Case Study in Puerto Rico." Paper presented at the Conference on Feminine Perspectives in Social Science Research in Latin America, Buenos Aires. Pp. 69-85 in June Nash and Helen Safa, eds., *Sex and Class in Latin America.* New York: Praeger, 1976. A Spanish version appears in María del Carmen de Leñero, *La mujer en América Latina,* vol. 1. Mexico City: SEP/SETENTAS, 1975.
1974b   *The Urban Poor of Puerto Rico: A Study in Development and Inequality.* New York: Holt, Rinehart and Winston.
1976   "The Changing Class Composition of the Female Labor Force in Latin America." Paper presented at the Conference on Women and Development, Wellesley College. Appears in *Latin American Perspectives* 4, no. 4 (Fall 1977): 126-136.
Saffioti, Heleieth Iara B.
1969a   *Profissionalização femenina: Professôras primarias e operárias.* Araraquara, Brasil: Faculdade de Filosofía, Ciencias e Letras.
1969b   *A Mulher na sociedade de classes: Mito e realidade.* São Paulo: Livraria Quatro Artes.
1974   "Relaciones de sexo y de clases sociales." Paper presented to the Conference on Feminine Perspectives in Social Science Research in Latin America, Buenos Aires, March. English version, pp. 147-159 in June Nash and Helen Safa, eds., *Sex and Class in Latin America.* New York: Praeger, 1976. A Spanish version appears in María del Carmen de Leñero, ed., *La mujer en América Latina,* vol. 2. Mexico City: SEP/SETENTAS, 1975.
Sánchez-Albornoz, Claudio
1960   *La España Musulmana.* 2 vols. 2nd ed. Buenos Aires: Editorial El Ateneo.
Sánchez, Luis Alberto
1963   *Historia general de América.* 2 vols. 7th ed. Santiago: Ercilla
Schmidt, Steffen
1974   "La mujer colombiana en una época de transición." Paper in draft. Ames, Iowa: Department of Political Science, Iowa State University.
1975   "Women in Colombia: Attitudes and Future Perspectives in the

Political System." *Journal of Inter-American Studies and World Affairs* 17, no. 4 (November): 465-496.

Schmink, Marianne
1974   "Dependent Development and the Division of Labor by Sex: Venezuela." Paper presented at the Conference of the Latin American Studies Association, San Francisco, March. Appears in *Latin American Perspectives* 4, nos. 1 & 2 (Winter and Spring, 1977): 153-179.

Signorelli de Marti, Rosa
1967   "Spanish America." Pp. 192-208 in Raphael Patai, ed., *Women in the Modern World*. New York: The Free Press.

Smith, A. J., and W. D. Ross
1912   *The Works of Aristotle*. London: Clarendon Press.

Soiza Reilly, Juan José de
1924[?] *Mujeres de América*. Buenos Aires: Librería Anaconda.

Stevens, Evelyn P.
1965   "Mexican Machismo: Politics and Value Orientations." *Western Political Quarterly* 28, no. 3 (September): 848-857.

1973a   "Marianismo: The Other Face of Machismo in Latin America." Pp. 89-101 in Ann Pescatello, ed., *Female and Male in Latin America*. Pittsburgh: University of Pittsburgh Press.

1973b   "The Prospects for a Women's Liberation Movement in Latin America." *Journal of Marriage and the Family* 35, no. 2 (May): 313-321.

Suárez, Flor
1975   *La movilidad ocupacional en Lima metropolitana*. Lima: Ministerio de Trabajo, Dirección General del Empleo.

Sullerot, Evelyne
1971   *Women, Society and Change*. Trans. from the French by Margaret Scotford Archer. New York: McGraw-Hill Book Company.

Taborga, Mercedes
1978   "Aspectos económicos del trabajo de la mujer." Pp. 41-65 in Paz Covarrubias and Rolando Franco, eds., *Chile: Mujer y sociedad*. Santiago: Fondo de las Naciones Unidas para la Infancia.

Tamayo Vargas, Augusto
1940   *Perú en trance de novela: Ensayo crítico biográfico sobre Mercedes Cabello de Carbonero*. Lima: Editorial Baluarte.

1965   *Literatura peruana*. 2 vols. Lima: Universidad Mayor de San Marcos.

Theobald, Robert, ed.
1967   *Dialogue on Women*. New York: Bobbs Merrill & Company.

Tinker, Irene S.
1974   "The Widening Gap." *International Development Review* 16, no. 4: 40-42.

1976   "The Adverse Impact of Development on Women." Pp. 22-34 in
        Irene Tinker and Michèle Bo Bramsen, eds., *Women and World
        Development.* Washington, D.C.: Overseas Development Council.

Toro Godoy, Julia
    1967   *Presencia y destino de la mujer en nuestro pueblo.* Santiago:
            Ediciones Maipo.

UNITAR (United Nations Institute for Training and Research)
    1975   "Women and the UN," special issue of the *UNITAR NEWS* 7, no.
            1.

United Nations Secretary General
    1970   *Implementation of the Convention on the Political Rights of
            Women.* United Nations, N.Y.: General Assembly, Twenty-fifth
            session. A/8132, December 15.
    1974   *Participation of Women in the Economic and Social Development
            of Their Countries.* United Nations, N.Y.: Commission on the
            Status of Women. E/CN.6/513/Rev. 1.

United States, Civil Service Commission, Federal Women's Program
    1969   *Study of Employment of Women in the Federal Government,
            1968.* Washington, D.C.: Government Printing Office.
    ———— , Department of Labor, Women's Bureau
    1968   "Fact Sheet on Women in Professional and Technical Positions."
            Washington, D.C.: Women's Bureau. Mimeographed.

Valenzuela Frías, Francisco, and Sonia Haeberle Bocaz
    1972(?) *Séptimo año básico—Ciencias Sociales. El hombre se organiza
            para vivir en sociedad. El hombre se organiza para gobernarse.*
            Santiago: Nascimento, n.d.

Vallier, Ivan
    1970   *Catholicism, Social Control and Modernization in Latin America.*
            Englewood Cliffs, N.J.: Prentice-Hall.

Vélez, Brunilda
    1964   "Women's Political Behavior in Chile." M.A. thesis, University of
            California, Berkeley.

Vexler, Erica
    1968   "El desafío de la mujer: Nuevo y eterno femenino." *Ercilla* 1740
            (October 23 to 29): 34-40.

Videla de Plankey, Gabriela
    1974   "Las mujeres pobladoras y el proceso revolucionario." Paper
            presented at the Conference on Feminine Perspectives in Social
            Science Research in Latin America, Buenos Aires, March.

Villalobos de Urrutia, Gabriela
    1975   *Diagnóstico de la situación social y económica de la mujer peruana.*
            Lima: Centro de Estudios de Población y Desarrollo.

Werth, Alvin, O.F.M. Cap., and Clement S. Mihanovich
    1955   *Papal Pronouncements on Marriage and the Family.* Milwaukee:
            Bruce Publishing Company.

Williams, Edward J.
>   1967   *Latin American Christian Democratic Parties.* Knoxville: University of Tennessee Press.

Youssef, Nadia Haggag
>   1973   "Cultural Ideals, Feminine Behavior and Family Control." *Comparative Studies in Society and History* 15, no. 3: 326-347.

Newspapers

La Crónica, Lima, September 1, 1924; January 31, 1925.

El Mercurio, Santiago, Chile, "La mujer en política," Revista del Domingo, March 26.

La Nación, Lima, January 12, 1925; November 3, 1954.

New York Times, November 10, 1968; April 17, 1969.

La Patria, Lima, July 20, 1915.

La Prensa, Lima, October 29, 1911; August 17 (1924a) and September 21 (1924b); June 18, 1965.

La República, Buenos Aires, June 15, 1925.

La Tribuna Nacional de Buenos Aires, July 11, 1925.

Index